BY H. G. JONES

THE RECORDS OF A NATION (1969)

FOR HISTORY'S SAKE (1966)

UNION LIST OF NORTH CAROLINA NEWSPAPERS, 1751–1900
(1963)

BEDFORD BROWN: STATE RIGHTS UNIONIST (1955)

THE RECORDS OF A NATION

H. G. JONES

THE RECORDS OF A NATION

THEIR MANAGEMENT, PRESERVATION, AND USE

WITH AN INTRODUCTION BY
WAYNE C. GROVER

ATHENEUM

NEW YORK

1969

To the Memory of
JOHN FRANKLIN JAMESON
and

WALDO GIFFORD LELAND,
*who led the movement for the establishment of the
National Archives*

To the Memory of
ROBERT DIGGES WIMBERLY CONNOR
and

SOLON JUSTUS BUCK,
*who carried the National Archives to world leadership
in fourteen short years*

To
WAYNE CLAYTON GROVER
and

ROBERT HENRY BAHMER,
*who extended that leadership to the management of
modern records*

And to
ALL THOSE WHO AIDED THEM

INTRODUCTION

IT IS NOW nearly 200 years since we set forth so boldly at Philadelphia to try our grand experiment in self-government. It is an obvious time for stock-taking and during the next few years the Republic will abound with orators looking at the record. This study asks that the statesmen among the orators look also at the records.

Dr. H. G. Jones, spurred on by a joint committee of historians and archivists concerned with the status and programs of the Federal Government's record-keeping organizations, has written the first full account of these programs since the establishment of the National Archives. This latter event, some readers will be surprised to learn, did not occur until our own generation. The archives are as old as the Republic, but the institutions established for their preservation and use are very recent indeed.

These institutions were created at a perplexing moment in the archival history of civilized society. Had the National Archives been established in 1914, when the efforts of its early supporters seemed on the verge of success, the newly formed archival profession might have absorbed the paperwork revolution, if not with more skill, at least with more aplomb. By 1934 the avalanche was already upon us.

Nineteen-fourteen, the end of an epoch, how wonderful and timely it would have been! Many of the older records were poorly housed and some had been ravaged by fire: the War Office, 1800, the Capitol, 1814, and far too many others; but there had been rescuers too. Neglected, true, crowded into hot and dusty attics by the ever-pressing business of today, but records were neither ignored, nor forgotten, nor wantonly destroyed. Congress, the Supreme Court, the old Executive Departments—State, War, Navy, Interior—took pride in their ancient archives.

The example had been set by the Founding Fathers themselves. No one could have been a more careful record-keeper than Charles Thomson, Secretary of the Continental Congress, and no one more solicitous for the safety and preservation of these prized records than George Washington. If the higher officials of the rambunctious nineteenth-century Republic forgot these examples, the clerks and scribes did not. Day after day, equipped with pen and ink and good rag paper, they copied the outgoing letters in heavy letter-books; folded and filed the incoming; penned the orders and reports; filled in the muster rolls and census returns; kept the journals and minutes and daybooks; prepared the abstracts and indexes and cross-indexes. It is a rich record of a confident people, spreading across a continent, making laws, handing down decisions, negotiating treaties, fighting wars, fostering agriculture and commerce and education, failing and succeeding, but keeping the experiment in self-government intact. We are heavily indebted to that legion of anonymous clerks and scribes who kept so carefully the record of the youthful Republic.

There might have been time in 1914 for a new archival profession to focus all its attention for a few years on the task of bringing these records together, arranging and repairing them, preparing the array of finding aids necessary to make them most useful. But even then the typewriter and telephone and carbon paper would have required some attention. And by the time the National Archives was finally established and staffed in the late Thirties, the machine-made revolution in record-keeping was in full flood.

The small archival staff recruited by the first Archivist of the United States had certainly expected to devote its full attention to the task of bringing together the older records of the Republic. They looked forward enthusiastically to the day when, for the first time, the Nation's archives could be made readily accessible to the people. But almost before they knew what was happening they found themselves giving an increasing amount of their precious time to emergency out-patient service for the records of the present. It wasn't simply a matter of reacting or being drowned. For the archivist-historians who made the first surveys, it appeared that the record was becoming as incoherent as it was massive. The archives of the future could be unintelligible.

This development had not been foreseen in 1914 or even in

1934. It resulted in the creation of a new field of professional specialization, records management, now generally recognized and supported both in government and in business. It also led to the reduction in status of the National Archives Establishment, which had been created as an independent agency. Because of the anxiety of archivists themselves, the National Archives was thrust into an organizational environment in which the internal business affairs of the government were of overriding concern.

The historians and archivists and educators who had labored so zealously for so many years for an archival agency with stature and status in the government structure were unprepared for this turn of events and did not like it. Until recently, they held their peace. At the annual meeting of the American Historical Association in 1966 a resolution, passed without dissent, invited the Organization of American Historians and the Society of American Archivists to join the Association in establishing a committee to "investigate and report upon the status of the National Archives in the Federal Government." Dr. Julian P. Boyd of Princeton University, the eminent Editor of the Papers of Thomas Jefferson and a former president of the Association, was designated chairman of the joint committee. Its other members, all leaders of distinction in the world of scholarship, are Dr. William T. Alderson, Director of the American Association for State and Local History; Professor Fletcher M. Green of the Department of History, University of North Carolina; Dr. H. G. Jones, State Archivist of North Carolina; Professor Louis Morton of the Department of History, Dartmouth College; and Professor David A. Shannon of the Department of History, University of Maryland. A valued member until his death in July 1967 was Dr. Kent Roberts Greenfield, formerly Chief Historian of the Department of the Army.

Dr. Jones, then Vice President and currently serving as President of the Society of American Archivists, was commissioned by the joint committee to prepare a detailed study of the organization, programs, and progress of the National Archives and its satellite institutions and activities. That study, together with the eloquent report of the joint committee itself, is now published in this book.

It is an important book, even an historic book. Like its sister institutions dealing with printed materials and museum objects, the Library of Congress and the Smithsonian Institution, the National Archives provides the leadership and the pattern for archival work throughout the Nation. In some degree, since American archivists were the first to face the technological revolution ushered in by new methods of documentation, the National Archives is pathfinder for its archival colleagues everywhere.

Statesmen, whether they be princes or presidents, members of Congress or members of the Chamber of Commerce, can be identified by the support they give to the underpinnings of civilized society. Our national archival organizations, conservators of the word as written and filed when the event took place, fall into this category. They keep the Nation's memory, the record of its errors and triumphs, the hard-won wisdom that comes from knowing what actually took place.

This book is addressed to statesmen. It asks for their support. It appeals unashamedly to their devotion to a record of self-government unparalleled in human history. It proclaims that the archives of the United States belong to the people, serve the civic needs of the public as importantly as the internal needs of government, and should be visible to the public not as "housekeeping" units of an unknown bureaucracy but as repositories of the accumulated archival wealth of a Republic whose past must truly serve as prologue.

It is an appeal that runs head on into certain principles of organization that have been sacrosanct in the Federal Government since they were propounded by the first Hoover Commission. There are signs that some academic members of the public administration guild may now be having their doubts about these sacred principles, but it is still popular in governmental circles to derogate boards and commissions and insist that truth and progress lie only in an hierarchical structure leading to an all-powerful, politically appointed Administrator. The President must keep everything within his "span of control" and all support services—recruitment of staff, budgeting, relations with the press and with Congress—must be centralized under this all-powerful Administrator's wing.

The National Archives system, serving all three branches of the Government and, through its Presidential Libraries, both major political parties, really should not be subject to partisan direction. Its institutions and programs need the support and guidance of leaders of both political parties, as well as of officials of the Judicial Branch and representatives of the educational community it serves. Its repositories need identity and visibility and status. This is the major conclusion of both the joint committee report and the Jones study.

It is whispered that without the patronage of the Administrator of General Services and the buildings and dollars under his command, the National Archives system would wither away. If that is so, we might as well forego the celebration of the bicentennial of the Republic. That kind of argument is an insult not merely to archivists and the Administrator himself, but to the form of government we celebrate.

The General Services Administration is a valuable organization with an impressive record and important functions to perform. The nationwide chain of Federal Record Centers that is now an inseparable part of the National Archives system probably could not have been organized so rapidly if it were not for the facilities available through GSA. But having said this, it is still possible to question whether GSA in the long run can provide the kind of leadership and environment that will best serve the Republic in the management, preservation, and use of its records.

In the final analysis it is a question of the regard the American people and their leaders hold for the great body of evidence which is the record of their achievement in self-government, the archives of the United States.

WAYNE C. GROVER
Archivist of the United States, 1948–1965

23 August 1968

PREFACE

THE CONTENTS of few books have been read, discussed, and debated by as many interested individuals as has the text of *The Records of a Nation*. The next-to-final draft was given searching analysis by my five colleagues on the Joint Committee on the Status of the National Archives, by the secretaries of the three organizations represented on the Committee, by two former Archivists and the present Archivist of the United States, by the heads of the offices—and a number of other officials—in the National Archives and Records Service, and by several outstanding historians vitally interested in the nation's archival program. The same draft was made available to the White House and to officials in the Bureau of the Budget and the General Services Administration. Many of these readers furnished detailed comments, which were taken into consideration in the revision of the text as it appears herein. This is not only one of the most thoroughly discussed studies to be published concerning the status of a federal program, it is also the first attempt to evaluate the particular status of the nation's program of managing, preserving, and using its documentary resources.

But let it not be assumed that *The Records of a Nation* represents a consensus of all those who have read and discussed its contents prior to publication. Far from it. I alone assume responsibility for what it reports and what it recommends. Nonetheless it should not be surprising that I am immensely pleased by the fact that the Joint Committee unanimously adopted the major recommendations of the study, that these recommendations have been endorsed verbatim by the governing boards of two of our sponsoring organizations and in an amended fashion by the third, and that my unofficial advisers outside of the National Archives and Records Service—and a number within NARS—have joined in this support.

This book is not a sensational exposé. It is not a full history of the nation's eventually successful effort to establish an archival program. It is not a study of all the record-keeping activities of the federal government. It is, instead, an effort to place in its historical setting a great educational, cultural, and service institution, whose light is shielded from the public by the bushel of organizational subservience. It is a report of the present status of the National Archives and Records Service. The findings of this study point to certain inescapable conclusions, which in turn dictate the divorce of the National Archives and Records Service from the General Services Administration and its reestablishment as the National Archives and Records Authority. This recommendation in no way justifies a characterization of the book as an attack on the General Services Administration or the National Archives and Records Service. On the contrary, within the resources at its command NARS has in the main developed programs unexcelled by any other nation. But these accomplishments must be measured not against the past but against the needs of the present and the future. These needs demand a new surge of imaginative planning at a time when traditional techniques of documentation are rapidly being replaced by highly complex new techniques, new concepts, new media.

The Records of a Nation is the result of thirteen months of research, investigation, interviews, and debates on the status of the archival and records management program of the federal government. While I assume total responsibility for the text, I must acknowledge the assistance of many interested persons both in and outside the federal government.

Because of their official positions, some persons who were helpful must remain anonymous. But I cannot refrain from publicly acknowledging the courage and assistance of the members of the Joint Committee on the Status of the National Archives, Chairman Julian P. Boyd and members William T. Alderson, Fletcher M. Green, Louis Morton, David A. Shannon, and the late Kent Roberts Greenfield, and several of my most trusted advisers: Wayne C. Grover, Archivist of the United States from 1948 to 1965; Lyman H. Butterfield, Editor of the *Adams Papers;* Ernst Posner, "dean" of American archivists; and Verner W. Clapp, former President of the Council on Library Resources, Incorporated. Robert H. Bahmer and James B. Rhoads, the former and present Archivist of the United States, respectively, were most cooperative in furnishing requested information and in making available to me records of the institution and in allowing members of the staff to express themselves freely during the data-gathering stages of my research. Paul L. Ward, Executive Secretary of the American Historical Association, co-operated fully with the Joint Committee. Christopher Crittenden, then Director of the North Carolina Department of Archives and History, generously granted me leave during the period of my work in Washington; and Julius H. Avant, my loyal assistant, went beyond the call of duty to coordinate the preparation of the numerous drafts and handle much of my correspondence. Mrs. Rea H. Battle and Mrs. Irene H. Hallman assisted in the typing, and C. F. W. Coker, Assistant State Archivist, relieved me of many routine duties during the course of my research. To them, and to others unnamed, I express my deep appreciation.

The original study was made possible by a grant from the Council on Library Resources, Incorporated, to the American Historical Assocation, neither of which is responsible for the findings or recommendations of this study.

H. G. JONES

Raleigh, North Carolina
August 1968

CONTENTS

PART ONE
Background: The National Archives, 1776–1949

PART TWO
The National Archives and Records Service, 1949–1968

PART THREE
The Future of the National Archives and Records Service

APPENDIX

ILLUSTRATIONS

Following Page 138

TABLES IN THE TEXT

PART ONE

BACKGROUND
THE NATIONAL ARCHIVES
1776–1949

I am very strongly of the opinion . . . that any legislation which makes it possible, now or hereafter, for any of the essential functions of the National Archives Establishment to be transferred to, or for the Establishment itself to be placed under the jurisdiction of any particular executive department, would not be in the interest of either economy or efficiency, but would handicap the National Archives Establishment in performing the duties required of it by law.

—R. D. W. Connor, *First Archivist of the United States, 1937*

A prerequisite of the judicious selection of records either for permanent preservation or for disposal is an appraisal of their value, and this appraisal can be made more readily and with greater assurance if the records have been arranged and administered with their permanent preservation or their disposal in mind. Arrangement usually takes place, however, when the documents are filed, that is, when they are first consciously considered as record material. From this chain of circumstances it becomes apparent that The National Archives must inevitably be concerned with the creation, arrangement, and administration as well as with the appraisal, disposal, and preservation of Government records, and that in order to perform its functions satisfactorily it must have a knowledge of the records that can come only from a continuous survey of them.

—Solon J. Buck, *Second Archivist of the United States, 1941*

Emphasis on the role of the National Archives in records management should not . . . be permitted to obscure the fact that the institution has other functions to perform. The National Archives is also responsible for preserving and making available for the use of the Government and the people the noncurrent records of the three branches of the Government—executive, legislative, and judicial— that are worthy of preservation. The selection of these permanent records and the fact that all phases of the management of current records vitally affect the job of preserving and controlling noncurrent records are the considerations that compel the American archivist to assume responsibilities for records management. It is especially this characteristic that distinguishes him from his European colleagues. But like them he is also the custodian of a priceless heritage—the memory of the National Government as it exists in the records of the various Federal agencies.

—Wayne C. Grover, *Third Archivist of the United States, 1949*

[1]

FROM DREAM TO REALITY,

1776–1941

The chief monument of the history of a nation is its archives, the preservation of which is recognized in all civilized countries as a natural and proper function of government. —Waldo Gifford Leland, *1912*

For a nation whose government is based upon a written constitution and laws to neglect its public records for a century and a half is remarkable in itself. For that same nation, once its conscience was awakened, to develop one of the world's foremost archival institutions in less than a generation is even more remarkable. Yet the United States of America endured the one and accomplished the other. This success justified the faith and perseverance of a handful of interested citizens, chiefly historical scholars, who conducted a noisy vigil over the documentary heritage of the nation while agitating, in every manner known to them, for the establishment of a national archival program. Though their predecessors—few in number and weak in political influence—had from time to time throughout the nineteenth century pointed to the government's neglect of its records, the long and often lonely, but eventually successful, battle was joined just after the turn of the century, when historians such as John Franklin Jameson and Waldo Gifford Leland turned their talented pens to the task. It was to the honor of the nation that its leaders were finally convinced and that Jameson and Leland lived to see their victory.

It may not be surprising that a newly independent people were too busy making history to pay adequate attention to the preservation of that history. Perhaps their youthful vigor led them to confidence in the future without regard for the lessons of the past. Or perhaps the problems of the times demanded so much effort that there was simply no time to consider the contents of the storage rooms. One keen observer attributes to political and administrative considerations the nineteenth-century archival backwardness of the United States, particularly the traditional —until now—American hostility to bureaucracy, the lack of "tangible" benefits from appropriations for archival purposes, and the tendency for the few available positions involving records to be filled by political hacks.[1] Yet there were heard occasional pleadings for this nation to care for its documentary heritage. Some—like Thomas Jefferson—looked to publication of the documents as a means of safeguarding them. Jefferson wrote: "Time and accident are committing daily havoc on the originals deposited in our public offices: the late war has done the work of centuries in this business: the lost cannot be recovered; but let us save what remains; not by vaults and locks, which fence them from the public eye and use in consigning them to the waste of time, but by such a multiplication of Copies as shall place them beyond the reach of accident. . . ."[2]

The work of men like Ebenezer Hazard and Peter Force in committing selected documents to print served a useful purpose,[3] but others recognized the value of the mass of original documents. During the Revolution the peripatetic Continental Congress, even when in danger, watched over its documentation so protectively that its records are more complete today than are those of the first few Congresses under the Constitution. For this demonstration of documentary preservation, Charles Thomson, the Greek scholar who became the "perpetual" secretary of the Continental Congress, may have been chiefly responsible, but it should not be forgotten that John Jay, president of the second congress of that body, wrote that he was "carefully arranging the state papers of Congress" as primary source materials for future historians.[4] So little care was given the records in the

1. Ernst Posner, "Archival Administration in the United States," in Ken Munden (ed.), *Archives and the Public Interest: Selected Essays by Ernst Posner* (Washington: Public Affairs Press, 1967), pp. 115–116.

2. Quoted in "Proposals for Printing by Subscription, A Collection of State Papers, Intended as Materials for An History of the United States of America. By Ebenezer Hazard, A.M.," in Ebenezer Hazard Papers, The Historical Society of Pennsylvania.

3. For a brief survey of American documentary publication, see L. H. Butterfield, "Historical Editing in the United States: The Recent Past," in L. H. Butterfield and Julian P. Boyd, *Historical Editing in the United States* (Worcester, Mass.: American Antiquarian Society, 1963), pp. 3–28.

4. David D. Van Tassel, *Recording America's Past: An Interpretation*

following two decades, however, that in 1810 a Congressional committee appointed to inquire into the condition of the "Ancient Public Records and Archives of the United States" complained that the early records were "in a state of great disorder and exposure; and in a situation neither safe nor convenient nor honorable to the nation." [5] The investigation led to probably the first definite attempt to provide space specifically for housing federal records—a general post office building with as many "fire proof rooms" as were needed for the deposit of the "public papers and records of the United States. . . ." [6]

If a nation or state needed justification for preserving its records, a New Englander uttered it. Richard Bartlett wrote: "To provide for the safe and perfect keeping of the Public Archives, is so obviously one of the first and most imperative duties of a legislature, that no argument could make it plainer to a reflecting mind." Everything that can be procured by money, he continued, "sinks into insignificance in comparison with the original records. . . ." [7] Interestingly enough, while Richard Bartlett, Lyman C. Draper of Wisconsin, David L. Swain of North Carolina, and others were goading individual states into action to preserve their written records,[8] the voices for archival preservation on the national scene were singularly ineffective, and it was not until the 1870s that considerable interest was exhibited in the halls of Congress. Even then it required a disastrous fire in a government building to initiate an investigation into the conditions of the records. A commission report led to a recommendation by President Hayes that Congress appro-

of the Development of Historical Studies in America, 1607–1884 (Chicago: University of Chicago Press, 1960), p. 33. Record-keeping by the Continental Congress is briefly reviewed in Harold T. Pinkett, "New York as the Temporary National Capital, 1785–1790: The Archival Heritage," *National Archives Accessions*, No. 60 (December 1967), pp. 1–11.

5. *Report of the Committee, appointed to inquire into the State of the Ancient Public Records and Archives of the United States, March 27th, 1810* (Washington: R. C. Weightman, 1810), p. 1.

6. Percy Scott Flippin (comp.), "The Archives of the United States Government: A Documentary History, 1774–1934" (unpublished typescript and scrapbook in 24 volumes, plus supplementary and index volumes, in National Archives Library), I, Preface, 1. These volumes will hereafter be cited as Flippin Collection.

7. Richard G. Wood, "Richard Bartlett, Minor Archival Prophet," *American Archivist*, XVII (January 1954), 14–15.

8. Ernst Posner, *American State Archives* (Chicago: University of Chicago Press, 1964), surveys the development of archival activities in the 50 states.

priate $200,000 for the construction of a "cheap building . . . as a hall of records . . . perfectly fire-proof. . . ."[9] Little attention appears to have been paid to the suggestion, however, until fires occurred in the War Department building in 1880 and 1881, after which the Senate finally passed a bill authorizing a hall of records. But it, like 42 others introduced between 1881 and 1912, failed to pass both houses in spite of the support of nearly every member of the Cabinet and of the various Presidents and in spite of an officially estimated 250 fires in government buildings in Washington from 1873 to 1915.[10]

Until the early years of the twentieth century the idea of a "hall of records" envisioned little more than a warehouse for the storage of records. Meanwhile, however, several states, beginning with Alabama in 1900, established agencies with programs not only of housing but also of systematically accessioning, arranging, describing, and making available for public use their public records. Historians, through the Public Archives Commission established in 1899 by the American Historical Association,[11] took a keen interest in archival preservation, and in 1909 the first annual Conference of Archivists met in conjunction with the Association's annual meeting. This activity coincided with a revival of archival advancement in Europe, but more importantly, with the coming on the scene of John Franklin Jameson,[12] editor for most of the time from 1895 to 1928 of the

9. *First Annual Report of the Archivist of the United States for the Fiscal Year Ending June 30, 1935* (Washington: Government Printing Office, 1936), p. 3. Annual reports of the Archivist hereafter will be cited as *Annual Report*, with number and year.

10. *First Annual Report, 1934–35*, pp. 2–3. Among these bills was one introduced in 1906 by Senator Henry Cabot Lodge that prophetically embodied in its proposals many of the provisions enacted into law in 1934. Senator Lodge's bill, S. 6728, 59th Cong., 2nd Sess., was referred to the Committee on the Library, where it died.

11. The activities of the Commission were reviewed in V. H. Paltsits, "An Historical Résumé of the Public Archives Commission from 1899 to 1921," in *Annual Report of the American Historical Association for the Year 1922*, I, 152 ff. Its reports were published in the various annual reports of the Association.

12. For biographical sketches of Jameson, see Elizabeth Donnan, Introduction, in Elizabeth Donnan and Leo F. Stock (eds.), *An Historian's World: Selections from the Correspondence of John Franklin Jameson* (Philadelphia: The American Philosophical Society, 1956), pp. 1–17; David D. Van Tassel, "John Franklin Jameson," in Clifford L. Lord (ed.), *Keepers of the Past* (Chapel Hill: University of North Carolina Press, 1965), pp. 81–96; and Ruth Anna Fisher and William

American Historical Review and from 1905 to 1928 head of the Carnegie Institution's Department of Historical Research. Jameson served both as the spiritual and practical spearhead in the movement that came to fruition three decades later. He more than any other man, ably assisted by his student, lifelong friend, and sometime colleague, Waldo Gifford Leland, may be considered the most influential single force in the drive for a national archives.[13] Leland was the theorist; Jameson, the confidant of congressmen and Presidents, dropped the seeds of archival preservation where they gradually took root.

It was Jameson who persuaded Carnegie's Department of Historical Research to sponsor the first survey of federal archives, which resulted in 1904 in the publication of Claude H. Van Tyne and Waldo G. Leland's *Guide to the Archives of the Government of the United States*.[14] Thus the first real guide to the records of the federal government was made possible by an outside professional agency, and it was this survey that gave new life to the movement for a national archival program by interesting professional historians in a documentary heritage that previously they hardly knew existed. Following as it did the graduate-school introduction of the new "scientific" research methodology, the publication of a guide to the federal records opened broad and challenging avenues of exploration for historians.[15]

At Jameson's urging, the American Historical Association took the lead in the movement for a national archives program

---

Lloyd Fox, *J. Franklin Jameson: A Tribute* (Washington: Catholic University of America Press, 1965).

13. For a biographical note on Leland, see Lester J. Cappon, "Waldo Gifford Leland, 1879–1966," in *American Archivist*, XXX (January 1967), 125–128. Leland's own writings, several of which are cited elsewhere in this study, comprise virtually an autobiography of this remarkable scholar.

14. Published by the Library of Congress, Division of Manuscripts. A revised and enlarged edition was published in 1907.

15. Still one of the best sources for reviewing the introduction of the new school of historical research is W. Stull Holt (ed.), *Historical Scholarship in the United States, 1876–1901: As Revealed in the Correspondence of Herbert B. Adams*, Ser. LVI, No. 4, of *The Johns Hopkins University Studies in Historical and Political Science* (Baltimore: The Johns Hopkins Press, 1938). See also Jurgen Herbst, *The German Historical School in American Scholarship: A Study in the Transfer of Culture* (Ithaca: Cornell University Press, 1965), and John Higham with Leonard Krieger and Felix Gilbert, *History* (Englewood Cliffs, N.J.: Prentice-Hall, Inc., 1965).

professionally directed by scholars, like those in European countries, rather than simply a storage building for records. The Council of the Association in 1908, complaining of the absence of "orderly keeping" of the federal records, appointed a committee to promote the establishment of such a program. Two years later the organization, noting that "the records are in many cases now stored where they are in danger of destruction from fire and in places which are not adapted to their preservation, and where they are inaccessible for administrative and historical purposes, and knowing that many of the records of the Government have in the past been lost or destroyed because suitable provision for their care and preservation was not made," petitioned Congress for the erection of a "national archive depository, where the records of the Government may be concentrated, properly cared for, and preserved." [16] Other scholarly and patriotic groups associated themselves with the petition.

Appearing before a House committee in 1911 in support of the petition, Jameson entered into the record an "elaborate history of the movement for a national archive building" and Waldo Leland's statement, "Present Condition of the Government Archives." [17] Leland, who had attended the International Congress of Archivists and Librarians in Belgium in 1910 and who had observed European archives, continued the argument in a published article in 1912 in which he wrote, "The chief monument of the history of a nation is its archives, the preservation of which is recognized in all civilized countries as a natural and proper function of government." [18] He proposed a "board of record commissioners" to have legal custody of archives and authority to make regulations regarding them and to "investigate the condition of the records of any office, in Washington or elsewhere, under the control of the federal government and to make recommendations respecting their preparation, preserva-

16. Quoted in *First Annual Report, 1934–35*, p. 4.
17. *Hearings Before Committee on Public Buildings and Grounds, House of Representatives, May 12, 1911, Relating to the Preservation of Government Archives* (Washington: Government Printing Office, 1911), pp. 3–25.
18. Leland, "The National Archives: A Programme," *American Historical Review*, XVIII (October 1912), 1. See also Leland, "Report on the Public Archives and Historical Interests of the State of Illinois," in Illinois State Education Building Commission, *Report* (Springfield: State Education Building Commission, 1913), p. 34.

tion, and use." Under the board would be the "archivist or keeper of the records," who would be assisted by a staff trained in history, government, and the principles of archival economy.[19] Leland estimated the annual accumulation of federal records at 60,000 cubic feet, a figure that was to be dwarfed by the 200,000 cubic feet being created each year by 1930, the shocking 4,000,000 cubic feet produced annually by 1953,[20] and the more than 4,500,000 cubic feet created in 1968.

The concerted movement generated great interest and met with apparent success when in 1913 Congress authorized the preparation of plans for a national archives building, the cost of which was not to exceed $1,500,000. Representing the far-sighted thinking of Jameson and Leland, the authorization stipulated that the planners inspect the most modern national archives buildings in Europe, a provision that was negated by the outbreak of war on the Continent. Three years later this restriction was officially removed, but before the plans could be completed the United States was drawn into the war, thus further delaying the project. Decisive action was not resumed until 1925, when President Coolidge specifically recommended additional buildings to house and protect the "employees and records" of the government. The following year Congress appropriated $6,900,000 (subsequently increased to more than $12,000,000) for a national archives building, which the Public Buildings Commission designated as "the third project in the triangle development" between Pennsylvania and Consti-

19. Leland, "The National Archives," p. 20. Leland's proposal for a "board of record commissioners" may have been influenced by the Lodge Bill of 1906, which was probably inspired by Jameson. See above, n. 10.

20. Robert H. Bahmer, "The National Archives After 20 Years," *American Archivist*, XVIII (July 1955), 200. Even the increasing quantity of federal records failed to result in Congressional action until 1881, when the first formal authorization for disposal permitted the Postmaster General to "sell as waste paper, or otherwise dispose of, the files of papers which have accumulated, or may hereafter accumulate in the Post-Office Department that are not needed in the transaction of current business and have no permanent value or historical interest. . . ." A similar authorization was extended to other executive agencies in 1889. In each case the agency head was required to submit to Congress a list of such records. By Executive Order No. 1499, March 16, 1912, the lists were required to be presented first to the Librarian of Congress for advice and approval. See Henry P. Beers, "Historical Development of the Records Disposal Policy of the Federal Government Prior to 1934," *American Archivist*, VII (July 1944), 184–196.

tution avenues on the north and south and Seventh and Ninth streets on the east and west. A ground-breaking ceremony for the building designed by John Russell Pope was held on September 9, 1931, and on February 20, 1933, President Hoover laid the cornerstone. Said the President:

> . . . there will be aggregated here the most sacred documents of our history, the originals of the Declaration of Independence and of the Constitution of the United States. Here will be preserved all the other records that bind State to State and the hearts of all our people in an indissoluble union. The romance of our history will have living habitation here in the writings of statesmen, soldiers and all the others, both men and women, who have builded the great structure of our national life. . . . Devoutly the Nation will pray that it may endure forever, the repository of records of yet more glorious progress in the life of our beloved country.[21]

The great structure was to be equipped with all the necessary facilities for the safe handling and for the physical preservation of archives that modern science could suggest. A total of more than 900,000 square feet of floor space, 90 percent of which was for documents, was provided for—space that, when finally shelved, could accommodate nearly 1,000,000 cubic feet of records. A country that for a century and a half had almost consistently neglected its documentary heritage now proudly displayed an archival facility equal in design, protection, and comfort to that of any other nation. The Archivist of the United States moved into the new building on November 8, 1935, though not all of the areas were ready for use for several more years.

The completion of the National Archives Building was an accomplishment of first magnitude, but had it not been for wise advance planning it would have offered little correction for the basic problem relating to the records—their orderly care, maintenance, and preservation or disposal. Jameson again exhibited

---

21. "Remarks of President Hoover at the Laying of the Corner-Stone of the National Archives Building, Washington, D.C., Monday, February 20, 1933, at 2:30 O'clock," in Flippin Collection.

foresight when, only a few days after the passage of the appropriation for the building in 1926, he wrote:

> . . . the objects for which we have sought such a building
> —security, suitable care, orderly arrangement, ease in laying hands quickly on what is needed for government use or by students, facility in using and good results from use— can not be secured by a building alone. There must be a high-grade organization, with expert personnel taken over from the contributing departments or secured by special search, and all necessary legislation toward this end ought to be put through in the next session of Congress, because a portion of the staff should be at work, well before the completion of the building, in doing all that can be done before hand to facilitate the transfer. If the organization of the archive service should wait till the building is ready, the service would be swamped in the beginning, and chaos produced, by the tumbling in of tons of records and papers which departments are in a hurry to get rid of.[22]

Fears that the huge building would be packed with canceled checks, requisitions, and other housekeeping records were not easily allayed, but Congressional wisdom in eventual passage of the National Archives Act in 1934 assured the second great achievement of the period—the establishment of an agency with authority to administer the records of all three branches of government and the selection of a dedicated group of scholars to administer the program. Fortunately the need for attention to the mass of records facing the new agency was recognized early. In 1930, for instance, a superficial survey estimated that there were in the federal government about 3,531,000 cubic feet of records—108,000 of them having been created prior to 1861, 923,000 of them representing the period from 1861 through 1916, and 2,500,000 feet having been accumulated between 1917 and 1930. Of these, the surveyors estimated fewer than 600,000 feet warranted permanent preservation.[23] Even so, the

22. Jameson to Senator Simeon D. Fess, June 23, 1926, quoted in Fred Shelley, "The Interest of J. Franklin Jameson in the National Archives: 1908–1934," *American Archivist*, XII (April 1949), 122.

23. Shelley, "The Interest of Jameson," p. 126. For other figures on accumulations of records during these periods, see *Fifteenth Annual Report, 1948–1949*, p. 8.

new building was designed to accept only a million cubic feet of records, and the problem of bulk obviously dictated the need for a long-range plan directed toward reducing the quantity of records thought to be of permanent value or adding archival space within a matter of years.

Despite the efforts of Jameson, Leland, and others to impress upon Congress the desirability of early archival legislation, passage of a national archives act came only after four years of bill drafting. As early as 1930, bills had been unsuccessfully introduced in Congress to establish the office of Archivist of the United States, but it was not until December 9, 1931, that the movement began in earnest. On that date Senator Reed Smoot of Utah introduced two bills that indicated that the organizational status of the proposed agency was a matter of debate. One, S. 689, would have provided for the Archivist to be appointed by the President by and with the advice and consent of the Senate. He was to be assisted by a National Archives Council, composed of himself, the Chairman of the Public Building Commission, Chairman of the Senate Committee on the Library, Director of Public Buildings and Public Parks, one of the secretaries to the President, and the Librarian of Congress. The bill also provided for an advisory committee made up of one representative designated by the head of each agency in the executive branch. Staff members were to be subject to the civil service acts. The bill required that all records dating prior to 1860 be transferred to the Archives, to be followed by additional five-year accumulations at the end of each five years.

That the Senator recognized differences of opinion on the proposed organization was reflected in his bill S. 692, introduced the same day, which would have provided for appointment of the Archivist of the United States by a National Archives Council "from among such persons as are qualified for the professional and scientific service, as defined in the Classification Act of 1923." The Council, as envisioned in this bill, was to be composed of two members of the Public Building Commission and its executive officer, the chairmen of the Senate and House Committees on the Library, the Librarian of Congress, and the Archivist, plus one representative appointed by the head of each agency transferring to the National Archives Building records exceeding 50,000 cubic feet.

These two bills, neither of which passed, are of interest

primarily because they point to the lack of a firm Congressional concept of the nature of a national archives. Both placed administrative authority in a National Archives Council, and neither provided for representation by the judicial branch. The composition of the Council, in fact, hardly represented cultural interests.

In 1933 Senator Henry W. Keyes of New Hampshire introduced a bill, S. 161, almost identical to Senator Smoot's second 1931 bill. It too never came out of committee.

In 1934, with the National Archives Building rapidly approaching completion, the urgency for an archives act was apparent during the second session of the Seventy-Third Congress. Several bills were introduced, but those of Representative Sol Bloom of New York (H.R. 8340 and 8910) and Senator Kenneth D. McKellar of Tennessee (S. 3110 and 3681) appear to have been the bases for committee discussion. Representative Bloom's first bill would have set up an Archives Commission to govern a United States Bureau of Archives, and the Archivist of the United States was to be appointed by the President by and with the advice and consent of the Senate. There was evidence that the bureau was to be placed in the Department of the Interior.

Apparently those most concerned with the establishment of the new agency—Jameson, Thomas P. Martin,[24] and others— recognized the defects of the Bloom bill, and two months later the New Yorker introduced his second bill. This provided for an independent agency, the National Archives of the United States, with an Archivist, to be appointed by the President by and with the advice and consent of the Senate, and a National Archives Commission, with limited powers, made up of the secretaries of the executive departments or alternates approved by the Archivist, the chairmen of the Senate and House Committees on the Library, the Librarian of Congress, the Secretary of the Smithsonian Institution, and the Archivist. H.R. 8910 passed the House in slightly amended form after Representative Kent R. Keller, Chairman on the Committee on Library, said that his committee had

sought the advice and counsel of prominent historians, archivists, and others qualified to give advice in the fram-

24. See, e.g., memo of Thomas P. Martin to Senator Tom Connally, February 24, 1934, in Flippin Collection.

ing of this proposed legislation. It has read and analyzed other legislation now in effect and governing archives in other governments; it has read and analyzed similar proposed legislation introduced by other Members of Congress, and has sought in every way possible to submit plans that will most nearly meet a complexity of problems, yet of such flexibility that will permit easy adjustment to future and unforeseen problems, and with such provisions that will make the operation and administration of the national archives effective.[25]

Meanwhile the Senate was considering Senator McKellar's bill, S. 3110, which provided for the same method of appointment of the Archivist, but with a National Archives *Council*, having the same composition as that provided in the second Bloom bill and acting as an advisory rather than an administrative authority. When the Bloom bill came to the Senate it was rewritten largely to conform to the provisions of Senator McKellar's bill. A conference committee recommended that the House accept most of the Senate's alterations.[26]

The act creating a National Archives of the United States Government,[27] approved by President Roosevelt on June 19, 1934, provided for an "Office of Archivist of the United States, the Archivist to be appointed by the President of the United States, by and with the advice and consent of the Senate," and other staff members to be appointed by the Archivist "solely with reference to their fitness for their particular duties and without regard to civil-service law . . . ; but any official or

25. 73rd Cong., 2nd Sess., *House Report No. 1156*, April 9, 1934, Public, Vol. II (Washington: Government Printing Office, 1934).
26. 73rd Cong., 2nd Sess., *House Report No. 2048*, June 15, 1934, Public, Vol. II (Washington: Government Printing Office, 1934). It is perhaps worthy of note that Jameson preferred the original provisions of Bloom's bill to those in McKellar's. He wrote: "It is true that on the whole, in the conference, the Senate bill prevailed over the House bill, and a pity it is 'tis true, for the House bill was distinctly better, and some of the provisions of the Senate bill, left in the residuum, are distinctly unfortunate. Still, they are no wise fatal or disastrous, and on the whole the act is a pretty good one." Jameson regretted that the position of Archivist had been exempted from the classification acts and that Senate confirmation of more highly paid assistants was to be required. See Jameson to Samuel Flagg Bemis, June 26, 1934, in Donnan and Stock (eds.), *An Historian's World*, p. 356.
27. 73rd Cong. 2nd Sess., P.L. 432; 48 Stat. 1112–1124.

employee with salary of $5,000 or over shall be appointed by the President by and with the advice and consent of the Senate."

Historians who were consulted in the framing of the act could be expected to distill from the experience of centuries one of its most far-reaching provisions, that conferring upon the Archivist of the United States a comprehensive responsibility for all records whether legislative, executive, or judicial, and commanding the full cooperation of all agencies of government in order to enable him to discharge his duty:

> All archives or records belonging to the Government of the United States (legislative, executive, judicial, and other) shall be under the charge and superintendence of the Archivist to this extent: He shall have full power to inspect personally or by deputy the records of any agency of the United States Government whatsoever and wheresoever located, and shall have the full cooperation of any and all persons in charge of such records in such inspections, and to requisition for transfer to the National Archives Establishment such archives, or records as the National Archives Council . . . shall approve for such transfer, and he shall have authority to make regulations for the arrangement, custody, use, and withdrawal of material deposited in the National Archives Building. . . .

The immediate custody and control of the National Archives Building were placed in the hands of the Archivist. The provision that this authority should also extend to "such other buildings, grounds, and equipment as may from time to time become a part of the National Archives Establishment" seems to have anticipated that additional repositories for the growing mass of records would be needed.

The National Archives Council was to be composed of the secretary of each of the executive departments of the government or an alternate appointed by him, the chairmen of the Senate and House Committees on the Library, the Librarian of Congress, the Secretary of the Smithsonian Institution, and the Archivist of the United States. It was to "define the classes of material which shall be transferred to the National Archives Building and establish regulations governing such transfer; and shall have power to advise the Archivist in respect to regulations governing the disposition and use of the archives and records transferred to his custody."

Other provisions included the creation of a National Historical Publications Commission and the requirement that the Archivist submit to Congress an annual report and a description of records "which appear to have no permanent value or historical interest, and which, with the concurrence of the Government agency concerned, and subject to the approval of Congress, shall be destroyed or otherwise effectively disposed of."

Organizationally, the three major provisions of the National Archives Act—the result of more than four years of legislative consideration—were (1) an independent National Archives, (2) an independent Archivist of the United States, appointed by the President by and with the advice and consent of the Senate, and (3) an advisory, not an administrative, National Archives Council. Interestingly enough, the composition of the Council did not include representation from the judicial branch—a defect that, at the time, should have been obvious to those familiar with the nature of custody and control of government records and of the balance-of-power theory of the United States.

Even before the passage of the National Archives Act historians were busy discussing possible candidates for the position of Archivist of the United States. The choice $10,000-per-year appointment—a high salary in 1934—would certainly be eyed by politicians; and historians, having been qualified to assist in the framing of the legislation, felt that they were also qualified to suggest the kind of Archivist who would lift the office above partisan politics. Above all, they believed that the office must be filled by a scholar. They found their candidate in Robert Digges Wimberly Connor, the first Secretary of the North Carolina Historical Commission and then Professor of History at the University of North Carolina. The ever-present Jameson, in conveying the recommendation to President Roosevelt, wrote:

. . . while the Executive Committee of the American Historical Association lays proper emphasis on successful experience in archive work, it is well aware that the business of being the first Archivist of the United States is primarily an administrative employment, and one requiring a combination of organizing power and personal tact.

In recommending Professor Connor they have had chiefly in mind the fact that he is a man of great administrative capacity, a man of force and character, who would wish and would be able to place the new institution on a high level and maintain it there, a man of affairs and action, yet one of quiet and agreeable ways, who has shown by his success in dealing with the North Carolina Legislature the tact and considerate spirit which a novel institution like the National Archives will require in its dealing with the various governmental organizations which will contribute to the Archives and which the Archives will serve.[28]

On October 10, 1934, the White House announced the appointment of Connor, who entered upon his duties immediately.[29] A staggering array of problems faced the first Archivist of the United States. Construction was still in progress on the National Archives Building and decisions had to be made on equipping it. There was no model archival agency from which lessons could be learned concerning the best and most modern facilities, for even most of the archives buildings of Europe were outdated, and there were few state archives with acceptable equipment. The views of archivists, historians, and designers were brought together in an effort to make the National Archives the best-equipped archival facility in the world.[30] Novel equipment was installed for work in photography, document restoration, cleaning, fumigation, and the handling of special record types. The most significant features of the National Archives were not the size, location, design, or sculptural and mural decorations, but rather the facilities with which it was

28. Jameson to President Franklin D. Roosevelt, July 14, 1934, quoted in Waldo Gifford Leland, "R. D. W. Connor, First Archivist of the United States," *American Archivist*, XIV (January 1953), 50.

29. The appointment was confirmed by the Senate on March 20 the following year. See R. D. W. Connor Journal (unpublished typescript in 6 volumes in the Southern Historical Collection, University of North Carolina Library, Chapel Hill), I, 132–134. For reminiscences of his early days as Archivist of the United States, see Connor's "Adventures of an Amateur Archivist," *American Archivist*, VI (January 1943), 1–18.

30. The shortcomings of the building were given a lengthy review in 1946 when the Open Conference on Administration considered "The National Archives Building—An Appraisal After Ten Years' Occupancy." See minutes of meeting of Open Conference on Administration, February 25, 1946.

equipped. Even so, the metal containers used in the early years were found to be unsatisfactory and ultimately had to be replaced by steel shelving and cardboard document cases.

A second major consideration was the staffing of the new agency. During the first four years all positions were exempt from the civil service acts, and had the President not supported Connor in his insistence upon professionals to assist him, the new archival program might have resulted in a maze of political appointments. In spite of Connor's bland denial years later,[31] political considerations were undoubtedly present, but in the main he gathered around him historians and a few trained archivists. Four years later he wrote:

> It may not be amiss at this time to make some note of the character of the personnel that has been obtained by appointing employees "solely with reference to fitness for their particular duties." Although academic achievements cannot be fully accepted as criteria for the determination of ability, particularly in the case of the administrative personnel, it is nevertheless significant that of the 319 employees on the staff of The National Archives at the close of the fiscal year [1938] no less than 160 held bachelor's degrees, 73 master's degrees, and 32 the degree of doctor of philosophy. Moreover, many of the employees do not regard their education as finished when they join the staff. The records show that, during the fiscal year 1938, 68 members of the staff were increasing their qualifications for archival work by attendance at local professional schools, colleges, and universities.[32]

The third and most vexing task facing the new National Archives was the development of principles and procedures for tackling the mammoth record problem. The accumulation of more than a century and a half totaled nearly 10,000,000 cubic feet of records scattered throughout the country. In order to provide a more accurate estimate and to locate the thousands of hiding places, a survey was begun that by 1939 had already identified in Washington alone 2,729,000 cubic feet of records, 17,737,000 feet of motion pictures, 2,346,000 photographic

31. Connor, "Adventures of An Amateur Archivist," p. 5.
32. *Fourth Annual Report, 1937–38*, p. 5.

negatives, and 5,495 sound recordings, located in 6,570 places, nearly a third of which were exposed to danger from fire, half to damage by filth, and many to the ravages of rain and vermin. Simultaneously the Federal Records Survey, with the full support of the National Archives, began a study of federal records outside of Washington.

Most of these records, of course, did not possess values sufficient to warrant their continued preservation, and therein lay the greatest task before the staff: the appraisal of thousands of series to determine which records could, with the approval of Congress, be disposed of and which of the residue could be accepted by the National Archives.[33] The extent of the problem was unique in the history of mankind. "Records management" was an unborn idea, and, indeed, the "archival profession" was little more than a small band of historians and a few toilers in state archival agencies and historical societies who had no published guidelines of significance. It is not too much, therefore, to credit to the National Archives the American origin of the profession of archivist and a major role in the later evolution of the specialty of the records manager. Though persons concerned with archives had met annually with the American Historical Association since 1899, they looked upon themselves as lonely workers in a specialized field, without a patron or a voice except through the historical profession. It is not surprising, therefore, that it was the staff of the National Archives, recognizing the need for the development of an archival profession with a body of literature upon which it could base its work, who joined with their colleagues in state and local organizations to organize the Society of American Archivists only two years after the passage of the National Archives Act. That society in 1938 inaugurated its quarterly journal, the *American Archivist*, which has been more instrumental than any single factor in bringing to maturity the long-needed profession.[34] The journal, along with the *An-*

33. Though their other contributions to the National Archives program were indispensable, historians, congenitally disposed to save everything, were sometimes an outright handicap in the development of appraisal standards and were largely responsible for an ambivalence that became more obvious when the National Archives extended its interests to preaccession phases of the life cycle of records. See p. 31.

34. Ken Munden, a recent editor of the *American Archivist*, has analyzed the history of the journal in "The *American Archivist:* The Measure of Its Success and Failure" (unpublished typescript of a paper

nual Report of the Archivist and National Archives informational and instructional publications such as the *Bulletins of the National Archives*, begun in 1936, and *Staff Information Papers*, first issued in 1938, made available to archivists the first substantial American contributions to the preservation and administration of archives.

Thus, without significant native experience and with just one English-language textbook on archival methodology,[35] the staff of the National Archives was forced to draw upon its own interest in and knowledge of history and government as the foundation upon which it developed principles and procedures for launching the nation's archival program. A review of the 34-year history of the institution reveals the remarkable soundness of the program that it developed; its principles and techniques have now been largely adopted by both public and private archival institutions in the United States and have exerted great influence even upon long-established archival programs throughout the world. Not the least accomplishment of the National Archives in its formative years, therefore, was its emphasis upon training—an emphasis that led in 1939 to the introduction of courses in archival methodology by Solon J. Buck and Ernst Posner at the American University. It was the latter institution that provided most of the formal archival training in the United States.[36]

It was only three years after the National Archives Establishment came into existence that it was obliged to defend its independent status against the first of a series of recurrent proposals aimed at the possible absorption of certain smaller agencies by larger ones. The fact that the National Archives was responsible for the records of all three branches of the federal government, and that this indispensable element of its responsibility had

---

read before the Society of American Archivists in New York City on October 8, 1965).

35. Hilary Jenkinson's *A Manual of Archive Administration* (London: Percy Lund, Humphries & Company, Ltd., 1937) had first been published in 1922; S. Muller, J. A. Feith, and R. Fruin's *Manual for the Arrangement and Description of Archives*, the "Dutch Manual," was not translated into English until 1940, when it was published by the H. W. Wilson Company, New York, with Arthur H. Leavitt as translator. The first American textbook on the subject—T. R. Schellenberg, *Modern Archives: Principles and Techniques* (Chicago: University of Chicago Press)—was not published until 1956.

36. See Chapter 10.

called for an independent status, suggested what the response to such a proposal would be. The Archivist, R. D. W. Connor, was both experienced in administration and fully conversant with the discussions among historians and others that had led to the creation of the National Archives as an independent agency. He therefore gave immediate and emphatic opposition to the suggestion: Congress intended that the National Archives should be the custodian of records of *all* agencies of the federal government and therefore independent of any executive agency. After outlining the reasoning behind the Congressional action he repeated, "It seems logical to assume from this analysis of the act creating the National Archives Establishment, that it was the intent of Congress to set it up as an independent establishment . . . to make it independent of any particular executive department or other agency except Congress." He continued, "Not only was this . . . the intent of Congress; it is also, tested by the experience of other nations as well as by the experience of many of the states of the American Union, the most efficient plan of archival organization and administration." He concluded:

> I am very strongly of the opinion . . . that any legislation which makes it possible, now or hereafter, for any of the essential functions of the National Archives Establishment to be transferred to, or for the Establishment itself to be placed under the jurisdiction of any particular executive department, would not be in the interest of either economy or efficiency, but would handicap the National Archives Establishment in performing the duties required of it by law.[37]

The force of Connor's logic was incontestable. To make so radical a departure from the plain intent of Congress was worse than illogical. It also flew in the face of experience. No mere concept of administrative efficiency could be permitted to deflect the object for which historians had labored so long and to which the Congress had so recently given legislative sanction. Connor was not only an experienced archival administrator acquainted

37. R. D. W. Connor to "The Chairman, Senate Select Committee on Government Organization," July 1, 1937, in Record Group 64, Records of the National Archives.

with the discussions that had taken place among historians and others about the kind of establishment required for the federal government, he was also the head of an independent agency with direct access to the White House and to the Congress. His emphatic opposition to an alteration in the status of the National Archives was effective. But when the threat to independence was renewed a decade later under similar and better organized drives for administrative efficiency, Jameson and many of his generation of historians, who regarded the state of the records of the nation as a peculiar professional responsibility, had passed from the scene. The then Archivist of the United States, Wayne C. Grover, newly appointed from the career service, made a valiant stand, but the forces against which he contended had been augmented tremendously and his allies in the historical profession correspondingly diminished. With the help of President Roosevelt in 1937, Connor and the National Archives Establishment won; without the help of either his professional colleagues or the then President, a later Archivist—and the nation—lost in 1949.[38]

When Connor submitted his resignation, effective September 15, 1941, President Roosevelt wrote: "As the first Archivist of the United States you have not only laid the foundation but have built the actual structure of an extremely important and permanent repository of American historical source material. Your record is one which will always be acclaimed with well-deserved appreciation." [39] The President did not attempt to chronicle the accomplishments of seven years of archival effort, nor will this study, but in no nation had there been accomplished theretofore such an archival success story as was written by the United States from 1934 to 1941. Already in the Archives were 330,000 cubic feet of permanently valuable records, dating from the earliest days of the republic; principles and practices were being developed for appraising, accessioning, arranging, describing, and making available for use those records,[40] and,

38. See Chapter 3.

39. President Roosevelt to Connor, July 20, 1941, in Connor Papers, Southern Historical Collection, University of North Carolina Library, Chapel Hill.

40. It was only in the latter part of Connor's regime and in the early years of Buck's that this methodology was developed along modern archival lines. When the National Archives began its work in 1934 the

indeed, reference services were totaling 1,000 calls per day to government agencies, historians, and researchers of all types; millions of cubic feet of other records had been inventoried and their locations made known; a presidential archives had been established that was to provide a precedent for the future preservation of the papers of the Presidents, who previously had often allowed them to be destroyed or dispersed; a training program had been instituted that would inure to the benefit not only of the National Archives but also of the state archival agencies; a national association of archivists had been formed and a scholarly journal had begun publication; and modern and scientific methods of archival preservation, restoration, and duplication were being formulated. The United States of America, a nation that for 150 years had largely ignored its documentary resources, had finally taken a giant step toward the goals proposed by historians three decades earlier.

---

principles and techniques of the archival profession were not well defined. In its first years the staff was organized along library lines, with units for cataloging, classifying, servicing, and appraising records.

[2]

THE NEW DIMENSION: THE EXTENSION OF

ARCHIVAL INTERESTS TO RECORDS

MANAGEMENT, 1941–1949

*We may assume that gradually the archivists will be-
come the nation's experts who must be consulted in all
questions of public record making and record keeping
and likewise become the trustees who will safeguard the
written monuments of the past, of the present day, and of
the future.* —Ernst Posner, *1940*

*The archivist is to the government as a whole what the
records officers . . . are to the individual agencies.*
—Philip C. Brooks, *1942*

*No longer can anyone concerned with efficient Federal
administration turn his back on the [records] situation.
It is like keeping an elephant for a pet; its bulk cannot
be ignored, its upkeep is terrific, and, although it can be
utilized, uncontrolled it is potentially a menace. As the
agency of the Government with chief responsibility for
Federal records, the National Archives would be remiss
in its duty to the Government and people of the United
States if it did not actively concern itself with this elephantine records management problem.*
—Solon J. Buck, *1943*

S OLON J. BUCK, Director of Research and Publications in
the National Archives, was appointed by President Roosevelt to succeed R. D. W. Connor as Archivist of the United
States. He assumed his duties on September 18, 1941, and for
the next seven years the agency underwent a gradual transfor-
mation from a passive records repository to a service agency for
the benefit of both the government and the public. It is probable
that the war encouraged rather than discouraged this transfor-
mation, which was attended by mixed blessings, but which was
nevertheless inevitable if the National Archives was to become
the active agent of documentary preservation in the United

States. A nationally known scholar before joining the National Archives in 1935, Buck had raised the Minnesota Historical Society, which he headed, to a position of leadership among state historical agencies. He was the kind of historian who could not avoid concerning himself with every detail involved in the production and servicing of records. Conventional scholars on the National Archives staff—and many outside—grumbled at his tendency to involve himself in details that seemed to them to be of little relevance to the duty of an archivist.

But Solon Buck had on his staff a number of young archivists who looked beyond the ancient records in their possession: They realized that the unique knowledge of the archivist could benefit public administrators in their handling of modern records, and they knew that improvements in current record-keeping practices would enhance the quality of future accessions while providing safer techniques for separating records of continuing value from those that did not warrant permanent retention. With their help, Buck turned out to be a far-sighted planner in directing his institution into the murky area of "records administration," the precursor of modern records management.[1]

The traditional archival phases of the National Archives Establishment's program suffered significantly from the depletion of the staff during World War II and from shortages of materials and equipment. In 1942 employees in the agency numbered 502 (including temporary and non-archival personnel), but more than half of these entered service or left for war work. Some replacements were found, but it is vital to note that not until 1959 did the staff assigned specifically to the archival function again reach its 1942 strength of 315. Measurably weakened in personnel, the agency did the best it could to continue work in the fundamentals of the archival program—ap-

1. For biographical sketches of Buck, see Theodore C. Blegen, "Solon Justus Buck—Scholar-Administrator," and Ernst Posner, "Solon Justus Buck—Archivist," *American Archivist*, XXIII (July 1960), 259–262 and 263–269, respectively. Posner wrote: "He knew that the problem of records, from the day they come into existence in the agency of origin until they are finally either disposed of or deposited in the archival agency, should constitute the subject matter of an integrated program—records administration."
Veteran archivists of the Buck era still debate whether he led the National Archives into records administration or whether he was pushed into it by a combination of the needs of the time and the convictions of certain members of his staff.

praising, accessioning, arranging, describing, and servicing the more than a quarter of a million cubic feet of archives already in its possession. Progress in these fundamentals failed to keep pace with the influx of additional records, and the program of analyzing, inventorying, and describing records fell further and further behind. But in times of emergency, reallocation of emphases is a necessity. Consequently the National Archives, like all government agencies, altered its program to meet the most pressing demands of wartime. Space in Washington was at a premium, and the National Archives Building became a temporary home for both records and personnel of other departments. Some of its most promising young professionals were transferred to other agencies to handle the mounting quantities of records created as a result of the war. Some of the publications of the National Archives were curtailed during the war, but staff members continued to contribute articles to professional journals, particularly the *American Archivist*. And, significantly, the annual report of the Archivist of the United States, always a remarkable document and one that has sorely been missed since 1949, was issued on schedule each year.

The demands of war led the Archivist to report in 1946:

> The flood of records coming into the building, doubling within 2 years the holdings of the National Archives, the fourfold increase in the demand for reference service, the necessity that steps be taken to effect an orderly records retirement program for the Government as a whole, and a serious reduction in staff combined to squeeze out such deferrable though necessary work as records analysis and description. For 4 years it received only such odds and ends of attention as could be spared, with the result that there was built up a tremendous backlog of records for which not even preliminary checklists had been prepared by the National Archives.[2]

It was estimated that 589,000 cubic feet of records in the building still had not been "checklisted." The institution faced the formidable task of reshaping and accelerating its program of arrangement and description.

2. *Twelfth Annual Report of the Archivist of the United States for the Year Ending June 30, 1946*, p. 26.

Thus Buck's administration, like Connor's before him, was characterized by conditions that frustrated attempts to maintain essential archival controls over the torrents of records flowing into the Archives. This frustration, though, carried a blessing in disguise, for many of the archivists, in analyzing their problems, did not fail to see that such conditions could be avoided in the future if the records were better made, filed, and maintained in the creating agencies. They were aware also that economy and efficiency could be served by a more orderly control over records. As early as 1938 Connor wrote, "The efficient appraisal by The National Archives of records of questionable value and the subsequent destruction of useless material occupying office and storage space has already effected a saving in space equivalent to the capacity of several buildings and a saving in dollars that is difficult to estimate." He added, "The removal of records from containers that either can be used again or have salvage value produces another type of financial saving." [3]

It would be a mistake, however, to place too much weight upon economy in the creating agencies as a force behind the extension of archival interests to current records. The overriding consideration was the need for better control over the records of the federal government as a means of facilitating the appraisal process and of directing to the National Archives, in an orderly fashion, those to be preserved permanently. It was the archivist's duty to bring about this control. He must go beyond simply caring for the records that he was able to gather into his building. He must, in fact, promote throughout the government a "records administration" program designed to eliminate many of the problems being created unnecessarily by agencies without guidance in their record-making and record-keeping practices.

Ernst Posner, who moved to the United States in 1939 and whose distinguished archival career is internationally known,[4] gave a theoretical basis for archival interest in "records administration" when in 1940 he wrote:

3. *Fourth Annual Report, 1937–38*, p. 38.
4. For an intimate biographical sketch of Posner, see Paul Lewinson, "Introduction: The Two Careers of Ernst Posner," in Ken Munden (ed.), *Archives and the Public Interest: Selected Essays by Ernst Posner* (Washington: Public Affairs Press, 1967), pp. 7–19.

The authority of archives administrations to examine records still in the custody of the government agencies will prove to be a first step that leads to even broader powers. If all the public records of a nation are one sole undivided *fonds*, the agencies that are destined to receive and keep them ultimately will be justified in claiming the right to give their advice as to how the files of government offices should be organized and kept from the beginning so as to insure a satisfactory original arrangement that will also be suitable for retention by the archives agencies.[5]

It was within the National Archives, however, that the best justification was made for a gradually expanding program of concern for the manner in which current records were being created and maintained. The *Annual Report* stated the case as follows:

A prerequisite to the judicious selection of records either for permanent preservation or for disposal is an appraisal of their value, and this appraisal can be made more readily and with greater assurance if the records have been arranged and administered with their permanent preservation or their disposal in mind. Arrangement usually takes place, however, when the documents are filed, that is, when they are first consciously considered as record material. From this chain of circumstance it becomes apparent that The National Archives must inevitably be concerned with the creation, arrangement, and administration as well as with the appraisal, disposal, and preservation of Government records, and that in order to perform its functions satisfactorily it must have a knowledge of the records that can come only from a continuous survey of them.[6]

Members of the National Archives staff proposed that retention and disposition "schedules" be completed for the records of all government agencies and that there be developed a "comprehensive Government records program" that would include the

5. Ernst Posner, "Some Aspects of Archival Development," *American Archivist*, III (July 1940), 172. The Posner quotation in the epigraph is also from this page.
6. *Seventh Annual Report, 1940–41*, p. 1.

encouragement of greater planning by Government agencies in such matters as the filing and the microfilming of their records. In relatively few agencies is any attention given as yet to deciding, when a document is filed, whether it is actually worthy of preservation as a record; and few agencies at the time of filing segregate the documents into groups that must be preserved for periods of 1, 5, 7, 10, or more years and those that must be preserved permanently. As a result, great masses of heterogeneous records accumulate. They cannot safely be destroyed in their entirety, for there are valuable documents among them; they cannot economically be kept in their entirety, for the valueless documents among them will occupy costly space; and they cannot be segregated into groups according to value without great expenditures of time and money.[7]

That the National Archives itself should tackle the records problem alone was never envisioned. As the 1941 *Annual Report* declared, "A basic requirement for the permanent solution of the problem of records administration is the development by the agencies concerned of programs for reducing the quantity of records accumulated, and The National Archives should be prepared to assist the agencies in planning such programs." The report added, ". . . the time is opportune for progress toward the solution of the whole problem of records administration. . . ."[8]

Already in several departments comprehensive records programs were being developed by professional archivists previously on the National Archives staff. A "Federal Records Conference," composed of files personnel throughout the federal government in Washington, had been organized "as an outgrowth of the activities of local members of the Society of American Archivists" and an "interdepartmental committee for records administration" was being considered by the Civil Service Commission. The latter organization evolved into the Interagency Records Administration Conference, first under sponsorship of the Civil Service Commission and later of the National Archives and Records Service.

It is worthy of note that each annual report of the Archivist

7. *Ibid.*, pp. 4–5.   8. *Ibid.*, pp. 6, 8.

after 1941 devoted its first substantive section to "Records Administration," and upon occasion this section amounted to nearly 10 percent of the entire report. In 1942 it was reported that additional funds had been obtained from Congress "to expand the program of records administration, which had existed for some time in embryo form," and that the National Archives had assisted in establishing a records program in the Tennessee Valley Authority.[9] The following year, noting that the government's records holdings had risen to 16,000,000 cubic feet, only half of which were in Washington, and that the rate of annual production was 1,000,000 cubic feet, the Archivist urged greater efforts toward solving the "elephantine records management problem."[10] He noted with satisfaction:

> Expansion of records management programs throughout the Government was accompanied by the drafting of experienced National Archives personnel to administer these programs. The Navy Department's Office of Records Administration and several subdivisions of that Office and of the Records Division of the War Department are headed by former members of the staff of the National Archives. Others are serving or have served in strategic records positions in the War Production Board, the Board of Economic Warfare, the War Relocation Authority, and the Petroleum Administration for War, and a number have been loaned upon request to conduct surveys, direct scheduling, or plan the installation of records offices.[11]

Among the archivists who did the yeoman work in developing the National Archives' records administration program was Philip C. Brooks. Addressing the Society of American Archivists in 1942, Brooks called for the appointment in every federal agency of a records officer whose responsibility would extend beyond the preservation and disposal of records. He said:

> If he is to attain maximum usefulness, the records officer should advise administrators in the planning of forms and procedures so as to prevent the creation of unnecessary

9. *Eighth Annual Report, 1941–42*, pp. 3–9.
10. *Ninth Annual Report, 1942–43*, p. 5. See epigraph, p. 24.
11. *Ninth Annual Report, 1942–43*, p. 9. See also minutes of meeting of Open Conference on Administration, July 3, 1944.

papers and to have records properly identified; he should study filing schemes in all their bewildering variety so as to apply them properly in diverse circumstances; he should train the personnel doing mail and records work, whether they are under his immediate supervision or not; he should know how to evaluate records from the legal and administrative points of view, depending on archivists to define research uses; and finally he should administer the whole retirement program. . . . The archivist is to the government as a whole what the records officers . . . are to individual agencies.[12]

Brooks further noted the reluctance with which some archivists of the old school admitted the need for archival involvement in modern records but pointed out that eight articles favorable to the new responsibility had already been published in the *American Archivist* during its first four years. He concluded:

Current records administration is to the archivist of today what the study of diplomatics was to the archivist of earlier times—and more. Authorities on the qualifications of archivists say that archivists, in order to apply the principle of provenance, should know the methods by which records in their custody are produced. The complexities of modern administrative documentation have so multiplied the technical facets of filing that many persons regard it as a mysterious cult to be either feared or blandly ignored. Neither attitude is consistent with the principle that the whole life history of records is an integrated continuous entity. No period in that history can be ignored. It is inevitable that the iniquity of omitting care for records as they accumulate shall be visited upon the third and fourth generations of later administrators, archivists, research students, and society as a whole.[13]

12. Philip C. Brooks, "Current Aspects of Records Administration," *American Archivist*, VI (July 1943), 162–163. See also Brooks, "The Selection of Records for Preservation," *American Archivist*, III (October 1940), 221–234; Commission on Organization of the Executive Branch of Government, *Records Management in the United States Government: A Report with Recommendations* (Washington: Government Printing Office, 1949), p. 31; and Buck, in *Tenth Annual Report, 1943–44*, p. 11.
13. Brooks, "Current Aspects of Records Administration," p. 164.

Archivists brought up in the stern school of experience in the National Archives carried their convictions like missionaries into the profession and later into business. Emmett J. Leahy, trained in the National Archives, in 1941 persuaded the Society of American Archivists to change the name of the committee of which he was chairman from that of Committee on Reduction of Archival Material to Committee on Records Administration.[14] Leahy's successor in 1945 as committee chairman was Philip Brooks, who prepared a brief manual on records administration that was finally published four years later under the title *Public Records Management*,[15] the best early statement of the need for archival participation in records management.

The passage of the Records Disposal Act of 1943, which with subsequent amendments authorized continuing disposal schedules for specified records common to all or many agencies, was a major achievement in which the National Archives participated. Still, the law failed to prevent the accumulation of 18,000,000 cubic feet of records by the end of the war. These records, scattered in hundreds of thousands of offices, depots, and warehouses throughout the world, were sufficient to fill eighteen buildings the size of the National Archives or to reach nearly to the top of the Washington Monument when stacked over an acre of ground. Apologetic because lack of staff and funds had made it impossible for the National Archives to conduct a records administration program "on a wholly adequate scale," the Archivist nevertheless in 1945 was encouraged by "the ever-widening circle of interest in records management both as an adjunct to efficient administration and as an aid to research."[16]

After the war many temporary agencies were liquidated and much attention was given to the appraisal of the records of those agencies with a view toward destroying records of no further value. President Truman issued an executive order in which he directed that each agency develop an active records management program and that the Bureau of the Budget "with the advice

14. *American Archivist*, III (April 1940), 123; IV (April 1941), 136; and V (June 1942), 59.
15. *Public Service Publication*, No. 103 (Chicago: Public Administration Service, 1949).
16. *Eleventh Annual Report, 1944–45*, p. 10.

and assistance of the National Archives" conduct inspections, require reports, and issue directives and regulations concerning the orderly disposal of unnecessary records.[17] This executive order was a major records management landmark. Hindsight suggests that it was not without its snare. Based upon a broad interpretation of the National Archives Act of 1934 and upon the principle enunciated by the Society of American Archivists in 1940 that the chief archival officer should have general supervision over the "making, administration, and preservation" of all public records,[18] the full responsibility outlined in the executive order should have been placed in the National Archives. This would have seemed particularly fitting in view of the fact that the concern was legitimately an outgrowth of the National Archives' advocacy of records administration programs for the preceding five years. Even so, the Bureau of the Budget was the executive agency with the necessary controls to force a degree of compliance by other federal agencies, and it was this power that appealed to the agency records officers. At the time there appears to have been no suspicion on the part of the Archivist that some day this leverage would be used as an argument for placing records management functions in a general services agency.[19]

The presidential order brought to the National Archives a "flood of calls for help," and an important milestone was reached: More records were destroyed during the year than were created. Buck wrote:

> The seemingly endless pyramiding of Government records, then, has come to a stop. Furthermore, it is not too much to expect that the efficient management of current records, promoted by records administration programs such as the National Archives has been advocating for the last 5 years, and a continued aggressive attack on the accumulations of noncurrent Federal records can in a rea-

17. Executive Order #9784 of September 25, 1946. In the same year Buck wrote, "The Bureau of the Budget also usually refers to us for a report on the feasibility of a project if an agency requests a substantial sum of money for microfilming" (Buck to George W. Brown, University of Toronto, March 11, 1946, in Records of the National Archives).
18. "The Proposed Uniform State Public Records Act," *American Archivist*, III (April 1940), 107–115.
19. See pp. 41 ff.

sonable length of time—perhaps 10 years—practically wipe out the backlog. That, of course, is one of the long-range objectives of the National Archives, but in our efforts to attain it we are faced with a real challenge. The appraisal of records, the burden of which rests upon the National Archives, becomes more and more complex as obviously useless material is eliminated and borderline and then valuable records must be appraised. This process of evaluation demands the highest professional competency. It requires knowledge of the Government and its functions and the imagination to foresee what uses Federal agencies may make of Government records, an understanding of the rights of United States citizens and of the records that must be kept to protect those rights, and a broad appreciation of the place of the Nation's archives in the totality of materials for research that is the cultural heritage of America. Now that the mechanics of disposal have been improved, the attention of the National Archives must be centered on this all-important problem of evaluation.[20]

To succeed Buck upon his resignation effective May 31, 1948, President Truman continued the example of his predecessor by appointing another competent scholar, Wayne C. Grover, as Archivist of the United States.[21] Grover thus became the first Archivist to have grown up in the profession. His experience was broadened when during the war he transferred to the War Department and established one of the outstanding records management programs in the government. Following the war he returned to the National Archives as Buck's chief assistant.

In assessing his predecessor's role in fostering improved records practices in the federal government, Grover wrote:

Abjuring the traditionally conservative attitude of archival agencies, the National Archives during Dr. Buck's administration entered the current records administration field. The Government's records problems, numerous enough before World War II, became acute with the outbreak of

20. *Twelfth Annual Report, 1945–46*, p. 15.
21. The danger of a political appointment raised its head in 1948 and again in 1953, but Presidents Truman and Eisenhower wisely heeded the appeals of professionals.

the war. It was obvious that leadership was needed to induce Federal agencies, especially the temporary ones, to apply modern money-saving and time-saving management methods to their record-making and record-keeping, to dispose of useless materials promptly, and to plan for the ultimate disposition of all their files. As the central agency with major responsibility for the welfare of Government records and as the eventual victim or beneficiary of the records management practices of Federal agencies, the National Archives took the initiative in encouraging and assisting other agencies to establish records administration programs. So effective were many of them that in 1947 [1946] the President ordered all Federal agencies to conduct records retirement programs.[22]

Solon Buck's administration thus projected the National Archives into an uncharted wilderness called "records administration." This audacity would have been unusual under any circumstances, but for it to come from the encouragement of a scholarly historian of Buck's stripe was extraordinary. Even most of the traditionalists on the staff who had not restrained their doubts early in the 1940s were forced by 1948 to recognize the validity of the argument that only through an orderly program of records creation and maintenance in the agencies could the archival establishment properly carry out its responsibility for all public records.

The 17-year administration of Wayne Grover, trained initially in the National Archives and experienced as an agency records manager, enlarged upon the concepts inherent in the 1943 disposal act and the 1946 executive order and adapted them to new circumstances and new challenges. Beginning about 1948, the term "records administration"[23] gradually gave way to "records management."[24] Thus the "Grover era"

22. *Fourteenth Annual Report, 1947–48*, p. 4.
23. The term was at the time generally defined as "correspondence management, with the emphasis on form letters, files management, mail management, records storage, documentation, and surveys and audits, but with the emphasis in all of these activities on records disposition" (Frank B. Evans, "Archivists and Records Managers: Variations on a Theme," *American Archivist*, XXX [January 1967], 48).
24. To some archivists and records managers there was no essential difference between what Buck called "records administration" and what

consummated the transition of the National Archives from an archival agency of the traditional kind to a true national archives and records administration.[25]

One of Grover's first interests was the acquisition of additional space, both for accessioned archives and for economical storage of records still in the agencies. Already the National Archives Building was bulging with more than 850,000 cubic feet representing most of the early records of permanent value, but hundreds of thousands of cubic feet of additional materials remained to be transferred. The space crisis had been foreseen at least as early as 1941, at which time President Roosevelt suggested to the Archivist the possibility that the War Department Building—the Pentagon—then under construction, might after the "emergency" be used as an "archives annex." Should this come to pass, Buck wrote, "The annex might well serve . . . as a temporary storage space for noncurrent records scheduled for destruction at a fixed time in the future, as a depository for records of doubtful value until the passage of time provides the answer to their ultimate fate, and perhaps as a permanent home for noncurrent records that are relatively inactive." [26] Buck also called attention to the great quantities of federal records located outside of Washington and suggested the possibility of field archives, thus anticipating by nearly a decade the development of federal records centers and regional archives.

Grover and his associates came to call "records management." Nevertheless the program after 1949 did add new dimensions—Federal Records Centers, for example—and new emphases, and it appears justifiable to use the terms in vogue at the various periods in the history of the institution. Beginning in 1955, "paperwork management"—encompassing the handling of papers before they are filed—became an officially recognized term.

25. Archivists disagree on the definition of the words "archives" and "records." Men like Leland, Buck, and England's Sir Hilary Jenkinson objected strongly to the narrowing of the definition of "archives" to records designated for permanent preservation. To them public records were archives regardless of their location or retention value. "Archives" and "records" represented words meaning exactly the same thing coming out of two different language sources. Buck, recognizing the advantages of using the word "records" instead of "archives" in communicating with laymen, nevertheless regarded as tautological the change of the name of the national program in 1950 to the "National Archives and Records Service," and once expressed the hope that after a while, when government officials had been sufficiently educated, the title could return to "The National Archives" as a name for the entire service.

26. *Seventh Annual Report, 1940–41*, pp. 5–8.

In 1944 Buck asked that future construction plans take into consideration a "public records building." [27] The next year he was more specific:

It is also highly desirable that the facilities available to the National Archives for the storage of records be expanded sufficiently so that it can assign to other agencies of the Federal Government secure, well-planned, inexpensive space for the temporary housing of records of continuing value that must be retained in their custody until they are no longer needed or until they have become sufficiently noncurrent to permit transfer to the custody of the Archivist. . . . One Government agency has stated that it would like to have the National Archives make available to it for 10 years space sufficient to accommodate 200,000 cubic feet of valuable records that must remain in its custody.[28]

Later in the same year an ill-fated bill was introduced in the Congress to authorize a building at Suitland, or elsewhere, at a cost not to exceed $6,500,000 "for the safe but inexpensive storage of records that must be retained for a while before they are destroyed or transferred to the National Archives—records that are now often housed in space for which the Government must pay high rentals." [29] The requested construction was not provided for, but within two years a portion of an existing building in Suitland was assigned to the National Archives, and the new Archivist held discussions with the Public Buildings Administration concerning the "possibilities for further space-creating construction in the building and for the construction of a Federal Records Center, to include permanent facilities for the storage and administration of both paper records and film." [30] This reference in the Archivist's annual report may have been the first upper-case use of the term "Federal Records Center," though the idea had been advanced years earlier.

Thus the concept of records centers, like that of records

27. *Tenth Annual Report, 1943–44*, p. 61.
28. *Eleventh Annual Report, 1944–45*, pp. 40–41.
29. *Twelfth Annual Report, 1945–46*, p. 46.
30. *Fourteenth Annual Report, 1947–48*, pp. 43–44. It is interesting to observe that a mammoth Federal Records Center has recently been opened in Suitland—20 years later.

management, was the product of a natural evolution. Already various federal agencies had established about a hundred individual low-cost records centers, and North Carolina in 1947 appropriated funds to its State Department of Archives and History for a new, specially designed records center for the housing of relatively inactive modern records.[31] The concept was, moreover, evidence of the growth of the concern of the National Archives for the efficient and economical management of the nation's records, a concern that had come a long way from the less sophisticated ideas expressed ten years before. The National Archives by 1949 was anxious to expand into a full-fledged staff service agency for all federal agencies as well as for the public. The hour was to come sooner than expected for the realization of an object long anticipated.

By no means all archivists—particularly those outside the National Archives—were happy with the widening of archival interests in the direction of current records management. If few spoke out, many maintained a painful silence while reading searchingly the warnings of a United Nations archivist in 1948:

> Among American archivists the cost [of archival involvement in records management] has been the abandonment of the tradition of scholarship and research, desertion of historiography, and renunciation of a broad intellectual comprehension of the records, particularly an understanding of how they relate to the world of reality beyond the walls of the repository. The professional archivist is atrophying. At one time, he was coming to be recognized on a coequal status, as the research partner of the historian, the economist, the administrator and scientist. It was considered of primary importance that the archivist should be able to render his documents, however complex and specialized, available and usable. Now it appears to be sufficient to house the records safely, to mechanize refer-

31. Fannie Memory Blackwelder, "The North Carolina Records Management Program," *North Carolina Historical Review*, XXXVI (July 1959), 346. Emmett J. Leahy is credited with establishing in the Navy Department the first identifiable "records center" about 1941. Herbert E. Angel, "In Memoriam: Emmett Joseph Leahy, 1910–1964," *American Archivist*, XXVII (October 1964), 508.

ence service on the documents, and to keep storage and maintenance costs down to a minimum by means of wholesale records destruction.[32]

Irving Schiller's concern was shared by other scholars whose contacts with the National Archives were limited to their roles as researchers and users of the records. This concern was not only legitimate, it was also prophetic. They foresaw the danger of overemphasis on one function at the expense of another, a danger that some qualified observers believe became a reality in the succeeding two decades. Part of the alarm resulted from a lack of familiarity with the professional problems of the archivist, but there was more than a grain of truth in the warning. What these doubters did not understand, however, was that there was also ambivalence among the leadership of the National Archives—an ambivalence that militated against the forecast of the traditionalists. Buck, Grover, and Bahmer, it should be noted with gratitude, did not trade their archival birthright for the magic of the words "economy" and "efficiency." They led the National Archives up the path that all public archival institutions must inevitably take if their programs are to encompass both present and future documentation as well as that of the past. But with a dogged determination born of their training as archivists, they guarded as best they could against a disporportionate emphasis upon preaccession phases of archival administration. If they were not always successful, it was because of forces beyond their control. Indeed the solution to the issues being faced in 1968 will determine whether Schiller's doleful predictions of 1948 yet become a reality.

32. Irving P. Schiller, "The Archival Profession in Eclipse," *American Archivist,* XI (July 1948), 229–230.

[3]

THE LOSS OF INDEPENDENCE, 1949

. . . any legislation which makes it possible, now or hereafter, for any of the essential functions of the National Archives Establishment to be transferred to, or for the Establishment itself to be placed under the jurisdiction of any particular executive department, would not be in the interest of either economy or efficiency, but would handicap the National Archives Establishment in performing the duties required of it by law.
—R. D. W. Connor, *1937*

. . . I object to having records and archives grouped with office desks, lamps, rugs, and other items of supply as if there is a fraternity of interest or identity of interest in the administration of the one with the other . . . .
—Robert H. Bahmer, *1949*

It should never be lost sight of that the National Archives is a dual purpose institution—a cultural agency and a service agency. Its strength will lie in keeping these purposes balanced through the years. . . . [O]ur cue should be to counter those forces [threatening to make the National Archives predominantly a government service agency] by emphasizing our cultural responsibilities to keep us from being submerged as an appendage to a larger service agency. We should not pull so hard to that side that we are likely to sever ourselves from the service responsibilities that we have developed, but we must emphasize that the cultural side exists and has its own justifications. . . . —Oliver W. Holmes, *1949*

THE RECORDS ADMINISTRATION PROGRAM of the National Archives from 1941 to 1949 was financed largely from the agency's regular budget and administered by its archival staff. In this sense the activities in the field of records administration were at the expense of the basic programs of accessioning, arranging, describing, and servicing the records of permanent value. The entire National Archives staff, including employees in non-archival work, in 1948 numbered only about 340—less than 70 percent of its size six years earlier. Moreover,

40

after nearly a decade of gradual extension of aid to other departments, the National Archives found that the problems relating to records still in the agencies were multiplying instead of decreasing. Though the liquidation of various wartime emergency agencies had led to disposal of great masses of records, and though a growing number of departments had established improved records programs, the federal government's record-making propensity indicated that never again would the nation's paperwork fall to its prewar level in either quantity or simplicity. Thus while the records administration program of the National Archives, encouraged by the Bureau of the Budget, was making identifiable contributions in meeting the most serious of the problems, it could not cope with the increasingly complex situation without additional legislation, funds, and personnel. The program, after all, had been based only on the authority of the National Archives to examine and appraise.

At this crucial point an opportunity presented itself for a high-level study of the nation's records problems. Congress in 1947 had established the Commission on the Organization of the Executive Branch of the Government, made up of a dozen distinguished Americans and chaired by former President Herbert Hoover, to undertake detailed studies of government programs and services. This Hoover Commission was in the process of appointing a number of "task forces" for specialized investigations. Early in 1948 Emmett J. Leahy, until 1941 a member of the staff of the National Archives, during the war the prime mover in the Navy Department's outstanding records management program, and subsequently founder of the National Records Management Council (a private New York corporation), suggested the need for a study of federal records problems.[1]

1. Leahy to Herbert J. Miller, undated but apparently written in January 1948, in Records of the First Hoover Commission, RG 264, National Archives. To the letter was appended a six-page proposal for a "task force on federal records problems" in which Leahy offered his "assistance or personal participation." As director of the Navy Department's records management program from 1941 to 1945, as organizer of the National Records Management Council, and as coauthor of an important textbook on the subject, Leahy was the father of the new profession. For a biographical sketch, see Herbert E. Angel, "Emmett Joseph Leahy, 1910–1964," *American Archivist*, XXVII (October 1964), 507–508. An Emmett Leahy Award is given annually by the magazine *Information and Records Management* to a man or woman "whose unique contribu-

Wayne C. Grover, then Assistant Archivist of the United States, endorsed the proposal for a study to resolve the following questions: (1) Where did staff responsibility for records management lie? (2) What were the respective responsibilities of staff agencies and operating agencies? (3) Should there be a new general records act? (4) What was the proper role of the intermediate records storage centers? [2] The Commission was impressed, and on April 12, 1948, it contracted with the National Records Management Council for a task force survey of federal records programs. Leahy himself directed the study. His consultants were Herbert E. Angel, Director of Office Methods for the Navy Department; Edward B. Wilber of the Department of State; Frank M. Root of Westinghouse Electric Corporation; and Grover himself for a few weeks (until his appointment as Archivist of the United States), after which he was replaced by his assistant, Robert H. Bahmer. Though only one formal meeting of the group was held, Grover, Bahmer, Angel, Wilber, and others were consulted frequently during Leahy's visits to Washington. The "Leahy Report," as the task force report was unofficially but appropriately named, was indeed Leahy's. It was submitted to the Commission on October 14, 1948, and was published in January 1949.[3]

Characteristically, the Leahy report began with an explanation of the proliferation of public records, which had made record-making and record-keeping "the greatest consumers of salaries, space, and equipment of all the housekeeping or service activities of the Federal Government." [4] The magnitude of the problem was stated in dollars: $1,000,000,000 was being spent each year on salaries of personnel engaged in handling records,

---

tions to records control, filing, and information retrieval have advanced the information and records management profession."

2. Robert W. Krauskopf, "The Hoover Commissions and Federal Record-keeping," *American Archivist*, XXI (October 1958), 375–376. See also Oliver W. Holmes, "The National Archives at a Turn in the Road," *American Archivist*, XII (October 1949), 339–354, and Wayne C. Grover, "Recent Developments in Federal Archival Activities," *American Archivist*, XIV (January 1951), 8.

3. Commission on Organization of the Executive Branch of the Government, *Records Management in the United States Government: A Report with Recommendations* (Washington: Government Printing Office, 1949). The document will hereafter be cited as Leahy, *Task Force Report*.

4. Leahy, *Task Force Report*, p. 2.

$154,000,000 was tied up in equipment, the annual rental value of space in which the records were stored was estimated at $27,000,000, and an additional $20,000,000 was being spent annually on space operation and maintenance.

The "attempts in program sponsorship" by the National Archives and the Bureau of the Budget were described as having been "sharply limited to the few phases of records management that most directly effect the isolation and eventual transfer of the small percentage of records which have permanent value and historical interest." Much more was needed, Leahy argued, in the form of a "central agency to undertake this staff function of developing a program, providing experienced counsel and expert assistance, and sponsoring training programs." Specifically, the report proposed an entirely new agency with authority over standards and controls for record-making and record-keeping, selective records preservation, scheduled records disposal, and transfer of records to records centers; application of tested methods, practices, materials, equipment, and machines; inspection of federal records and requiring reports as to their management; training programs directed at improving the effectiveness and technical knowledge of personnel assigned to record-making and record-keeping; and standards and controls for physical, legal, and security safeguards of all federal records. It recommended the establishment of central records centers to serve all agencies and the consequent reduction of the "more than 100 duplicating and overlapping records centers established in the last 10 years by less than a score of the departments and agencies." It estimated that 2,000,000 cubic feet of records then in office buildings could be placed in records centers alongside the 6,000,000 already in agency centers at an annual saving of $6,500,000.

The proposals, though more far-reaching, were not unlike others suggested earlier by the National Archives. The greatest surprise of the Leahy report, therefore, was not that it suggested a broader staff service program, but rather that it did not propose the placement of that responsibility in the National Archives. Instead, it recommended that "a Federal Records Administration be established and that the existing National Archives Establishment become an integral part thereof." [5] His

5. Leahy, *Task Force Report*, p. 8. Leahy wrote in the report, "If at this time or in the future, a department of general administration is

reasoning, Leahy reported, was based on the assumption that to place the new responsibilities in the National Archives would "change the character and scope of the National Archives so radically as to create, in fact, a new kind of agency." After all, he wrote, the "essential specialized function of The National Archives is limited to only 5 percent of Federal records," and the "95 percent of Federal records outside The National Archives present primarily a management rather than an archival problem." [6] What Leahy failed to see was that it was he who proposed to "change the character and scope of the National Archives so radically as to create, in fact, a new kind of agency." He advocated a disavowal of the nurturing principles that had ushered in the new profession and such exemplars of its techniques as himself. He was advocating, in brief, not the principle of continuity but the principle of separation. It was, furthermore, no argument to say that the specialized function of the National Archives was limited to only 5 percent of federal records. Connor and Buck had seen this long before Leahy did, and he could use it as an argument only by forgetting entirely the insistence of Buck, Brooks, and others on the principle that responsibility for that 5 percent could be met effectively only by being involved in decisions concerning the other 95 percent.

Though professing to continue the National Archives "as an integral and vital" part of the centralized agency, the Leahy report actually sought to subordinate it to a Federal Records

---

established, the inclusion of the Federal Records Administration therein should be considered." This was in direct conflict with Leahy's sentiments expressed subsequently when he said, ". . . my preference, a personal preference but not that of the Commission, is an independent agency." Quoted in Interagency Records Administration Conference, *Report of Seventh Meeting, 1948–49 Season, March 18, 1949: The Report of the Hoover Commission on Records Management* (mimeographed), p. 16. Cited hereafter as Interagency Records Administration Conference, *Report of March 18, 1949.*

6. Leahy, *Task Force Report*, p. 24. A new records act was proposed as the second major recommendation. Such an act would consolidate and improve existing laws by defining records and fixing responsibilities for their making, keeping, and disposal. The third proposal was "That each department and agency of the Federal Government be required by law, or by resolution of the Federal Records Administration Council approved by the President, to appoint or designate a qualified records management officer to plan, develop, and organize a records management program. The minimum content of a records management program should include tested controls of record making, record keeping and selective records preservation" (*Ibid.*, p. 11).

Administrator.[7] The case for the management of records centers by a new centralized agency rested on the premise that the records in such centers would "present primarily a management rather than an archival problem," that their handling involved techniques that were "administrative rather than archival," and that this handling should be done "for the most part by clerical and administrative employees rather than professional archival assistance." Only by creating a new Federal Records Administration, Leahy argued, could the management of great quantities of records in the records centers be coordinated "with the objectives and requirements of the National Archives." Leahy's error has been amply demonstrated by the effective management of the records centers since 1949 by the National Archives and Records Service.

The report of the task force, delivered to a powerful commission, whose work was supported by an influential and well-organized group called the Citizens' Committee for the Hoover Report, was not the sort of dispassionate analysis of the two main responsibilities of the National Archives concerning records that Buck had set forth in his far-reaching statement of 1941.[8] It made little attempt at appraising the substantial progress of the National Archives Establishment in records administration. It belittled the very significant contributions of the National Archives during the preceding decade in the particular area that it described as a mammoth national problem. It clinched the argument by glowing promises of savings to the amount of $32,000,000 per annum if only tested managerial techniques were applied to hacking away this administrative

7. The office of the Archivist of the United States as then constituted was to be abolished and its authority transferred to the Federal Records Administrator, who was to be appointed by the President by and with the advice and consent of the Senate. The "records and the professional staff" of the National Archives were to be placed "under the general direction of an outstanding archivist selected in accordance with Civil Service Regulations. . . ." (Leahy, *Task Force Report*, pp. 9–10). That this was indeed subordination was admitted by Leahy himself: "In honesty I've got to admit that the bulk of this Agency's [i.e., "a Federal Records Administration or . . . a Records Management Bureau in the Office of General Services"] problem is management rather than archival and that the Archives should be under it. . . ." (Interagency Records Administration Conference, *Report of March 18, 1949*, p. 16).

8. See p. 28. The task force began its work in April and completed its report in October.

jungle of records programs in the federal agencies. In brief, the Leahy report was an exercise in salesmanship. With commendable candor, Leahy himself later was quoted as conceding the fact: ". . . the Task Force Report is not a treatise on records management. It is not a textbook on records management. It is an action document and covers those things which it was considered necessary to call to the attention of the Commission, and to sell the Commission." [9]

And so it was and did. The devices of salesmanship required only the presentation of necessary information—necessary, that is, to persuade the Hoover Commission to adopt a particular recommendation. Such devices of salesmanship had been employed successfully in the business community by the author of the report. They were now wielded with equal effect upon a public commission whose mandate was economy in government. Under the impact of these carefully chosen arguments, Herbert Hoover, who as President had dedicated the National Archives to its dual responsibilities of service to government and to posterity,[10] was persuaded to lend his great influence to the primary goal of economy. Arguments of a countervailing tendency addressed to the other great purpose for which archives exist were either not solicited or not regarded. The crucial opportunity to affect legislation dealing with all aspects of the records problems of the nation thus came at an inauspicious moment. Had this opportunity presented itself a decade earlier or a decade later, there can be little doubt that the subsequent history of the National Archives would have been quite different, its achievements in both areas of its responsibility more impressive. Leahy's argument that the proposed expanded records management activities be placed not under the Archivist of the United States but rather under a new Federal Records Administrator was, therefore, reactionary, a brake upon efficiency and not a promoter of it. However well intended, it was an undeserved, ill-conceived, and potentially disastrous blow to the agency that had been the first to advocate an efficient program of records administration and the most constructive single force toward its accomplishment. Such was the ironic reward for the achieve-

9. Leahy's statement was published in Interagency Records Administration Conference, *Report of March 18, 1949*, p. 16.
10. See p. 10.

ments of the National Archives in this area since the Archivist of the United States first defined the goal in 1941.

The task force report, published in January, caused anxiety enough, but it was only a committee proposal, and there was hope among archivists that the Hoover Commission would not accept its recommended organizational changes. Nevertheless, Leahy's emphasis on records management as a *management* function naturally suggested to the Commission its candidacy for inclusion in a general services agency that was already being contemplated. Consequently the Commission's report on an Office of General Services,[11] published in February, scrapped the idea of an independent Federal Records Administration in favor of creating a "Records Management Bureau in the Office of General Services, to include the National Archives."

The Hoover Commission's recommendations created a state of frustration in the leadership of the National Archives. For years the institution had worked toward the general goals advocated by the task force report in relation to records management and records centers. Now, however, the National Archives was faced with a proposal that it become an adjunct to a new central staff agency with broader authority than had ever before been suggested. The result of this dilemma was that members of the National Archives staff exhibited contradictory attitudes in their vain effort to retain identity as an independent agency. Adoption of a firm stand was made more difficult by conflicting opinions among the leadership. Some, never happy with the agency's dabbling in records administration, proposed a retrenchment and an all-out drive to reestablish the National Archives as simply an archival repository. Others, painfully aware of both the theoretical and practical necessity of archival involvement in records management, proposed, in accordance with the recommendation in the task force report, that an effort be made to incorporate the broadened program in the existing National Archives Establishment. Anguished soul searching and discussion occupied the top staff members throughout the first half of 1949.

11. Commission on Organization of the Executive Branch of the Government, *Office of General Services: A Report to the Congress, February 1949* (Washington: Government Printing Office, 1949), pp. 5–9.

As early as January 28, Grover, who had succeeded Buck the previous year as Archivist, suggested to Chairman Hoover that any centralization of records management activities could best be performed within the framework of the National Archives, a going organization with experience in the field.[12] Nevertheless, the Hoover Commission's report on an Office of General Services stated that "A new central records service is needed to consolidate and reduce the records centers which various Government agencies now operate, and to direct the work of these regional records centers along with that of the National Archives in Washington," and recommended establishment of a Records Management Bureau in the proposed Office of General Services.[13] Concern among archivists now turned to alarm. Dismayed by the Hoover Commission proposals, top staff members at an Archivist's Conference on February 15 expressed a tentative willingness to wash their hands of records management activities as the only means of preventing their institution from being thrown into the government's new housekeeping agency. Even the Archivist himself was quoted as saying that "we should stop pretending we are experienced in records management techniques and . . . we should get out of such activities." [14]

Such sentiments, however, appear to have been only the result of the disappointment caused by disclosure of the Commission's recommendations, and not a result of an objective consideration of the role that the National Archives had played during the previous eight years. Within a few days, in fact, the task of calmly considering the views of the leadership and the formulation of a staff paper on the matter was assigned to T. R. Schellenberg, Program Adviser, and Arthur E. Young, Archival Procedural Officer. Among those who counseled against surrender of the principle of archival involvement in records management were Oliver W. Holmes, formerly Program Adviser but

12. Cited in Krauskopf, "The Hoover Commissions," pp. 381–382.
13. Commission on Organization of the Executive Branch of the Government, *Office of General Services: A Report to the Congress, February 1949*, pp. 5, 8.
14. Quoted in minutes of a "Discussion at the Archivist's Conference, February 15, 1949" (typescript), in dossier titled "Transaction: 049–106. Formulation of recommendations with respect to the Hoover Commission Report on 'Records Management in the United States Government,' " Records of the National Archives. This source will hereafter be cited as Dossier 049–106.

then Director of the Natural Resources Records Division, and Collas G. Harris, Director of Administrative Services. The former had already written that the dual purpose of the National Archives—as a cultural agency and as a service agency—must continue to be "balanced." [15] Harris claimed fathership of the "Records Administration Program launched by the National Archives and approved by the Bureau of the Budget . . . in the early forties," and wrote further, "I still believe that it is a proper function of the National Archives to engage in records administration activities and hope it is not too late for this very important activity to be an objective of the National Archives." [16]

Another staff member, Harold Hufford, wrote that the Leahy report "merely iterates established principles and purposes long practiced by the National Archives and, in that respect, contributes nothing to the solution of records problems." He continued, "The archival function is a 'records management' function. The National Archives is vitally interested in Government records from the time they are created—interested in them as possible archival material—until they have been studied, sorted, and the chaff weeded therefrom." He noted that most of the records management programs in government had been started by archivists like Angel, Alldredge, Bishop, Brooks, Beach, Bourne, Claussen, Darter, East, Claus, Shipman, Grover, Bahmer, and Leahy himself. [17]

The 51-page Schellenberg-Young report, released on March 3, was the most responsible document to appear in connection with the Hoover Commission proposals concerning the National Archives. Its main thrust was that while archival administration could not be effectively divorced from records management, the professional functions of the National Archives should not be subordinated to managerial functions. It stated:

> When records are removed from offices to storage areas, archival methods are involved in every phase of their handling and are more applicable than current records management practices. The transfer of records, their place-

15. Statement of Oliver W. Holmes, January 26, 1949, in Dossier 049–106. See epigraph, p. 40.
16. Harris to T. R. Schellenberg, February 28, 1949, *ibid.*
17. Harold Hufford to Thad Page, February 28, 1949, *ibid.*

ment in the stacks, the development of controls over them, their processing, and their storage require "archival" techniques more than "records management" techniques. The importance of "archival" methods is accentuated whenever the records to be preserved include permanently valuable records, and whenever the processing of the records includes processing for purposes of permanent preservation. The processing for administrative and legal purposes should be done by agency personnel under proper professional disposition standards established by professionally-trained archivists. The inclusion of professionally-trained archivists on the staffs of the records depositories is thus vital to their effective operation.[18]

The Commission, Schellenberg and Young charged, "proposes an organization in which the professional [archival] functions are subordinated to the management functions. It makes a professional body (i.e. the National Archives) become a subordinate and passive recipient of records which a management agency decides should be kept. . . . It emphasizes management functions and management techniques in the work of the records centers."

With the Schellenberg-Young report in hand, the leading people in National Archives held a two-day meeting on March 8 and 9. The momentary panic that manifested itself three weeks earlier had dissipated, and those who had counseled withdrawal from records administration activities expressed second thoughts. There seemed to be a consensus that the National Archives could ill afford to reverse its philosophy of archival interests in the entire life span of records. The Archivist, noting that if the institution remained a dual cultural and service agency it could hardly "escape the evils" that go with being one, suggested that perhaps the Bureau of the Budget might carry on staff records management functions closely allied with office management activities, and that the National Archives retain its records retirement responsibilities. He proposed that the Ar-

18. T. R. Schellenberg and Arthur E. Young, "Recommendations with Respect to the Hoover Commission Report on 'Records Management in the United States Government,' " March 3, 1949 (mimeographed), p. 37, *ibid.*

chives support a move to "give statutory strength to the agencies' records management programs, including the management of depositories." The National Archives could then "maintain a quasi-independent status similar to that of the Smithsonian Institution, keeping to the National Archives its organic and other statutory authority, and relying on OGS only for budgetary and other central assistance." He suggested that the National Archives should fight for the *status quo ante* while at the same time making a strong argument for building up records management programs in the agencies. The National Archives could operate such of the depositories as necessary to hold permanently valuable records, and the field centers could be operated through the cooperation of the Bureau of the Budget, the Public Buildings Administration, the agencies themselves, and the National Archives.[19]

On March 18 the Interagency Records Administration Conference held a panel discussion on the Hoover Commission recommendations on records management. Participants included Robert H. Bahmer, Deputy Archivist; Philip C. Brooks, a former member of the National Archives staff but then with the National Security Resources Board; and Leahy. Following Leahy's defense of the recommendations, Bahmer forcefully objected to the absorption of the National Archives by another agency. He said:

> The point I wish to speak on briefly is a very limited one, but it is an important point to the archivist, particularly to those archivists in the National Archives—one we feel is so vital that we want it called to the attention of everyone concerned with giving a New Look to records management in the Federal Government. We don't want it to go by default. That point is the position of the National Archives in the proposed Bureau of Records Management in the proposed Office of General Services. My comments would probably bear equally on the proposed Federal Rec-

19. "Discussion at the Archivist's Conference, March 8 [and 9], 1949: Recommendations with Respect to the Hoover Commission Report on 'Records Management in the United States Government'" (typescript), *ibid.* These "minutes," which were often in the language of the minute-taker rather than the speaker, were prepared by Arthur E. Young.

ords Administration. . . . There are logical and convincing grounds for maintaining that the National Archives ought to continue its independent status in the Government scheme of organization. If one analyzes the National Archives Act, and studies the deliberations that lead [*sic*] to the passage of that act, I think it is clear that the intent was to establish an agency that would have a certain jurisdiction over the records of all three constitutional branches of the Government; legislative, executive and judicial. In the considerations that preceded the Act, it was perceived that there were clearly limitations on the power of Congress to exercise authority over records that were created under the authority of the President. On the other hand it was perceived that there were clearly limitations on the power of the President to exercise authority over records created under the authority of the Congress. To achieve what one person has called a matured national purpose of having one archives for the United States Government, the problem was solved by the creation of a National Archives Council and the Office of the Archivist, the National Archives Council having on it representatives of the legislative and executive branches. . . . My point is that it is representative of the two branches of the Government. I think you are familiar with the provisions of the National Archives Act. They give the Archivist of the United States charge and superintendence over the archives and records of the whole Government of the United States[,] "legislative, executive and the judicial and other." You are familiar with the Archivist's authority as concerns the establishment of rules and regulations for use and access to records; an extremely important authority in dealing with the three branches of the Government. You are familiar also, I am sure, with the authority of the National Archives Council relative to the establishment of the classes of records appropriate for requisitioning by the Archivist of the United States. I don't need to stress those points.

I think it is clear that the National Archives and the National Archives Council are quite different from the usual executive agency whose lines of authority are wholly to the Chief Executive. This fact should not be overlooked in any proposal to place the National Archives and the Archivist and the Archives Council, in the proposed Office of General Services, which has as its announced mission the administration of certain housekeeping functions, I want to underline the last words *"general to the executive departments and agencies of the Government."* It is unwise, I think, to contemplate the establishment of separate archival agencies for the three branches of the Government but that possibility should not be dismissed lightly, if there is taken away from the National Archives, the Archivist and the National Archives Council, their legal basis for dealing with the three branches of the Government. I don't deny, of course, that Congress and the President can change the situation as they will. All I can ask is that they be fully aware of the problem with which they are dealing. Congress and the President can place the responsibility now exercised by the Archivist and by the National Archives Council in anyone's hands. They can give it to the Director of the District of Columbia Incinerator Plant if they want to. They can give it to the Director of the Office of General Services. It is my feeling, however, that on reflection they will leave the present happy arrangements just as they are.

A second point that argues the undesirability of the transfer of the functions and responsibilities of the National Archives to the Office of General Services, relates to the Archivist's functions relative to the evaluation of records. In this matter the Archivist, I think it is clear, acts as the agent of the Congress, making recommendations to that body on proposals for the disposal of records submitted to him by the agencies and departments. I think the Archivist was given that authority because it was felt that his special professional competence fitted him to do the job. I do not think it was intended that his action should be reviewed by any other agency in the executive branch. Unless the Archivist's review, insofar as recommendations to Congress are concerned, is final, the basis, the real basis, for an independent and objective appraisal is gone. If the Archivist is placed under the Administrator of the Office of General Services and his recommendations conflict with the recommendations of his boss, it's clear as to whose recommendations will in the end prevail.

In this respect I think I should comment, in the nature of an objection in part, to one statement in the Hoover Commission's Task Force report, to the effect that the essential specialized function of the National Archives is limited to 5% of the records in existence. That figure is probably correct insofar as the total volume of records that will ultimately be transferred to the custody and administration of the Archivist [is concerned]. It should be pointed out, however, that that 5% is selected, cooperatively, of course, with agency records officials, from the total volume, by the process of evaluation and appraisal. The Archivist is vitally interested in all of the records since from the total mass he must select that core to be preserved to document the functioning of the agencies of our Government. This selection or evaluation process is one of the essential specialized functions of the Archivist.[20]

Upon the invitation of President Truman, Archivist Grover on March 21 transmitted his formal comments on the Hoover Commission recommendations. He concurred wholeheartedly in points 2 and 3 of the recommendations, which called for a new records act and the establishment of expanded records management programs in each department and agency. He then devoted seven pages to opposition to the inclusion of the National Archives in the proposed Office of General Services. "It is my conclusion," he wrote, "that the National Archives Council and the National Archives, because of their responsibilities and functions, are unique as to status in the Federal Government and should be given a position similar to that recommended for the Smithsonian Institution." He pointed out that Congress in 1934 had considered various possible locations of the National Archives and had concluded that, because its responsibilities extended to all three branches of government, the agency should occupy a position wholly under neither the executive nor the legislative branch. The National Archives Council, he pointed

20. Interagency Records Administration Conference, *Report of March 18, 1949*, pp. 8–10. See also *ibid.*, p. 20. The Bahmer quotation in the epigraph is from this same source.

out, was therefore made representative of both branches. "To place the National Archives and the Archivist of the United States in the proposed Office of General Services, which has as its mission the administration of certain housekeeping functions *general to the departments and agencies of the Executive Branch*, would disregard the responsibilities which the Archivist and the National Archives Council have concerning the archives of the Legislative and Judicial Branches," he wrote.

Should the Hoover Commission's proposed reorganization be carried out, Grover argued, the concept of the Archivist as the final arbiter in questions of disposal would be nullified. Congress had assumed, he wrote,

> that the professional competence of the Archivist fitted him to perform this review and that his recommendations, although of necessity properly coordinated, should be unreviewed by any other Executive agency. The transfer of the responsibility for the evaluation of records to the Director of the Office of General Services, even though this official might delegate it to the Archivist who presumably would be a part of his staff, would in any conflict of opinion remove completely the basis on which an objective and independent appraisal can be made.[21]

The Archivist expressed lack of enthusiasm for Leahy's proposal for central operation of records centers. He saw few potential savings accruing from elimination of individual agency records centers, and doubted if all agencies would be willing to transfer their records to centers organized and run by a government-wide authority. He felt that the existing Federal Records Center in Suitland, Maryland, could take care of records of agencies desiring such storage, and that if field records were not being properly cared for, the National Archives, in cooperation with the Public Buildings Administration and the agencies concerned, could "without additional authority take the initiative in

---

21. "Statement Relating to the Hoover Commission Report on Records Management," accompanying Grover's letter to the President, March 21, 1949, in Dossier 049–106. Grover might have explained that the training and experience of an archivist give him this "professional competence" to act as the agent of posterity in determining what documentation is to be preserved.

planning for additional records centers in the field, perhaps on a regional basis."

Grover found no justification for placing central staff authority over records management in a Records Management Bureau. Instead, he wrote, "There are some practical reasons . . . which could justify the location of a small records management staff group in the National Archives, as a separate unit of this agency." His reasons were (1) The National Archives, as the long-run beneficiary of improved records management programs in the agencies, would give the activity maximum support. (2) Any improvements in the procedural aspects of selective records preservation would be closely related to the substantive activities of the archival staff of the National Archives. (3) The National Archives could serve the legislative and judicial branches, as well as the executive agencies. "The National Archives receives many calls for technical assistance and advice on current records management practices from . . . agencies," he continued. "It complies with requests as well as it can. A small staff group especially trained, not in the archival aspects of such work but in its management aspects, would be better." [22]

But this powerful protest, reflecting the considered judgments of the Schellenberg-Young report and discussions in the National Archives, was to no avail. The Commission's final report recommended the creation of a Bureau of Records Management in the proposed general services agency and the transfer of the National Archives and its allied functions to that bureau. [23]

Several bills already under consideration by the Congress were amended to carry out the recommendations of the Hoover Commission by providing for the creation of a General Services Administration incorporating supply, property, and records functions. However, the bill that passed the House on June 8—H.R. 4754—omitted provisions for both the creation of a Bureau of Records Management and the transfer of the Archivist's responsibility for submitting disposal requests to Congress. Conceding that the die had been cast against continued

22. Grover to the President, March 21, 1949, *ibid.*
23. Commission on Organization of the Executive Branch of the Government, *Concluding Report: A Report to the Congress, May 1949* (Washington: Government Printing Office, 1949).

independence, the National Archives now sought to save as much as possible by persuading the Senate to accept the bill passed by the House. In a letter to the chairman of the Senate committee considering the legislation, Robert H. Bahmer, Acting Archivist, restated the opposition of the National Archives to the removal of the Archivist's appraisal authority and the creation of a Bureau of Records Management.[24] Concerning the development of records centers, Bahmer wrote: "I believe that the National Archives Establishment . . . in cooperation with the Public Buildings Administration and the agencies concerned, should take the initiative in planning for additional records centers in the field, perhaps on a regional basis. I do not think that this activity would warrant the creation of a new Records Management Bureau." He continued:

> It is worth noting that practically all of the major agency records centers now in existence were established under the supervision of personnel who received their training in the National Archives. While it is true that many of the operations in the records centers do not require a professional archival staff, it is equally true that these operations would benefit from archival advice and assistance. One of the major objectives of the records centers is the systematic destruction of records of temporary value. In the evaluation and appraisal of this material, the assistance of the professional archivist is essential.

Bahmer then turned his attention to the proposal that a small staff be provided to promote government-wide improvements and economies in records management: "I agree wholeheartedly that a small, central staff group of this kind is needed. I do not agree that the need for such a group justifies the establishment of a new bureau. Its activities, which should not be as broad as Mr. Leahy defines them, could well be performed within the framework of the National Archives Establishment." He endorsed a proposed act to define the objectives of the records management program and to require the preparation of disposal schedules, the establishment of intermediate depository operations, and the improvement of record-keeping practices; but

24. Bahmer to Senator John L. McClellan, June 28, 1949, in Dossier 049–106.

such a system, he said, "should be built around the National Archives Establishment. . . ."

Whether Bahmer's letter had any influence is doubtful, for the Senate bill—S. 2020—was passed, sustained in the conference committee, agreed to by the House, signed by President Truman, and thus became law. It removed virtually the last vestige of the Archivist's statutory authority by transferring even his disposal responsibilities to the Administrator.

Section 104 of the Federal Property and Administrative Services Act of 1949 [25] provided that, effective July 1, 1949:

(a) The National Archives Establishment and its functions, records, property, personnel, obligations, and commitments are hereby transferred to the General Services Administration. There are transferred to the Administrator (1) the functions of the Archivist of the United States except that the Archivist shall continue to be a member or chairman, as the case may be, of the bodies referred to in subsection (b) of this section, and (2) the functions of the Director of the Division of the Federal Register of the National Archives Establishment. The Archivist of the United States shall hereafter be appointed by the Administrator.

(b) There are also transferred to the General Services Administration the following bodies, together with their respective functions and such funds as are derived from Federal sources: (1) The National Archives Council and the National Historical Publications Commission, established by the Act of June 19, 1934 (48 Stat. 112), (2) the National Archives Trust Fund Board, established by the Act of July 9, 1941 (55 Stat. 581), (3) the Board of Trustees of the Franklin D. Roosevelt Library, established by the Joint Resolution of July 18, 1939 (53 Stat. 1062) and (4) the Administrative Committee established by section 6 of the Act of July 26, 1935 (49 Stat. 501), which shall hereafter be known as the Administrative Committee of the Federal Register. The authority of the Administrator under section 106 hereof shall not extend to the bodies or functions affected by this subsection.

(c) The Administrator is authorized (1) to make sur-

25. P.L. 152, 81st Cong.

veys of Government records and records management and disposal practices and obtain reports thereon from Federal agencies; (2) to promote, in cooperation with the executive agencies, improved records management practices and controls in such agencies, including the central storage or disposition of records not needed by such agencies for their current use; and (3) to report to the Congress and the Director of the Bureau of the Budget from time to time the results of such activities.[26]

The ignominious end to the National Archives Establishment as an independent agency carried with it a tragic illustration of the dangers facing an institution that is forced to depend upon its own strength and reason in combating undesirable legislation. While the record reveals an unimaginative role of opposition to the proposals of the Hoover Commission by the National Archives itself, it also reveals the total absence of assistance on the part of its friends who were in a position to come to its aid. The cultural community—particularly the American Historical Association and the Society of American Archivists, one the father, the other the offspring of the National Archives—was not called upon for help. There was simply no communication between the two worlds on this fundamental change in the agency that historians had done so much to create. Earlier, professional historians assumed responsibility for exploring the condition of the nation's archives and for compiling reports, guides, and calendars—experience that fitted them to become archivists. They brought about the creation of the National Archives and furnished its leaders. But once they discovered that the problems of reduction and retention could not be solved unless archivists assumed some responsibility for the whole archival process from beginning to end, the academicians as a whole washed their hands of responsibility and retreated to their proverbial ivory towers. In short, historians and the academic world were utterly indifferent to what was going on, and no effective effort was made to enlist their aid.[27]

26. 63 Stat. 381.
27. The first mention, in a professional journal, of the dangers facing the National Archives appeared in the April 1949 issue of the *American Archivist* (p. 205). The fourteen-line report noted that "The Commission's report, although circulating to a small group of officials, is still

The speed with which the drastic changes were made, it may be argued, prevented effective marshaling of the forces of historians and archivists. It may be pointed out that the Leahy report was not published until January, the first Hoover proposal for a Records Management Bureau in an Office of General Services not until February, and the final Hoover Commission report was not released until May. Furthermore, neither the Hoover Commission nor Congress afforded an opportunity for interested parties to be heard—an inexplicable procedure in a matter of such far-reaching implications. Nevertheless, as early as October 1948 the direction of the Leahy report was becoming evident, and it was known that legislation to create a general services agency was being considered by Congress for months prior to its eventual passage. It may also be pointed out that there were no hearings on the revised bills, which had been amended to incorporate essentially the Hoover Commission proposals, and that there was no general debate upon the floors of the Congress.[28] These facts, however, do not absolve historians and archivists generally, and in particular the three organizations sponsoring the present study[29] from an obvious case of indifference and/or negligence. If the leaders of the professions were not aware of the threats inherent in the legislative proposals, they must have been oblivious of much of what was taking place in their fields of interest. Furthermore, if they were not informed, their colleagues in the National Archives failed in their duties by not calling the crisis to their attention. Whatever the reason, and wherever the fault, the historical and archival professions reflected a state of impotency ill-becoming the successors of Jameson and Leland.[30]

---

confidential as this journal goes to press." The October 1949 issues of the *American Historical Review* (p. 261) and the *American Archivist* (p. 429) carried brief reports on the new legislation.

28. Holmes, "The National Archives at a Turn in the Road," pp. 349–350.

29. The American Historical Association, the Organization of American Historians (then the Mississippi Valley Historical Association), and the Society of American Archivists.

30. Jameson had died in 1937; Leland, 70 years old in 1949, was Director Emeritus of the American Council of Learned Societies. At least some efforts were made by National Archives personnel to enlist opposition of other agencies to the Hoover Commission's proposals for centralizing records management and centers in a general services agency: e.g., Kenneth W. Munden, "The Hoover Commission's Report on Records

Happily for the National Archives, the Congress had not gone along with the Hoover Commission's recommendation that a records management bureau be set up in the new General Services Administration, and for the next several months the leadership of the National Archives convinced Jess Larson, newly appointed Administrator of General Services, that the proper course was to continue the records management program under the Archivist so that it could be better coordinated with the archival program. The dual responsibility of the new "service" was recognized in the title given it by General Services Administration Order No. 27, issued December 1, 1949, which created the present National Archives and Records Service. This action salvaged much.

There was a tendency for the leadership of the National Archives to look upon the momentous change of 1949 with mixed emotions. The loss of independence was a serious blow to the morale of the staff, to the pride of the profession, and to the standing of the institution among the cultural agencies of the world. The relatively calm acceptance of the *fait accompli* on the part of the National Archives staff, therefore, appears to have resulted from a determination to make the best of an unhappy situation. In a remarkably dispassionate discussion of the subject, the Archivist, Wayne Grover, in his last annual report as head of an independent agency, looked optimistically into the future when a more forceful records management program could be inaugurated in keeping with the spirit of the act creating the General Services Administration. At the same time, he cautiously wrote:

> Emphasis on the role of the National Archives in records management should not, however, be permitted to obscure the fact that the institution has other functions to perform. The National Archives is also responsible for preserving and making available for the use of the Government and the people the noncurrent records of the three branches of the Government—executive, legislative, and judicial—that are worthy of preservation. The selection of these perma-

Management: A paper read before the seminar of Historical Records Section, DRB, AGO, on 7 April 1949" (Washington: Departmental Records Branch, Adjutant General's Office, 1949, mimeographed).

nent records and the fact that all phases of the management of current records vitally affect the job of preserving and controlling noncurrent records are the considerations that compel the American archivist to assume responsibilities for records management. It is especially this characteristic that distinguishes him from his European colleagues. But like them he is also the custodian of a priceless heritage—the memory of the National Government as it exists in the records of the various Federal agencies.[31]

He stressed the need for additional staff in the National Archives proper, calling particular attention to the desirability of accelerating the work of appraisal, arrangement, description, and preservation.

A veteran staff member, Oliver Holmes, undertook an objective analysis of the meaning of the absorption of the National Archives by the General Services Administration almost before the reorganization was effected. He saw the success or failure of the change as depending upon the Administrator and his successors. If the Administrators recognized the importance of the professional autonomy of the Archivist, the marriage could be a happy one. Holmes wrote:

What is important is that the professional head [of the National Archives] and the Administrator [of General Services] should meet in friendly give and take in the formulation of policy and program, and then that the functions involved in carrying out a professional program should be delegated back to the professional head. There can be no half and half business about this. Records management must be included in this unified program. It has made progress only as it was led by a professional group and dominated by the professional spirit. Records management in the agencies and in the intermediate records centers must be coordinated and harmonized with the work in the National Archives—must be a professionally controlled activity throughout the life history of the records. That is

31. *Fifteenth Annual Report of the Archivist of the United States for the Fiscal Year Ending June 30, 1949*, pp. 3–4.

the meaning of the revolution through which we have passed. Let there be no mistaken impression that it was the opposite—that the entire program was to be deprofessionalized. Failure and a quick relapse to the old situation would follow.[32]

He expressed apprehension lest officials of the superior agency, in whose hands all power now resided, give precedence to the broadened program of records management "to the extent that obligations of the National Archives to culture and scholarship will be relegated to a lesser rôle—in budget matters, in choice of personnel, and in emphasis in planning and programming."

Holmes saw potential advantages that might eventually outweigh the dangers inherent in the new status of the National Archives. To be under the same roof with services controlling space and equipment might well lead to the acquisition of more and better suited space and equipment for both archival materials and noncurrent records. "Through the controls now given the General Services Administration over intermediate records centers, the whole complex situation can be worked on as one problem," he optimistically wrote. He also expressed the hope that the weight and influence of a larger agency might be brought to bear toward securing more funds for the "normal, traditional activities of the National Archives."

The act creating the General Services Administration envisioned detailed legislation to implement the archival responsibilities placed in that agency. Such legislation—the Federal Records Act of 1950 [33]—was signed into law by President Truman on September 5, 1950. It repealed the National Archives Act of 1934, as amended, and placed in the office of Administrator of General Services virtually all national archival and records management authority.

Even the admitted inclusiveness and strength of the new statute and the need for many of its provisions hardly relieved the heartache among professionals as they repeatedly read the words "The Administrator shall. . . ." His archival authority

32. Holmes, "The National Archives at a Turn in the Road," pp. 350–351.
33. P.L. 754, 81st Cong.; 54 Stat. 483.

was firmly established in the opening section: "The Administrator shall have immediate custody and control of the National Archives Building and its contents. . . ." Then, after reconstituting the National Historical Publications Commission to include membership from all three branches of government plus two members from the American Historical Association and two from the public at large, the act abolished the National Archives Council and replaced it with a Federal Records Council, with which the Administrator was to "advise and consult with . . . a view to obtaining its advice and assistance. . . ." Inclusion of representation from the judicial branch was designed to placate criticism of the 1934 legislation that had omitted such representation, but professionals were quick to note that the new Council was a very weak body. It could only give "advice and assistance" when asked for them. Furthermore, though in theory the Administrator may have been given authority over the records of the legislative and judicial branches, practically speaking he had no control over those records except insofar as the two branches were willing to grant it. Because there was no policy-making body representing all three branches, and because the general authority of the General Services Administration extended only to the executive branch, the Archivist—to whom the Administrator delegated day-to-day supervision of the archival functions [34] —was in no stronger a position than he had ever been previously with respect to the records of the Congress and the Judiciary.

Together, the Federal Property and Administrative Services Act of 1949 and the Federal Records Act of 1950 constituted a statutory demotion of both the National Archives and the office of Archivist of the United States. The former removed from the list of federal agencies the respected title "The National Archives." The latter removed from the laws of the land, except with regard to several minor capacities, the equally respected title "The Archivist of the United States." At last, as incredible as it seemed at the time and as incongruous as it is obvious today, the documentary heritage of the United States, from the

34. These responsibilities were delegated by Administrator Larson to the Archivist in September 1950. See Herbert E. Angel, "Federal Records Management Since the Hoover Commission Report," *American Archivist*, XVI (January 1953), 14–15. There had been two previous delegations—on July 1, 1949, and on December 12, 1949.

Declaration of Independence to the treaty terminating World War II—and beyond—had been relegated to an agency having charge of "working space," "supplies," "excess property," and "motor pools." [35]

35. *Annual Report of the Administrator of General Services for the Fiscal Year Ending June 30, 1966*, p. vii.

PART TWO

THE NATIONAL ARCHIVES AND RECORDS SERVICE

1949-1968

TABLE I

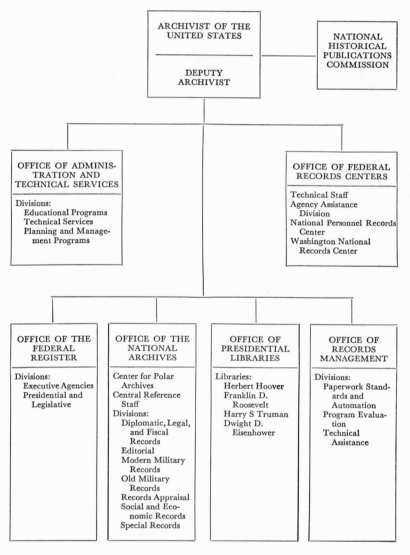

ARCHIVIST OF THE UNITED STATES

DEPUTY ARCHIVIST

NATIONAL HISTORICAL PUBLICATIONS COMMISSION

OFFICE OF ADMINIS-TRATION AND TECHNICAL SERVICES

Divisions:
Educational Programs
Technical Services
Planning and Manage-
ment Programs

OFFICE OF FEDERAL RECORDS CENTERS

Technical Staff
Agency Assistance
Division
National Personnel Records
Center
Washington National
Records Center

OFFICE OF THE FEDERAL REGISTER

Divisions:
Executive Agencies
Presidential and
Legislative

OFFICE OF THE NATIONAL ARCHIVES

Center for Polar
Archives
Central Reference
Staff
Divisions:
Diplomatic, Legal,
and Fiscal
Records
Editorial
Modern Military
Records
Old Military
Records
Records Appraisal
Social and Eco-
nomic Records
Special Records

OFFICE OF PRESIDENTIAL LIBRARIES

Libraries:
Herbert Hoover
Franklin D.
Roosevelt
Harry S Truman
Dwight D.
Eisenhower

OFFICE OF RECORDS MANAGEMENT

Divisions:
Paperwork Stand-
ards and
Automation
Program Evalua-
tion
Technical
Assistance

NATIONAL ARCHIVES AND RECORDS SERVICE
Organization Chart, June 30, 1968

INTRODUCTORY NOTE

S INCE THE establishment of the National Archives and Records Service in the General Services Administration in 1949,[1] the Service has been divided into several major administrative units. The chronological creation of these units is of little concern at this point, and it is sufficient to note that in 1968 NARS comprises, in addition to the Office of the Archivist of the United States, six operating "offices" and one commission: the Office of the National Archives, the Office of Presidential Libraries, the Office of the Federal Register, the Office of Records Management, the Office of Federal Records Centers, the Office of Administration and Technical Services, and the National Historical Publications Commission. Each of the "offices" is headed by an Assistant Archivist, with the exception of the Office of the Federal Register, which is headed by a Director; the staff of the National Historical Publications Commission is governed by the Commission, which appoints an Executive Director, who in turn works under the supervision of the Archivist of the United States in his capacity as Chairman of the Commission. In the following chapters each of these units, with the exception of the Office of Administration and Technical Services, will be discussed separately. Although activities relating to repair, photographic reproduction, and exhibit of documents are assigned for supervision to the latter office, they are inseparable functions of the archival program and will be included with the National Archives for purposes of discussion.

During the fiscal year ending June 30, 1967, the staff of the National Archives and Records Services numbered about 1,900. Funds available during the same year amounted to approximately $18,549,000 from the following sources: $16,314,000 from regular appropriations, $375,000 from ap-

1. See p. 61.

TABLE II

Personnel Paid from National Archives Appropriations, 1935–49
and
NARS "Operating Expenses" Appropriations and Personnel Paid from NARS Appropriations, 1949–68
(Dollars in Thousands)

Fiscal Year	Administrative Services Avg. Pos.	Administrative Services Funds	Service Direction † Avg. Pos.	Service Direction † Funds	National Archives Avg. Pos.	National Archives Funds	Nat. Hist. Publ. Comm. Avg. Pos.	Nat. Hist. Publ. Comm. Funds	Presidential Libraries Avg. Pos.	Presidential Libraries Funds	Records Management Avg. Pos.	Records Management Funds	Record Centers Avg. Pos.	Record Centers Funds	Federal Register Avg. Pos.	Federal Register Funds	Total Avg. Pos.	Total Funds
1935	25				15										2		42	
1936	73				87										15		175	
1937	97				139										15		251	
1938	101				218										16		335	
1939	107				220										16		343	
1940	114				246										16		376	
1941	117				257				9						16		399	
1942	99				315				14						20		448	
1943	95				270				11						25		401	
1944	88				197				10						26		321	
1945	84				212				10						28		334	
1946	80				219				9						27		335	
1947	82				220				10						40		352	
1948	68				220				11						39		338	
1949	66		66	$264	236	$ 978			13	$ 53					43	$167	358	$ 1,462
1950	Services provided by GSA		6	$ 57	268	$1,117			13	$ 55	2	$ 15		$ 205	46	$195	335	$ 1,644
1951			20	$ 136	272	$1,255	1	$ 9	13	$ 64	22	$ 145	87	$ 1,017	47	$212	462	$ 2,838
1952			28	$ 202	283	$1,400	2	$ 25	13	$ 61	46	$ 287	342	$ 2,454	42	$218	756	$ 4,647
1953			27	$ 192	263	$1,309	4	$ 36	14	$ 65	44	$ 317	497	$ 2,707	44	$231	893	$ 4,857

1954	26	$201	251	$1,425	4	$ 38	12	$ 61	48	$ 333	536	$ 3,844	44	$233	921	$ 6,135
1955	27	$224	246	$1,337	6	$ 45	12	$ 64	41	$ 316	514	$ 3,423	44	$234	890	$ 5,648
1956	28	$252	243	$1,421	8	$ 52	11	$ 65	36	$ 318	564	$ 3,828	42	$257	932	$ 6,193
1957	28	$266	236	$1,431	8	$ 55	12	$ 75	47	$ 429	587	$ 4,041	43	$261	961	$ 6,558
1958	28	$312	284	$1,790	8	$ 54	22	$142	56	$ 569	612	$ 4,318	43	$307	1,053	$ 7,492
1959	28	$356	329	$2,295	9	$ 65	23	$168	56	$ 611	669	$ 4,884	46	$335	1,160	$ 8,719
1960	28	$495	331	$2,339	9	$ 68	24	$180	59	$ 650	1,329	$ 8,605	45	$323	1,825	$12,659
1961	29	$503	335	$2,578	9	$ 71	30	$351	64	$ 788	1,316	$ 8,869	49	$378	1,832	$13,538
1962	30	$553	342	$2,637	9	$ 77	35	$294	70	$ 864	1,273	$ 8,461	50	$400	1,809	$13,286
1963	31	$556	347	$2,783	9	$ 86	36	$326	69	$ 921	1,251	$ 8,604	51	$418	1,794	$13,694
1964	31	$618	328	$2,856	9	$ 92	46	$380	70	$ 996	1,219	$ 8,954	51	$427	1,754	$14,923
1965	31	$663	351	$3,042	9	$114	52	$560	71	$1,045	1,196	$ 9,248	51	$478	1,761	$15,150
1966	31	$734	355	$3,132	10	$119	53	$612	65	$1,147	1,150	$ 9,560	52	$500	1,716	$15,804
1967	30	$646	378	$3,399	10	$127	55	$614	79	$1,229	1,170	$ 9,921	55	$545	1,777	$16,481
*1968	29	$654	355	$3,425	10	$126	60	$692	80	$1,300	1,175	$10,500	55	$568	1,767	$17,265

* Estimated
† Archivist, Regional Directors, and their staffs

propriations for grants, $820,000 from trust funds, $162,000 from private sources, $663,000 from reimbursable services, and $215,000 from transfers. Of the personnel, about 1,700 were paid from direct appropriations, 80 from trust funds, 60 from reimbursable funds, and the remainder from other sources.

TABLE III
National Archives and Records Service

Distribution of Work Time Spent by Functions *
Fiscal Year 1968

	Total		Headquarters		Field Office	
	Avg. Pos.	*Per-cent*	*Avg. Pos.*	*Per-cent*	*Avg. Pos.*	*Per-cent*
Archival Work	526	100	438	83	88	17
Preservation & Reproduction	113		113		–	
Arrangement & Finding Aids	130		130		–	
Reference	150		150		–	
Records Appraisal	10		10		–	
NHPC	14		14		–	
In Records Centers	25		–		25	
In Presidential Libraries	84		21		63	
Records Management	121	100	87	72	34	28
Program Development	16		16		–	
Agency Evaluations	11		8		–	
Technical Assistance	28		12		16	
Agency Surveys	66		51		15	
Record Centers	1,211	100	15	1	1,196	99
Accessions	257		–		257	
Disposal	44		–		44	
Reference	814		–		814	
Other	96		15		81	
Federal Register	55	100	55	100	–	–
Service Direction	29	100	10	34	19	66
TOTALS	1,942	100	605	31	1,337	69

* These figures include nearly 200 positions paid from nonappropriated funds.

These figures, when compared with the staff of 358 and appropriations of $1,462,000 in 1949,[2] reveal a substantial increase during the past 18 years. The increases, however, reflect largely the *new* or *expanded* responsibilities assumed

2. The 1949 figures reflect only *direct appropriations;* they do not include funds from trust funds and other sources that furnished additional employees. See Table II.

since 1949—in records management, records centers, and presidential archives. Records centers alone account for about 60 percent of both the staff and budget. In contrast, for the National Archives proper, appropriations have more than tripled but the staff has increased only 50 percent.

Upon the retirement of Wayne C. Grover in 1965, GSA Administrator Lawson B. Knott, Jr., appointed Robert H. Bahmer to the position of Archivist of the United States. Bahmer, educated as a historian and, like his two immediate predecessors, the holder of a Ph.D. degree, joined the National Archives staff in 1936 as one of the examiners who conducted the original surveys of records in the Washington agencies. He subsequently served as the head of one of the records divisions in the Archives and during the war assisted in developing the War Department's records management program. He then returned to the National Archives and served as Deputy Archivist until his appointment as Archivist. Upon Bahmer's retirement in March 1968,[3] Administrator Knott appointed James Berton Rhoads, who also holds a doctorate in history, who served nearly two decades in various NARS positions, and who was Deputy Archivist under Bahmer.

3. For a tribute to Bahmer upon his retirement, see *Congressional Record*, CXIV, March 6, 1968, H-1742.

[4]

THE NATIONAL ARCHIVES, 1949–1968

Support for archival operations is difficult to come by. To this I can testify from 30 years of experience in the Federal Government in this field. I know of no activity that lays any claim to importance in the field of the humanities that is so niggardly supported by tax money as the archival operations of the United States. . . .
—Robert H. Bahmer, *1966*

It was a good feeling to have instilled in one at the start of a trip through the United States and it was reinforced by the city of Washington itself, with its massive, dignified marble buildings out of which come the decisions of the land; its archives commemorating the American past; its monuments to our heroes; its burial ground for the men who made our freedom possible—all of them combining to give one the feeling of permanence and solidity.
—Philip Kunhardt, *1967*

THE WISE DECISION of the first Administrator of General Services to establish the Office of Records Management as coordinate with the National Archives served as a precedent when additional "offices" were created. These actions permitted the National Archives to maintain to a considerable degree its own individuality within the National Archives and Records Service. The new activities during the years following 1949, however, could not but demand an increasing part of the attention of the Archivist of the United States and his immediate staff. These new areas of responsibility not only took time in day-to-day supervision, they also required attention in the budget-making process. It was only natural, therefore, for some members of the National Archives staff to feel that, because of the impressive economies promoted by the records management program, the emphasis of the leadership of NARS appeared always in the direction of records management and records centers. Economy and efficiency became the most popular topics of discussion in budget hearings, for they are subjects that appeal to many executive and legislative leaders who have little

74

interest in the records of the past. Thus the expansion of NARS was viewed with conflicting emotions among some professionals, for the new areas of concern inevitably contributed to their feeling that the cultural functions of the National Archives were not receiving the emphasis they deserved.

That the feeling was not groundless is borne out by comparative staff and budget statistics. While appropriations for the entire service increased from 1949 to 1968 by more than 1,100 percent, funds appropriated just for the National Archives increased less than 400 percent. During the same period the staff of NARS, paid from appropriated funds, increased by 500 percent [1] while that of the National Archives increased only 50 percent. These comparative figures, coupled with the vastly increased demands upon the National Archives from both government and the public, leave little room for doubt that the anxiety expressed in 1949, that within GSA the National Archives would not receive the attention and support that it would enjoy as an independent agency, was well founded.

The National Archives is responsible for the appraisal of all federal records and the accession, preservation, reproduction, rehabilitation, arrangement, description, and servicing of the permanently valuable records of the federal government.[2] Its holdings amount to 895,807 cubic feet of textual records (probably over 2,000,000,000 pages of writing), 3,620,000 still pictures, 1,551,000 maps and charts, 64,900 reels of motion pictures, 34,300 sound recordings, and thousands of reels of microfilm. Almost all of these are unique items in contrast to the holdings of a library, and consequently not subject to the

1. Records centers, of course, represent the lion's share of this increase, the staff having grown from zero in 1949 to nearly 1,200 in 1967. NARS, incidentally, figures that if records centers absorbed by the Service had remained under supervision of the individual agencies, 1,758 employees would be required. The Bahmer quotation in the epigraph, p. 74, is from *Proceedings of the Conference on the Utilization of Archival and Educational Resources [at Sacramento State College, September 17, 1966]* (Sacramento: Telefact Foundation, 1967), p. 57. The Philip Kunhardt quotation on the same page appeared in his article, "This Is My Land," *Life*, June 2, 1967, p. 20D.

2. Activities relating to repair, photographic reproduction, and exhibit of documents are assigned for supervision to the recently established separate Office of Administration and Technical Services, but since they are inseparable functions of the archival process, the work of the Technical Services Division will be included in the following discussion of the Office of the National Archives.

economies of cooperative cataloging as are books in a library. Items were called for from these holdings 566,700 times during fiscal 1967.[3] The public at large, however, does not have an opportunity to observe the stacks areas and consequently has little concept of the magnitude of the documentary mass behind the masonry walls. Even serious researchers often get no farther than the Search Room, where records are made available for study. Perhaps the architect of the building should have provided for a glassed-in opening through which the 1,200,000 visitors who come annually to the Exhibit Hall could get a peek at the bulging stacks and their contents. All too many come and see the Declaration of Independence, the Constitution, the Bill of Rights, and a few hundred other documents on display, then leave with no idea of the additional cultural wealth of the nation housed in the core of the great structure.

The work of the National Archives is carried on by about 414 employees, only 355 of whom are paid from NARS appropriations.[4] Some of these serve on a Central Reference Staff, but most of them are assigned to one of seven divisions: Editorial, Records Appraisal, Diplomatic, Legal, and Fiscal Records, Modern Military Records, Old Military Records, Social and Economic Records, and Special Records. The others are on the staff of the Office of Administration and Technical Services. Of the total, approximately 112 employees hold professional classifications of archivist or historian with salaries ranging from Grades 5 through 16, the median being Grade 11, with a beginning salary of $9,657; and about 117 are subprofessional archives assistants ranging from Grades 4 through 10, with the median slightly above Grade 5, the initial salary of which is $5,565. The remainder of the staff members are largely in clerical, technical, and housekeeping classifications. Of the 274 employees assigned to the Office of the National Archives,[5] there are only 132 holding earned college degrees—17 Ph.D.s, 43

3. *Administrator's Annual Report, General Services Administration, Fiscal Year 1967*, p. 24. This publication is cited hereafter as *GSA Annual Report.*

4. Of these, approximately 120 employees in preservation and reproduction and a few others in specialized functions are assigned for supervision to the Office of Administration and Technical Services.

5. This excludes personnel in preservation and reproduction and a few other specialized functions assigned to the Office of Administration and Technical Services.

with a master's degree, and 72 with a bachelor's degree as their highest academic attainment. In a scholarly institution this proportion of college graduates to its total staff strength is low and represents a sharp downtrend since 1938, when, out of a staff of 319, there were 265 college graduates, of whom 32 had Ph.D.s, 73 had a master's degree, and 160 held a bachelor's degree.[6] As a matter of fact, there are fewer than 30 staff members in the whole of NARS with the earned doctorate.[7]

The present total staff strength of the National Archives is convincing evidence that the institution has not grown in proportion to the demands upon it. Even though, as has been pointed out, the budget of the Archives has increased nearly fourfold in the past 18 years, most of this increase has been a result of salary adjustments characteristic of both government and business.

If the financial support of the National Archives has remained beneath its needs, demands upon its staff have increased annually. As a result of the shortage of office space in the government buildings, more than 909,000 cubic feet of records had been accepted in the building by 1950. This liberal accessioning policy meant that many records were accepted prior to adequate appraisal. It thus imposed upon the institution the necessity for a continual reevaluation of its holdings and the elimination of records of less than permanent value. The establishment of Federal Records Centers offered the safety valve. Many of the records of continuing administrative value but without historical significance were removed from the Archives Building to the centers. Other record groups of mixed values were also transferred, and in the centers they were analyzed, segregated, and those of permanent value set aside either for return to the Archives or for retention in the centers for regional research. By 1952 the total cubic footage had decreased to 793,000, and by 1957, to 775,000. Only through this device was the National Archives able to make room for additional archival materials steadily arriving at its dock. Accessions in the past ten years

6. See p. 18.
7. Two factors partially account for the reduction in the proportion of degree-holders: (1) the availability of the "academic proletariat" looking for jobs in 1938, and (2) the trend in archival agencies with large holdings of modern records to use more nonprofessional personnel in various stages of the work.

have again filled the building to capacity, the holdings now totaling approximately 900,000 cubic feet. In order to make room for additional records of prime research value, some 250,000 cubic feet now in the National Archives—mostly those in restricted or low-reference categories—are currently being transferred to the new Archives Branch in the Federal Records Center in Suitland, Maryland.

The physical task of moving hundreds of thousands of cubic feet of documents in and out of the National Archives was strenuous enough, but the more difficult job was the continuous reappraisal of records already in custody, the accessioning of additional materials, and the arrangement, description, and preservation of both. Accustomed to receiving, without publicity or public notice, truckload after truckload of files from the federal agencies, the National Archives in 1952 took particular pride in the arrival of the three great charters of American freedom—the Declaration of Independence, the Constitution, and the Bill of Rights.[8] These documents, transferred from the Library of Congress in keeping with the purpose of the National Archives as the repository of federal records, were given specially designed display facilities in the Exhibition Hall, where they have since been viewed daily by thousands of visitors. The National Archives, then less than two decades old, could pause to review its accomplishments. Wrote the Archivist:

> The completion of the transfer of older records together with certain recent events has transformed the National Archives into what its name implies and what it was originally intended to be—a repository of all historically significant records of the national Government and one of the important national centers of historical research. Recognition of its transformation is already evident by the increasing number of scholars who come from all parts of the world to study the rich resources in its charge or to learn its archival techniques.[9]

8. National Archives, *Facts for Visitors to the National Archives* (Washington: National Archives, 1966), p. 4. These documents had been in the Library of Congress since 1921, when they were transferred from the Department of State. See David C. Mearns, *The Story Up to Now: The Library of Congress, 1800–1946* (Washington: Library of Congress, 1947), p. 191.
9. *GSA Annual Report, 1951–52*, pp. 70–71.

The tracing of the history of the National Archives after 1949 is infinitely more difficult because of a casualty caused by the loss of independence. The fifteen numbers of the *Annual Report of the Archivist of the United States*, published from 1935 through 1949, chronicled the birth and development of America's incomparable program. Each issue was more than just a report of the problems, accomplishments, and failures of the previous year; it was a source document itself, enunciating, clarifying, and expounding upon the evolving principles and techniques of archival administration. Appendixes carried an assortment of literature not readily accessible to archivists: statutes, reports, accessions, guides, professional contributions of the staff. And, to the delight of readers, most of these reports were thoroughly indexed. But, alas, when the National Archives was relegated to the position of a bureau in a larger agency, the annual report, published for the use of the National Archives itself and for the public that it served, was one of the first casualties. Grover's report for 1948–49 marked the end of this remarkable series, and effective in fiscal 1950, the *Annual Report of the Administrator of General Services* incorporated a section titled "National Archives and Records Management." From the 99-page report of the Archivist in 1945–46, the story of the institution, including its newly assigned duties, dropped to 24 pages in the GSA report for 1949–50 and 15 pages in 1956–57. By 1965–66 this section, now headed only "Records Management," amounted to less than four pages of text plus two photographs. This incredible demise of the most useful series of official reports on the archives of the United States has been a loss beyond calculation, for it has deprived the government and the scholarly and professional communities—and ultimately the public—of an account of the one agency responsible for the nation's documentary heritage. Its loss has been all the more tragic because the end came at a time when the archival programs were making unequaled progress in new areas of service, public knowledge of which was as much needed as was the story of earlier archival developments as told in the reports of Connor and Buck.[10]

10. The demise of the Archivist's annual report demonstrates one of the incongruities in the placement of NARS in the General Services Administration. The latter agency was created to serve other government

As has been said, the absence of detailed reports since 1949 makes it necessary for anyone tracing the archival program to turn, with disappointing results, to alternate sources: the meager sections of the GSA annual reports, news notes in the *American Archivist*, statistical summaries in the voluminous records of the National Archives itself, and the memory of staff members.

The administration of archives involves a complex series of interrelated activities that include (1) appraisal, (2) repair, rehabilitation, and reproduction, (3) arrangement and description, and (4) reference.

APPRAISAL

THE most important single responsibility in an archival program is its appraisal function through which records are evaluated for the identification of those of continuing value. Federal appraisal archivists have the most difficult responsibility of all: They exercise virtual life-and-death authority over the nation's records. It is they who decide what records are to be recommended to Congress for disposal; it is they who act as prognosticators of the future by determining what documentary evidence of the government will be preserved. This responsibility must be exercised only by mature historian-archivists, who cannot make wise decisions by a stop watch. Their evaluation often requires on-the-spot examination of records in the agencies and in the Federal Records Centers. Theirs is a judgment based upon knowledge and thought. It is they who decide which of the 26,000,000 cubic feet of records in the federal government are to be retained, a responsibility that cannot be delegated to lower-level personnel.

In an address before the American Historical Association and the Society of American Archivists in 1961 the Dominion Archivist of Canada said:

The archivist . . . is called upon . . . to practice the difficult art of prophecy. He must attempt to anticipate

---

agencies. It has no particular obligation to the public in general or to the special clientele of the National Archives. NARS has a double mission—to serve both government agencies and the people.

needs. Out of a vast mass of material, a high percentage of which must be destroyed, he must try to identify and retain those items that are most likely to be of interest and significance in the years to come. Unlike the historian, the archivist cannot place any convenient subjective limitations on his field of interest. Somehow or other he must find means to pass judgment on the probable value of source material that may relate to virtually any aspect or period of the history of the state or country with which his institution happens to be concerned. Recently, for example, I found myself judging the value (both historical and commercial) of contemporary copies of some highly important seventeenth-century correspondence relating to New France, trying to determine which records relating to Canadian service personnel who served in the First World War should be retained in original form, and worrying about the fate of the papers of a former cabinet minister whose death was expected day by day. In two of these three instances time was a matter of importance, and this point is worth noting. Sources can wait for the historian for years, but if they are to be there to await his pleasure, some archivist may have to make up his mind in a hurry and act quickly in order to secure and preserve them.[11]

This understatement of the awesome duty of the archivist touches upon the most frustrating and misunderstood aspect of his work. It is the responsibility that has widened the chasm between the writing historian and the archivist in recent years. The former, personally concerned largely with the records relating to his specific research project, often observes the gaps in documentation and prefaces his work with a haughty reprimand to those who allowed some of the trivial—and all too often some of the vital—materials to be destroyed. Letters declining invitations, for instance, comprise huge blocks in the correspondence of a public official. Even the most conservative archivist is likely to authorize their destruction, though accepted invitations may be retained. Yet, to the biographer, the refusal of the official to attend the luncheon of a business group while agreeing to ap-

11. W. Kaye Lamb, "The Archivist and the Historian," *American Historical Review*, LXVIII (January 1963), 385–386.

pear before a labor union may be of considerable significance. Thus to an individual researcher such letters declining invitations are worthy of preservation. So may be receipts, canceled checks, and even the much-maligned laundry slips. At some point, though, the researcher in modern materials suddenly is confronted with such a mass of materials that even he will agree that a limitation must be set on what is to be kept. The archivist is the limit-setter, not only because the laws of his nation or state place that responsibility upon him but also because he is—or is supposed to be—trained for the task. Where, and on what scale of judgment, does he set the limit? Only the archivist who has been numbed by the pressure of rapid decisions is insensitive to the awesomeness of his task. A historian-archivist with impeccable credentials writes:

> To me there is something truly awful in having to make the decision as to what the historian of the future generation is to know. . . . Obviously the decision should be made by someone with training and experience in historical research. I have known commercial records management services to recommend the destruction, as useless, of material of priceless historical value, actually protected by the statutes of the State. On the other hand, historians sometimes ask us to preserve material so bulky that any knowledge of records management costs demonstrates such a policy to be impractical.[12]

Holding in his hands the disposition of public records, the archivist is no less than a censor. His initials on a schedule or disposal list can mean that the documentary evidence of an event, a decision, or a consideration is consigned to the pulp mill or to the incinerator. By one flick of the pen he can decide that the present and future will be denied knowledge of a particular matter except through the undependable memory of any surviving participants. He can remove from the eyes of posterity a page or a volume of history. He can even falsify history by

12. Clifford K. Shipton, "The Reference Use of Archives," in Rolland E. Stevens (ed.), *University Archives: Papers Presented at an Institute Conducted by the University of Illinois Graduate School of Library Science, November 1–4, 1964* (Champaign, Ill.: The Illini Union Bookstore, 1965), p. 69.

selecting for preservation documents that put one official in a favorable light while showing another as a villain. Or he can mark for destruction records unfavorable to one point of view while preserving those supporting another. Even a curator of private manuscripts can distort history by assiduously collecting the papers of those active in one political or social or economic faction while displaying no interest in persons supporting other causes. Thus a manuscript repository may be found hard at work gathering in materials of civil rights groups while keeping their hands clean of the records of organizations of the far Right. A university archivist may, to his own satisfaction, decide that one administration was better than another and concentrate on preserving materials to support his belief. In short, an archivist can, if he does not live up to his creed, wittingly or unwittingly perform the role of a censor or propagandist. It was with this danger in mind that the Archivist of the United States promulgated "The Archivist's Code," which contains the following principle:

> The archivist must realize that in selecting records for retention or disposal he acts as the agent of the future in determining its heritage from the past. Therefore, insofar as his intellectual attainments, experience, and judgment permit, he must be ever conscious of the future's needs, making his decisions impartially without taint of ideological, political, or personal bias.[13]

The intellectually dishonest archivist is rare, but any custodian may feel subtle pressures. A governing board of a manuscript repository may object to accepting the papers of a "subversive" individual or organization, just as a library board may object to the display of certain books or periodicals; it may frown upon the acquisition of records of Right-wing elements because the repository might get a reputation for conservatism; it may propose public acknowledgment of gifts from certain quarters while giving no publicity to those from other donors. Tax-supported repositories may avoid certain collections for fear of legislative antagonism. Individuals may "plant" scurrilous

13. *The Archivist's Code*, para. 2.

material in a repository for the purpose of discrediting others.[14]

The prospect of an archivist intentionally violating his trust, while always a possibility, causes far less anxiety than the inevitability of unfortunate decisions made through the pressure of quick judgments or without adequate knowledge. The only defense—and, of course, it is not absolute—is proper training, adequate knowledge, reasonable time for consideration, personal examination and observation of the records, and a sixth sense that combines the rare talents of prophecy and realistic economy. The archivist in the first place is supposedly a historian with a wide knowledge of history and government. That is the primary desideratum. This knowledge may be acquired in ways other than graduate training, but such training is highly desirable because it acquaints the prospective archivist with the realm of historical research and researchers, a familiarity that is essential in his decision-making. Indeed, this acquaintance cannot end with formal education; the archivist must keep abreast with current research so as to anticipate future trends. Ideally, the appraisal archivist should be thoroughly familiar with the daily activities of the reference staff by either participating in searchroom activities or by studying registration records. Oftentimes it is the appraisal archivist who can be of greatest assistance to a researcher, particularly when records to be used have not yet come to the archives.

But general knowledge of history and government is not enough. When the archivist undertakes the appraisal of records, he engages in intensive research on the agency that created and used the records, thus acquiring firsthand knowledge of the history, organization, and functions of that agency and the uses and abuses undergone by the records themselves. This knowledge, added to his familiarity with current and probable

14. An instance such as the latter occurred recently in a Southern state. A citizen, opposed to the editorial policy of a local newspaper, found a Union Army document authorizing the editor's grandfather to cross the lines during the Civil War. She obtained a photocopy of the document, then sent it to the State Archives. It was dutifully accessioned, but careful note was made as to its donation. Shortly thereafter the institution received—just before Christmas—an order for multiple copies of the document. The photocopies, it was later learned, were distributed to "prove" that the editor's grandfather had been a "Yankee sympathizer" —about the most vitriolic accusation that can be made in some areas. Thus the donor had accomplished her purpose: She now was circulating "irrefutable evidence" from the State Archives.

research, fits him in varying degrees for his critical analysis of records.

Thus, ideally, the appraisal archivist knows history and government, is familiar with past and current research, and is thoroughly cognizant of the history of the agency whose records he is appraising and of the records themselves. If he meets this characterization, he has the basic credentials for determining what records have continuing value for research. Even so, he is handicapped: He cannot be a specialist in all subjects, and he is unlikely to be a specialist in even a few subjects. He will not, therefore, carry into his work an intimate knowledge of the diverse subjects for which the records may be consulted in the future. His decisions as to what to keep and what to destroy, therefore, may be questioned by individual researchers on specific subjects. There is no way out of this dilemma, for it would be impracticable to envision the consultation of thousands of specialists to advise in the appraisal of the records of, for example, the Department of State. A good appraisal archivist, however, may very well call on one or more outside consultants for advice in judging the retention value of certain record series.

The magnitude of his problem, resulting from the mass of records being created currently, may force the appraisal archivist into a race against time. If this happens he is likely to take short cuts that open the way for disastrous decisions. He may not study the administrative history of the creating agency and thus fail to comprehend its role in government. He may not consult with specialists in the subject field. But more than this, he may very well attempt to judge the value of the record series without personally inspecting and analyzing the records, whether they be in the agency or in a records center. While it is true that many types of records, because of their duplication or commonplaceness, may be judged simply by title and description prepared by someone else, many others defy appraisal except by on-the-spot evaluation. In the latter cases the archivist must read portions of the files, study their provenance and arrangement, observe their use over a period of time, and oftentimes schedule them for an additional period of observation in a records center.

No federal record, of course, can be legally destroyed until it has been adjudged of no continuing value by the archival agency. From 1934 to 1943 *ad hoc* appraisals of record series were undertaken by the National Archives when requested to do so by the originating agency. This cumbersome and wasteful procedure, under which as many as 73,000 series were appraised in one year, has largely been replaced since 1943, when Congress authorized continuing disposition schedules that permit accumulations of records in an appraised series to be disposed of without the necessity of repetitive reappraisals. As a result of the new act, 95 percent of all federal records on hand in 1955 were covered by authorized continuing schedules that had been appraised by the National Archives insofar as the disposal items were concerned. By 1962 a survey indicated that less than 5.4 percent of records being created annually by major government agencies were yet to be appraised or scheduled. A natural outgrowth of the evolving appraisal procedure has been the preparation of comprehensive agency records-retention plans after the work of each agency is scrutinized, function by function, and the records of archival value created by each function are designated. In this manner agencies are alerted at the time the records are created and filed to those of their records that have archival value. In the past five years the NARS appraisal staff has developed 136 retention plans and has conducted studies of a number of broad classes of records found in more than one agency. Meanwhile the number of record series submitted annually by the agencies for appraisal has decreased to fewer than 3,000.

Thus great progress has been made in the mammoth task of designating those of permanent value from among the nearly 5,000,000 cubic feet of records created each year. Yet there is a need to accelerate this progress and to provide for more frequent review of existing schedules and for the policing of their execution. Based upon the present complement of 15 appraisal archivists, the completion of retention plans for the remainder of the agencies is projected for 1972. In April 1968, however, the strength of the division dropped to 10 employees, due in part to vacancies and in part to budget restrictions. It is highly doubtful, therefore, that this projection can be met. Furthermore, there should be a continuing review of existing plans and constant attention to changes occurring in the organization of the agencies and in the structure of the records. Many agencies establish new series of records each year, discontinue others, and change the make-up of still others. The functions of an agency may change. Research trends change from time to time. Records this year judged to be of no value to research may, within a few years, become important for new studies. No retention plan can be adopted and shelved; all schedules must be restudied periodically.

Without adequate manpower in the appraisal unit, there is the possibility that too much reliance may be placed on the records officer in each agency. Many of these officers are well qualified in training and experience, and some of the agencies have archivists on their staffs. But the particular function of a records officer is to make recommendations as to administrative value for his own agency. He may not always take into account the interest of other agencies or the public. On the other hand, the appraisal officer representing the Archives must consider, in addition to historical values, administrative and legal needs of his government as a whole. There is no one else to take this responsibility. An agency records officer sometimes does not describe records so that their historical value can be ascertained easily by the archivist. In these cases the appraisal archivist must go into the agency and physically and intellectually inventory the records, study their contents, measure their reference frequency, and evaluate their potential historical value while at the same time assisting the agency records officer in evaluating long-range administrative usefulness. The need is also great for special studies in problem areas that relate to records common to more than one agency—for example, dockets in regulatory agencies, medical records, and the like.

One of the weakest aspects of the appraisal program, in the opinion of the division head, is the absence of a satisfactory dialogue between appraisal archivists, records managers, and electronic data-processing experts. Cooperative projects between the Records Appraisal Division of the Office of Records Management need to be increased, for it is within the area of the creation of records that the problems of appraisal should first be tackled.

Finally, there is a need for more policing of the execution of schedules. Again, too much may be left to the agency records officers. Although the authority of the National Archives is limited, its careful monitoring of agency records retention and disposition programs can be an effective force in the execution of the schedules. Ideally, there should be a team of National Archives appraisal archivists assigned to each of the larger agencies. Several smaller agencies could be assigned to one team. By serving as continuing liaison teams between the National Archives and the records officer in each agency, these archivists could develop a mutually beneficial relationship. The National Archives would gain by acquiring a better acquaintance with the permanently valuable documentation of the agencies, and the agencies would gain by being reminded constantly of the importance of archival principles and procedures in the creation, maintenance, and preservation of that small percentage of their total documentation that must be retained for posterity.[15]

To do better the job that it has done credibly in the past and to do those things that are necessary if more of the hazards are to be removed from the awesome responsibility of selecting the permanent documentation of the American government, the National Archives needs additional personnel in its Records Appraisal Division. The need is all the greater in the face of the rapid development of regional archives and of automated methods of record-making that will require insights into new dimensions of documentary preservation.

PRESERVATION AND REPRODUCTION

BECAUSE repair, rehabilitation, and photographic reproduction are all technical in nature, and because of the frequent substitution of reproductions to eliminate wear and tear upon originals, the National Archives looks upon these activities as being parts of one broad function called preservation and reproduction. Preservation, in this context, involves cleaning, flattening, repairing, and restoring original records to permit their continued use. Reproduction—usually by photographic means—involves

15. For additional comments on appraisal in the Federal Records Centers, see Chapter 8. The work of records appraisal in the federal government is discussed in greater detail in Harold T. Pinkett, "Identification of Record[s] of Continuing Value," *Indian Archives*, XVI (1965–66), 54–61.

(1) making copies for reference in the Search Room, thus permitting the withdrawal of deteriorating originals from public use, and (2) furnishing copies in response to requests by government agencies or the public. The staff assigned to the preservation and reproduction functions numbers about 120, mostly technically trained personnel.

A century and a half of neglect had its deleterious effect upon the records of the United States. Many of the records that survived fire, water, pests, and human abuse required immediate attention upon their acceptance in the National Archives. Records made of mass-produced wood-pulp paper after the Civil War often contained their own seeds of destruction. The Woodruff file, which during the same period generally superseded the earlier method of "bundling" papers, contributed its own perniciousness by exposing folded edges to excessive wear and tear.

It was appropriate, therefore, for the nation's archival institution to be provided with the finest document restoration facilities available. The construction of these facilities coincided with the development of a new method of laminating deteriorating papers by means of cellulose acetate foil and tissue and the demise of the traditional method of repairing documents with silk and paste. The National Archives pioneered in lamination, and after considerable hesitation, adopted the technique of deacidification as a means of removing the harmful agents within the paper itself prior to lamination.[16] Following removal of these agents and reinforcement of the original document by the application of acetate foil, tissue, heat, and pressure, the paper is capable of an extended life. The 117,000 sheets [17] laminated and 157,000 sheets deacidified by the National Archives in fiscal 1967, however, indicate that not a great deal of priority is currently being given to this method of rehabilitation. This deemphasis is in sharp contrast to the trend in leading state archival institutions. More time in the National Archives appears to be spent on

16. This technique was pioneered by, among others, William J. Barrow of Richmond, Virginia, whose "Barrow Method" has been adopted by many leading archives and manuscript repositories. Barrow died August 25, 1967.

17. This equals the expected production of about 8 full-time workers, based upon the North Carolina Department of Archives and History's output of nearly 17,000 sheets deacidified and laminated per employee per year.

flattening documents—a disagreeable and tedious but essential procedure for the proper boxing (or "packing," in National Archives terminology) of records. In the same year 782,000 sheets were flattened.

These figures are not overly impressive when it is recalled that a survey in 1959 estimated that 13,000,000 sheets of records in the Archives needed rehabilitation and that the figure would increase by at least 5,000,000 sheets each ten years.[18] Even these figures, however, were clearly underestimates. A veteran staff member believes that more than 20 percent of the holdings—or around 400,000,000 sheets—need rehabilitation of some kind, not counting a substantial quantity of materials in Federal Records Centers that may need similar treatment. In particular, federal court records and Indian agency records, housed in the centers, are in need of rehabilitation.

Because the cost of lamination is high,[19] a program of "preservation microfilming" was instituted as a means of reducing the handling of fragile originals. This practice permits the substitution of microfilm for research use, and the originals are either withdrawn completely or permitted to be used only in special instances. It might be noted that, while researchers are not always pleased with this substitution of microfilm for the originals, the furnishing of information on microfilm eases the task of the reference staff. One reel of film, for instance, may contain the carded service records of several hundred Civil War soldiers. By making available the film copies in a reading room, the work of the staff is greatly reduced. However, these advantages do not eliminate the obvious fact that original records continue to deteriorate whether or not they are in daily use. The mere substitution of reproductions of valuable documents, therefore, is not in all cases a solution to the problem of preservation.[20]

Microfilm was used in the National Archives as a means of reproduction as early as 1936. Repeated requests for copies of

18. *GSA Annual Report, 1958–59*, p. 28.
19. The cost varies from 25 cents to 45 cents per sheet.
20. The problem of deterioration has not been restricted to paper records. Motion pictures and microfilm on a nitrate base were serious problems—because of deterioration and the danger of fire—until they were transferred to safety-base triacetate film. Many flat film negatives made of the same dangerous material had to be copied.

the same records led to a logical conclusion: Wear and tear on the documents, the time of staff members, and the cost of copies could all be reduced by devising a plan whereby the National Archives would retain the master negative film of records frequently requested by researchers and institutions. Accordingly, in 1940 the Archivist announced a program of preparing "file microcopies" from which duplicate film copies would be sold at about one-fifth the price of the initial filming. Among the purposes of the program were "the wider distribution of the documents photographed, which is in effect publication of them, and . . . the assurance of the preservation of the contents regardless of the fate of the documents themselves." [21] The United States entry into World War II added justification for the distribution of copies. President Roosevelt gave his blessing "to the duplication of records by modern processes like the microfilm so that if in any part of the country original archives are destroyed, a record of them will exist in some other place." [22]

Microfilm publications progressed slowly until 1948, when the Rockefeller Foundation made a grant of $20,000 to the National Archives Trust Fund for the acceleration of the program. By 1965 more than 1,200 separate microfilm publications, each including from one to hundreds of reels, had been completed. By mid-1967 approximately 92,000 rolls of microfilm publications master negatives were available, and during fiscal 1967 alone, 5,494,832 linear feet of duplicates were sold. The largest single body of materials thus far filmed—more than 16,000 rolls—is captured German records. Understandably, the most popular series of microfilm publications are the federal census schedules, but frequently copied series also include diplomatic dispatches, territorial papers, Civil War service records, and Indian Office records.[23]

Selection of materials for filming is based largely upon refer-

21. *Seventh Annual Report of the Archivist of the United States for the Fiscal Year Ending June 30, 1941*, p. 36.
22. President Roosevelt to R. D. W. Connor, February 13, 1942, in *American Archivist*, V (April 1942), 120.
23. The best available history of the microfilm publication program is Wayne C. Grover, "Toward Equal Opportunities of Scholarship," *Journal of American History*, LII (March 1966), 715–724. For an account of its beginnings, see Preston W. Edsall, "The File Microcopy Program of the National Archives," *Journal of Documentary Reproduction*, IV (March 1941), 9–14.

ence demands, though the condition of originals continues to be considered. Scheduled for filming in the near future are the Revolutionary War collection and the Freedman's Bureau records. Some of the earlier census schedules are being refilmed for improved copies. Officially, the National Archives views microfilm publications as bridging the gap between costly printed source materials and the great mass of unpublished documents.[24] For professional archivists, however, the program has more profound characteristics. Wrote Ernst Posner:

> I consider this one of the most incisive steps in the philosophy and practice of the archival profession. In preparing film negatives of series of outstanding research value and making copies of them available at nominal cost, the National Archives has abandoned monopoly of some of its most important holdings and has thrown them open to the use of scholars and searchers, regardless of personal merits and qualifications. This is basically a final break with the archivist's proprietary attitude toward his records, a democratization of the archival reference service that constitutes an entirely new departure.[25]

This unprecedented contribution to the increase and diffusion of knowledge has expressed an urge to end once and for all the notion that public records "belong" to anyone other than literally everyone who has a need to use them. There is something quintessentially American about it, and it is the final and logical realization of Jefferson's injunction to multiply copies of documents rather than fence off the originals as a means of saving them.

The progress of the National Archives microfilm publication program should be continued and expanded in line with a plan adopted in 1965. Microfilm publication is the cheapest known means of reproduction, and for the scholar, photographic duplication exhibits a characteristic peculiarly superior to any other type of publication: It visually duplicates the original. Letter-

24. National Archives, *List of National Archives Microfilm Publications, 1953,* p. v. The most recent edition of this *List* was published in 1966; supplements were issued in 1967 and 1968.
25. Ernst Posner, "The National Archives and the Archival Theorist," *American Archivist*, XVIII (July 1955), 211.

press publication has its own justifications and advantages that in no way reduce the importance of microreproduction. Indeed, the two go hand in hand, one supplementing the other.

The microfilm publication program need not be restricted to manuscript materials, for the authority of the archival institution also extends to printed documents of the government that are, by definition, public records. The institution has proposed that it be given funds to provide for a microfilm publication of Congressional hearings, 1789–1950, most of which have been printed. Another much-needed project is a microfilm edition of the printed documents of the First through Fourteenth Congresses, 1789–1817. The Library of Congress has at length brought together and put under fair—though not yet perfect—bibliographical control an enormous mass of these ephemeral materials and has, it is believed, much the largest collection in existence. The holdings of the National Archives need to be searched for publications that can fill the gaps in the Library of Congress collection. Once a complete set has been located, these materials ought to be filmed. Whether the actual filming is undertaken by the National Archives or the Library of Congress —or cooperatively—is unimportant. The point is that here is a body of printed matter of such significance that the two national repositories of federal documentation have a duty to make them available to other research institutions; and the National Archives, through its microfilm publication program, is in a position either to sponsor or to cooperate with a project toward that end. The study of the early republic has been seriously handicapped by the anarchy existing among its printed documents and by the utterly unsatisfactory character of the selective reprinting of these documents in the *American State Papers*. A microfilm edition of the early legislative documents would contribute greatly to the overcoming of that handicap.

Reproduction in the National Archives is by no means limited to microfilm. Almost every copying method is utilized to provide copies for the Archives itself, for the government, and for the public. In fiscal 1967, for instance, 634,138 electrostatic copies were made, more than half of them for the public. In addition, 59,406 feet of electrostatic copies were made in roll form, and about 40 percent of these were in response to public orders. Photostatic copies totaled 21,391, about 60 percent of which went to the public. The year's production of the photographic laboratory included the making of 24,301 photographs, 7,575 copy negatives, 11,069 slides, 11,788 aerial prints, and 3,008 prints from microfilm. Motion picture production amounted to 41,932 feet of negatives, 32,877 feet of master positives, and 460,032 feet of projection prints. Finally, 1,685,400 feet of sound tapes were reproduced. With the exception of the tapes, public orders accounted for a large proportion of the reproductions.

Because there has been little coordination of audiovisual materials in the federal government, the Archivist in 1966 appointed a special assistant to study the matter. A preliminary survey suggested a major role for the National Archives in the future establishment of a central information and sales point for federal audiovisual materials, a central motion picture stock footage library for nondefense federal agencies, and an office to advise and assist federal agencies in producing and distributing audiovisual materials under grants and contracts. These plans deserve early implementation through adequate funding.[26]

Because of its facilities and the skill and experience of its staff, the National Archives is called upon continuously for technical assistance to federal agencies and to nonfederal institutions concerned with documentary reproduction. It immediately exhibited concern when minor instances of deterioration of microfilm were recently reported by other institutions. Technicians on its staff are working closely with the National Bureau of Standards and with film manufacturers in formulating improved manufacturing, processing, and storage specifications to insure increased film longevity, and the new Archives Branch in Suitland, Maryland, is equipped with specially designed vaults to provide proper conditions for the preservation of the master film copies.[27] New developments are occurring in the highly special-

26. Jim Gibson, "New Initiatives of the National Archives in the Area of Audiovisual Records," typescript of a paper delivered at the annual meeting of the Society of American Archivists, Santa Fe, N.M., October 19, 1967.

27. Among the useful papers resulting from investigations into the permanency of microfilm is C. S. McCamy and C. I. Pope, *Summary of Current Research on Archival Microfilm* (Washington: National Bureau of Standards [N.B.S. Technical Note 261], 1965). Later reports are carried in *National Micro-News* and *NMA Journal*, published by the National Microfilm Association. Significantly, film processed in the National Archives had not shown signs of deterioration.

ized field of microphotography and other types of reproduction, however, and in spite of past accomplishments, much remains to be done. As in so many other instances, additional manpower will be required to enable the National Archives to meet the demands made upon it.

ARRANGEMENT AND DESCRIPTION

THE librarian classifies and catalogs books. The archivist arranges and describes records. The control procedures of the two professions are so different that training for one may, in some instances, become a hindrance to the work of the other. Nonetheless, the aim of each is identical: to facilitate the location of a desired item in the shortest possible time. The whole purpose of archival preservation is the availability of the records for reference, but reference is possible only if the hundreds of millions of individual items in the National Archives are so arranged and described that the staff and researchers can locate what they are looking for. Even the principles of provenance, continuous custody, and original order—the archivist's trinity—do not solve this problem, because most official records require, if not some rearrangement, certainly a review of their arrangement. Furthermore, finding aids prepared in the agencies of origin, even when available, are often unsuited to the needs of the archivist and the researcher. One of the most important and time-consuming tasks of the archivist, therefore, is the continuing preparation of progressively more detailed finding aids.

In seeking an American counterpart of the European record "fond," the National Archives devised the concept of the "record group," defined as a "major archival unit established somewhat arbitrarily but with due regard to the principle of provenance and to the desirability of making the unit of convenient size and character for the work of arrangement and description and for the publication of inventories." [28] A record group may encompass all of the accessioned records of a small agency; the records of a large department may be divided into two or more

28. National Archives, *Glossary of Records Terminology* [*Draft*] (Washington: National Archives and Records Service, 1956), p. 24.

record groups. A complex record group will be further divided into several subgroups. Arrangement and description proceeds from the general to the particular for each record group. The National Archives descriptive program, as outlined by its Finding Aid Committee in 1941, was to include a summary guide and a more detailed general guide to all of the records of the repository, special guides to records covering particular subjects and classes, a descriptive preliminary inventory and eventually a final inventory of the records in each group, and detailed and special lists describing either what records are available on a particular subject or what subjects are covered by particular records.[29]

Immediately upon receipt of the first contingent of records from an agency, the staff of the National Archives prepares two documents: an *Accession Inventory*, which serves as the legal document transferring custody, and a *Record Group Registration Statement*, which is a sort of "birth certificate" giving the record group a name and a number, defining its boundaries, and summarizing holdings. These are basic administrative controls that are not intended primarily to serve as finding aids.

The basic finding aid is the descriptive *Preliminary Inventory* for each record group. This document contains "information on the character of records in terms of their administrative and functional origins; their types; their chronological, geographical, or subject-matter coverage; their relations to other records; and their arrangement."[30] Records are described by *series*—a body of records filed together because of some connection arising out of their creation and use. A series may contain records arranged under a single filing system or kept together because they relate to a particular function or have a particular physical form. Thus the descriptive preliminary inventory treats units of records, not discrete items, and the series description—usually one paragraph —gives the series title, period covered, quantity, and a summary of the type of information contained in the unit.

The preparation of these descriptive inventories proceeded

29. See, e.g., *Staff Information Circulars*, Nos. 14 and 15, *The Preparation of Preliminary Inventories* and *The Control of Records at the Record Group Level*, and *Staff Information Papers*, No. 17 (rev.), *The Preparation of Lists of Record Items*.

30. T. R. Schellenberg, *Modern Archives: Principles and Techniques* (Chicago: University of Chicago Press, 1956), p. 208.

slowly. Though many more had been prepared in rough form, only 22 had been published and distributed to the public by 1949. The progress had been so limited, in fact, that Wayne Grover, in the last annual report that he was permitted to issue, wrote:

> The lack of finding aids is basically uneconomical, since it leads to the expensive regathering of information already in existence or to the time-consuming repetition of experience already gained and documented in existing records. The National Archives has as its goal the completion of preliminary inventories on the records now in its custody within the next 5 years. To prepare these basic and elementary controls will require a considerable increase in the staff.[31]

These hopes for a "considerable increase in the staff" and for completion of preliminary inventories in the following five years were in vain, for during that period only 53 inventories were published, the preparation of some of which had been done prior to 1949. By 1962, faced with the facts that many record groups were without even unpublished preliminary inventories and that altogether only about 135 inventories had been published, a major policy change was made, and to carry out the new policy, the staff was reorganized. For all but selected groups of records, the *descriptive preliminary inventory* gave way to the *title preliminary inventory*, which omitted the series descriptions. A title inventory, referred to by members of the staff as a "quickie inventory" or "preliminary preliminary inventory," usually lists only the title and number of the series, inclusive dates, quantity, and arrangement. The difference between the descriptive inventory and the title inventory can be understood best by comparing entries in these two types of finding aids.

Here, for instance, is an entry in the descriptive preliminary inventory to Record Group 142, Records of the Office of the Chief of Finance (Army):

JOURNAL OF UNITED STATES MILITARY ACADEMY AC-
COUNTS. 1895–1905. 1 vol. 2 in.   <u>37</u>
Accounts of disbursing officers stationed at the United

31. *Fifteenth Annual Report, 1948–49*, p. 6.

States Military Academy between 1895 and 1900, show-ing receipts, expenditures, and balances. Arranged chrono-logically under name of disbursing officer. These accounts are followed by accounts for the Post Exchange, 1904–5, "incidental and miscellaneous expenses," and similar kinds of accounts. The volume also contains a few entries for accounts not relating to the Military Academy. Later dis-bursing officer accounts may be found in entry 38.

In striking contrast are the following entries in a title prelimi-nary inventory, that of the Textual Records of the Office of the Quartermaster General (Record Group 92):

I. Philadelphia Supply Agencies, 1795–1858.

BOUND VOLUMES OF THE PHILADELPHIA SUPPLY AGEN-CIES. 1795–1858. ca. 600 vols. 70 ft.   <u>2117</u>
Unarranged.

CORRESPONDENCE, REPORTS, RETURNS, BILLS, AC-COUNTS CURRENT, STATEMENTS, RECEIPTS, VOUCH-ERS, AND CONTRACTS ("COXE AND IRVINE PAPERS").
1794–1842. 204 ft.   <u>2118</u>
Unarranged.

The 1962 decision to substitute title inventories for descrip-tive inventories, resulting from insufficient personnel for the job as outlined in the National Archives' instruction booklet, *The Preparation of Preliminary Inventories*, was an expedient de-signed (1) to accelerate the preparation of less definitive finding aids and (2) to allow the use of subprofessionals, working under the direction of archivists, in certain phases of the descrip-tive process. The new policy did speed up the preparation of title inventories for internal use by the National Archives staff, but it had the opposite effect upon the *publication* of inventories. For the years 1963–67, inclusive, only 20 inventories were pub-lished—just 4 more than were published in 1949 alone. In fact, in 1968 preliminary inventories are available in published form for fewer than half of the approximately 400 record groups in the National Archives, though a good many more have been prepared for internal use. But finding aids available only on the shelves or in the drawers of the National Archives are of little value to the researcher at Cambridge or Berkeley who needs to determine what materials the National Archives may have for use in his particular project. To make a researcher come to Washington and then wade through hundreds of pages of type-written lists after he arrives is hardly fair, especially when many of these lists are in the form of title inventories lacking series descriptions and therefore of substantially less value to the re-searcher.

The original plan for finding aids called for the eventual preparation of a *Final Inventory* for each record group. The use of the word "final" was unfortunate, for both the historian and archivist know that no finding aid can truly be labeled "final." Nonetheless, and despite a declaration by the Archivist in 1968 that this concept was dropped "25 years ago," the National Archives has continued to promise to replace the preliminary inventories—both title and descriptive—with more adequate in-ventories, whether these be called "Final Inventories" or just plain "Inventories." In fact, each preliminary inventory pub-lished prior to 1964 carried the following statement in its fore-word:

These inventories are called "preliminary" because they are provisional in character. They are prepared as soon as possible after the records are received without waiting to screen out all disposable material or to perfect the arrange-ment of the records. They are compiled primarily for inter-nal use, both as finding aids to help the staff render efficient reference service and as a means of establishing adminis-trative control over the records.

Each preliminary inventory contains an introduction that briefly states the history and functions of the agency that accumulated the records. The records themselves are de-scribed series by series, that is, by units of records of the same form or that deal with the same subject or activity or that are arranged serially. Other significant information about the records may sometimes be given in appendixes.

When the record group has been studied sufficiently and the records have been placed in final order, the preliminary inventories will be revised and the word "preliminary" dropped from the title of the revision. Meanwhile, as occasion demands and time permits, special reports, indexes, calendars, and other finding aids to the record group will be prepared.[32]

Beginning in 1964 and continuing to the present time, the following statement has been carried over the Archivist's name in the preface of each published inventory:

> The first step in the records-description program of the National Archives is the compilation of preliminary inventories of the material in some 350 record groups to which the holdings of the National Archives are allocated. These inventories are called "preliminary" because they are provisional in character. They are prepared as soon as possible after the records are received without waiting to screen out all disposable material or to perfect the arrangement of the records. They are compiled primarily for internal use, both as finding aids to help the staff render efficient reference service and as a means of establishing administrative control over the records.[33]

It is clear, therefore, that the National Archives has never considered and does not now consider the preliminary inventory —descriptive or title—as being adequate and that, furthermore, it plans to issue revised inventories without the prefix "preliminary" in their titles. But it is equally clear that the descriptive program faces a staggering task: (1) Preliminary inventories need to be prepared for record groups that have not yet been brought under this level of finding aid control. (2) Title inventories need to be converted into descriptive inventories and published. (3) Because of increased knowledge of the contents of the records, changes in their arrangement, and reappraisal and subsequent disposal of some series, previously published inventories need to be revised, updated, and republished. (4) The National Archives must fulfill its promise to the historical profession and to the public to proceed to produce, as rapidly as

32. Ralph E. Huss (comp.), *Preliminary Inventories Number 159: United States Government Documents Having General Legal Effect* (Washington: National Archives and Records Service, 1964), p. iii.
33. Katherine H. Davidson (comp.), *Preliminary Inventories Number 160: Records of the Smaller War Plants Corporation* (Washington: National Archives and Records Service, 1964), p. v.

possible, "final" inventories, regardless of what they are called, when the "preliminary" inventorying is finished.

While inventories are the basic finding aids devised by archivists, they are not intended to serve as catalogs, calendars, or indexes. The inventories, therefore, must be supplemented by other types of aids. Twenty-one *Special Lists* of incalculable value have been prepared, typical of which are the 175-page *List of Documents Concerning the Negotiation of Indian Treaties, 1801–1869*, published in 1949, and the 217-page *Population Schedules, 1800–1870; Volume Index to Counties and Major Cities*, published in 1951. These lists identify specific records available on selected subjects and lead researchers directly to them. They serve the reference staff as quick locators and as tools that allow a researcher to decide what records he needs to see. They go so far beyond the inventories that their usefulness can hardly be compared. Unfortunately, no special list has been published since 1965.

Another valuable aid to researchers is the special *Guide* to a specific type of records. By early 1968 five such guides had been published: to materials on Latin America, genealogical records, federal archives relating to the Civil War, Civil War maps, and federal records of World War II (two volumes); [34] and seven more are in various stages of preparation. Their compilation and publication have been painfully slow. For example, the *Guide to Materials in the National Archives Relating to Alaska*, begun in 1962 and planned for issuance during the Alaska Purchase centennial, will not be ready at least until 1970; and the *Guide to the Archives of the Government of the Confederate States of America*, planned for release during the Civil War centennial, will appear three years after that observance has passed.

During and immediately following World War II, more than 40 *Reference Information Papers*, each dealing with some special subject on which records were found in several different record groups, were published. Most of these were part of a crash program to make the experience of World War I available to World War II agencies. This series virtually has been discontinued, though one paper, titled *Material in the National Ar-*

34. More than 50 *Guides to German Records Microfilmed* were published from 1958 through 1967 plus 3 volumes to the records of the Italian Armed Forces.

chives Relating to the Independence of Latin American Nations, was expected to be issued in 1968.

Keeping current and in print a general guide to all of its holdings is one of the most difficult tasks of any archival institution. The first such guide to the records of the National Archives was printed as an appendix in the *Annual Report of the Archivist* for 1936–37, and an expanded version was first separately published in 1940 under the title *Guide to the Material in the National Archives*. Finally, in 1948, the 684-page *Guide to the Records in the National Archives* was published, giving a brief entry for each of 224 record groups. This essential but now rusty tool, covering only half of the life span of the National Archives, has long been out of date and out of print. It is fundamental to any intelligent use of the records; yet it is a dubious aid in directing the researcher to the records that he needs. Hence it adds strain on the reference staff of the Archives and frustrations for scholars who really try to do their homework conscientiously. A new edition has been under preparation since 1965, but its date of publication cannot be predicted. An updated guide should include numerous things not found in the old one: a historical sketch of the Archives, a description of its far-flung activities, a chart of its organization, a guide to the use of the records, and a list of its publications both in and out of print. Now that substantial bodies of records have been published on microfilm, the description of each record group should be accompanied by a listing of what portions have been published in print or in microfilm, together with their serial numbers in the program and an indication whether pamphlet guides to the films are available. Equating record groups with published inventories, special lists, microfilm publications, and pamphlet guides can thus be made less exasperatingly difficult.

No phase of the National Archives program demonstrates more clearly the need for additional manpower than does the arrangement and description function. Twenty-seven years after the inauguration of a realistic finding aid program, veteran staff members estimate that really satisfactory preliminary inventories have been prepared for fewer than 75 percent of the approximately 400 record groups, and fewer than 45 percent of the groups are covered by published inventories. Only 21 special lists, 5 guides (other than guides to World War II enemy records on microfilm), and 44 reference information papers have been published thus far. The general guide to the records of the National Archives has been out of date and out of print for many years, and though a new guide is under preparation, its publication date cannot yet be predicted. Only about 125 staff members—approximately 30 percent of the personnel in the National Archives—are at work on arrangement and description, and the situation may get worse rather than better. The 1967 Program Memorandum reports that because of the necessity of rearranging the records in the National Archives following the transfer of a quarter of a million cubic feet of infrequently used records to the Archives Branch in Suitland, "Manpower requirements for the arrangement of records [during the period 1969–73] will continue to exceed the averages for years in the recent past. These additional needs will continue to be drawn from time that would otherwise be used for preparing finding aids." [35] An immediate, substantial increase in manpower is necessary in the finding aid program if the National Archives is to live up to its promise to make the records of the nation conveniently accessible to the American people. After all, as the 1967 Program Memorandum frankly admits, "Unpublished lists, prepared primarily for internal use by the staff, are of practically no value in popularizing the records (i.e., making known to the public their existence, contents, historical value, etc.)." [36]

REFERENCE SERVICES

The typical user of federal archives is oblivious to the problems of appraisal, preservation, reproduction, arrangement, and description. He is concerned only with having handed to him in the well-lighted, quiet, pleasant, and comfortable Search Room the records in which he is interested. Whether he is a government official, a scholar, a genealogist, or just a curiosity seeker, he wants information, either in oral or in written form. He is likely

35. National Archives and Records Service, 1967 Program Memorandum (typescript), V.B., Pt. II, p. 9.
36. *Ibid.*, p. 6.

to be in a hurry, and he expects the reference staff to be able to supply him with the desired records or information without delay. To furnish this service to him is the ultimate aim of any archival institution. The responsibility for furnishing it is entrusted to the reference staff, a body of archivists with a combination of virtues not likely to be required of any other group. For, in addition to a wide knowledge of history and government, the reference archivist must know the records of the institution, be able to furnish desired items without delay, and demonstrate a spirit of public service and friendliness that never betrays his frustrations arising from overwork, impatience of patrons, inadequate finding aids, and incorrectly shelved records. If there are saints among archivists, they most certainly are reference archivists who carry out their duties with a smile.

Even saints, though, cannot fulfill the objectives of an archival institution unless the records have been properly arranged and described. Successful reference services, therefore, are dependent upon the tedious, analytical, and time-consuming work of other archivists, who seldom meet the patrons of the institution—the using public—unless and until they are assigned to the reference function. Some archival institutions, failing to recognize the truth of this observation, pour more and more of their resources into reference, thus compounding an already serious problem by allowing the backlog of arrangement and description work to grow while they attempt as best they can to serve the immediate needs of the public. At some point the tragic lesson is learned: More and more staff time is being spent searching for more and more records for more and more people with less and less success. Probably no archival repository in the nation is sufficiently staffed to permit it to do a first-rate job of accessioning, preserving, arranging, describing, and making available its records. Lacking the manpower to do this job, one might suggest that the repository should close its doors, bring all of its holdings under control, prepare definitive finding aids, and then reopen with a large reference staff thoroughly familiar with the records and their contents. Such a procedure, of course, is impracticable. The only sensible alternative, therefore, is for the institution to place first things first, offering all public service that it can afford to give without neglecting the essential prereference activities.

All of this leads up to the dilemma facing the National Archives: How much of its resources should be allocated to the reference function? According to the 1967 Program Memorandum, the institution devotes 55 percent of its human resources to making materials available to researchers and to supplying information from the records. Thus, after allowing for personnel assigned to such functions as preservation, reproduction, etc., nearly twice as many employees are engaged in reference service as are assigned to arrangement and description—an extraordinary situation. At first glance these statistics suggest that the cart is before the horse. But the picture changes when one is reminded that in the National Archives nearly 600,000 reference services are rendered annually, or nearly 4,000 per reference staff member—a production figure perhaps matched by few other archival repositories in the nation.[37] Substantial relief in the finding aid program, therefore, cannot be obtained by diverting professional staff members from the reference function. Yet the strain on the reference staff will continue to increase unless that relief in the arrangement and description activities can be found so that more and better finding aids can be produced.

Reference activities have undergone several structural changes during the life of the National Archives. The most recent reorganization has tended to centralize these services in the public Search Room, which, it is encouraging to note, maintains a schedule generous enough to permit researchers to work at night. Several research scholars interviewed during the course of this study expressed preference for the earlier procedures whereby they were directed to the divisions maintaining custody over the records in which they were interested. These scholars contend that the division staffs are more familiar with their holdings and are, consequently, of much greater aid to researchers in suggesting additional sources pertinent to their interests. If these opinions are valid, researchers—particularly those on projects of considerable significance—should be informed that they may still request referral to the record divisions. This would not alter present procedures; it would simply

37. The National Archives figures that each call for information costs the government $2.30. A "reference service" is defined as a consultation, a letter replying to an inquiry, an oral reply, or an item of records furnished in the Search Room or loaned to the agency of origin.

make more generally known to serious researchers their privilege of assistance from the division staffs. The recent reorganization appears to have given the mistaken impression that all reference service must be conducted from the central Search Room.

The question of how much time reference archivists should devote to a particular request for assistance can never be answered. Every request has its own justification, but the reasonableness of the request must be determined by the archivist handling it. The furnishing of information from the nation's "strongbox" cannot involve unlimited time and effort. Priorities must be established, even if they are arbitrary. It may indeed be reasonable for a staff member to spend days or even weeks furnishing the Department of Justice information from the federal records for use in a case defending the government against claims, but it is certainly unreasonable to expect the same archivist to spend several hours trying to document the service of one Civil War soldier unless that documentation is of importance beyond a descendant's desire to qualify for membership in a patriotic organization. All manners of requests fall in between those two examples—and many outside of them—and to each must be applied the rule of reason weighed against the public responsibilities of the National Archives. But to all requests there should be an answer, whether oral or by mail, and that answer should reflect the dignity of the institution by giving whatever information can be furnished with reasonable time and effort and by suggesting further sources that the inquirer may search either in person or through his agent. The National Archives, sometimes with considerable backlogs of correspondence awaiting answers, follows the commendable and necessary policy of replying to all inquiries as quickly as possible. As in many repositories of public records, genealogical inquiries relating to census and military records comprise the greatest proportion of letters received. Out of necessity, simplified answers are furnished to this kind of inquiry, usually by filling in preprinted forms. Efforts are made, however, to provide individually typed replies to inquiries involving less routine types of reference.

Some long-time patrons of the National Archives say that the quality of reference services has deteriorated since the beginning of World War II. While this is probably incorrect, there are

106

several circumstances that may account for this impression. First, the holdings of the Archives have increased threefold, and satisfactory finding aids have not been prepared for all of these additional records. Consequently the reference archivists are sometimes faced with servicing records whose contents are not known to them. Second, the increase in the size of the staff and of the holdings of the institution since the early years has at times led to organizational changes that have tended to fence off reference archivists from some of the earlier phases of the archival process, again promoting unfamiliarity with the contents of the records. The present system of periodically rotating work assignments has, in the opinion of the Archivist, lessened this handicap. Third, well-trained scholars—professional historians —were more in abundance among the reference staff prior to World War II. With fewer records to handle and with a broader academic education, these scholars may have been of more assistance to their colleagues who came in as researchers. Furthermore, with graduate degrees dangling from their names, they were often of equal rank with the professorial visitors and thereby enjoyed their confidence. Finally, the contrast between the pay scales of federal archivists and college professors, particularly until the past year or so, has had an effect on lowering the educational attainments of the staff as a whole, and positions formerly filled by archivists with master's and doctor's degrees are now often occupied by those with only the bachelor's degree. Regardless of the reference archivist's knowledge, his standing in the eyes of all too many academicians still depends upon his university degrees. While there is little justification for this sort of academic snobbishness, archival administrators must recognize its existence and seek to overcome it by providing salaries and working conditions that will attract well-educated archivists.

Of potentially great significance to reference services in the National Archives is the possible application of automated techniques to its finding aids. Analyses are now being conducted to determine if the controls over the accessioned archives can be handled by a machine system. If so, one can envision an automated record that provides descriptive, use, and provenance controls over records down to the series level. Such a record would permit the automated accumulation of statistics on holdings and use and would bring into one central retrievable record all of the major elements of information about each record group. It would also be capable of establishing relationships for material in different records, as well as indexing substantive information from record group, subgroup, and series titles. For the Presidential Archives, one might envision a system structured along the lines of the Library of Congress' manuscript procedures.[38]

With the effective establishment of regional archives in the Federal Records Centers, it is not beyond reason to anticipate a future control network with a computer in one location and "on-line drops" located in all of the branch archives. Thus a call from Harvard University to the Waltham Federal Records Center concerning the location of certain records could result in Waltham's querying the NARS system and furnishing the information promptly. It is also possible that the NARS system might be tied in, either directly or manually, with the proposed national information network being discussed by librarians. In short, the possibilities may be limitless, though obviously the National Archives needs to concentrate first on the application of automation to its own holdings.

A word of caution, however, must be interposed. An automated record built on series titles in inventories could be a snare and a delusion unless those inventories are reviewed and revised where necessary and unless the descriptions of additional accessions are kept up to date. Series titles must be correct and must give adequate clues to the subject content of the records. The automated record will be only as reliable as are the inventories. Unless carefully and intelligently used, it could throw out false leads, thus increasing rather than decreasing reference costs.

To aid the present study of automated techniques, the Council on Library Resources, Incorporated, announced in 1967 a grant of $40,000 to NARS "for a 2-year project to develop and apply a computer program for indexing finding aids to archival and

38. See Frank G. Burke, "The Application of Automated Techniques in the Management and Control of Source Materials," *American Archivist*, XXX (April 1967), 255–278. This issue of the archivists' journal contains several other useful articles on information retrieval and automated processes. See also Burke's article, "Automation in Bibliographical Control of Archives and Manuscript Collections," in Dagmar Horna Perman (ed.), *Bibliography and the Historian* (Santa Barbara, Calif.: Clio Press, 1968), pp. 96–102.

manuscript materials." [39] The amount is to be more than matched by NARS appropriated funds. This is another instance in which forward-looking programs have obtained support from outside the government. It reflects, on the one hand, the niggardliness of the government in furnishing funds essential to the responsibilities of the national archival institution, and, on the other hand, the continued benefaction of the Council on Library Resources, which, under the presidency of Verner W. Clapp,[40] has shown more interest in archival development than any other private organization in the United States.[41]

SUMMARY

Two more topics are appropriate for discussion here: the relations of the National Archives with other archival agencies and manuscript repositories in the United States, and the need for the establishment of an archives of machine-readable records.

From its inception the National Archives has been the repository of the records of the federal government. It was never intended to be anything else. In that capacity it has developed remarkably harmonious relations with state, local, academic, and private archival and manuscript repositories. It has contributed immeasurably to the archival profession, and its experiences and resources have been shared throughout the land—indeed, throughout the world.

These good relations have been promoted by the wise leadership of the National Archives since its creation. The National Archives has been, in effect, a partner in the promotion of improved archival practices. It has avoided attempts to dictate or to influence unduly. It has recognized its role as the archival agency of the federal government and has contented itself with lending its advice and assistance when such were requested by nonfederal agencies and institutions.

39. *Library of Congress Information Bulletin*, XXVI, August 10, 1967, p. 538.
40. Clapp retired on August 31, 1967.
41. Among nonfederal archival projects supported by the Council have been a study of state archival programs, the preparation of a history of archives in the western world, and the forthcoming publication of papers on archives and records center buildings and equipment.

But another characteristic of the National Archives has contributed greatly to its good relations with other archival institutions. That characteristic derives from the act creating the National Archives. The institution is concerned with the records of the *federal* government. It was given no statutory authority outside that field. There has not been, therefore, a conflict of interest between the National Archives and smaller repositories in the states. There has been no real competition between the federal archival program on the one hand and the programs of the state, local, and nonpublic repositories on the other.

This clear line of demarcation between the concerns of the federal and other programs must be maintained, but there exists a danger that the importance of the line may be forgotten. One threat has arisen from the actions of a few federal officials—particularly the district court officers—who have, through a strange ignorance of the law, turned federal records over to nonfederal repositories. Such transfers are clearly illegal, and it is the responsibility of the National Archives, carrying out its statutory requirements, to bring these records back into federal custody. Instances of alienation of federal records have not been widespread, but they have been frequent enough to warrant a continuing program of informing all federal officials—particularly those outside of Washington—of the statutes and schedules governing their records. In return, the leadership of the National Archives is taking an increasingly reasonable attitude in situations involving federal records that were alienated from proper custody many decades ago. Its choice not to appeal the decision in the case of the Lewis and Clark Papers [42] indicates that the concern of the National Archives will be the preservation of such records rather than a narrow interpretation of the law as to their custody. In the words of a former Archivist, ". . . so long as these bodies of archival materials have been in responsible institutional custody, with provision for proper care and access, we have never sought their replevin. . . ." [43] With improvements in the education of archivists and of federal officials, and with expanding knowledge of basic archival princi-

42. For a layman's account of the significance of the case, see Calvin Tomkins, "Annals of Law: The Lewis and Clark Case," *The New Yorker*, October 29, 1966, pp. 105 ff.
43. Robert H. Bahmer to H. G. Jones, September 6, 1967.

ples, the problem of alienation of federal records may be expected virtually to disappear.

But there is another side to the coin. The National Archives, under a provision of the Federal Records Act,[44] may now accept "documents, including motion-picture films, still pictures, and sound recordings, from private sources that are appropriate for preservation by the Government as evidence of its organization, functions, policies, decisions, procedures, and transactions." Like so many laws, this one is susceptible to either a broad or a narrow interpretation. Wisely—very wisely—it has been exercised with discretion and restraint, and it must continue to be so exercised. It was never the intention of the provision to enable the National Archives to duplicate the role of the Library of Congress and other repositories in the collection of private papers of general interest; it was designed to permit the Archives to receive materials having direct bearing upon the "organization, functions, policies, decisions, procedures, and transactions" of the federal government. Thus the act in no way was intended to open the door for the institution's competition with established repositories for nonfederal materials. In only one instance has the National Archives actively sought private materials; that instance relates to records of polar explorations, activities dependent largely upon federal sponsorship.[45] The matter of accepting private papers in Presidential Archives is, of course, another story with another set of circumstances.[46]

The National Archives was conceived as the repository of the records of the federal government. In that capacity it has its hands more than full. It must continue the enlightened policy of referring prospective donors of personal collections to the institutions better qualified to handle and preserve private materials —the Manuscript Division of the Library of Congress and the many state, local, and nongovernmental repositories throughout the country. To attempt to compete with them would be to extend already overburdened resources to still another activity and to damage seriously the relations between the National Archives and these repositories. The National Archives needs

44. Section 507(e)(2).
45. There has been created recently in the Office of the National Archives a Center for Polar Archives.
46. See Chapter 7 for comments on this subject.

friends, and the surest way to make enemies is to commit the fearful power of a federal agency to competition in activities already being performed satisfactorily by other institutions.[47]

Even with its hands more than full in carrying out its traditional duties, the National Archives now must face and master a new challenge, a challenge brought on by modern technology. It must, in short, undertake a broad new program that may in a century or more dwarf in richness if not in size its present holdings. Indeed, it is not beyond reason to anticipate that many of the textual records now in the Archives will at some future date be converted to a new medium of information retention and retrieval.[48]

During his more than 4,000 years of record-making, man has progressed from one medium of recording to another. Even so, the clay tablet was used for more than 2,000 years, and paper has continued to be the most common medium for recording for 1,000 years. Beginning in the last half of the nineteenth century, new inventions such as the typewriter, carbon paper, and duplicating machines ushered in a period of mass production of paper records, a proliferation that has led to demands for alternate means of recording information. Consequently, traditional media for record-making are rapidly being supplemented; macroscopic paper records are giving way to machine-readable, highly compact tapes and other media. The computer, capable

47. In 1949, when a problem arose over the accessioning of motion picture films, the National Archives and the Library of Congress agreed upon a solution under which the former would not seek nonfederal films and the latter would transfer to the National Archives federal films then in its possession. (See *American Archivist*, XII [July 1949], 304.) The 1955 amendment to the Federal Records Act apparently nullified this wise agreement. GSA Order NAR 1848.8, issued June 8, 1967, included regulations concerning the allocation of records and papers between the National Archives and the Regional Archives. It did not, according to the former Archivist of the United States, establish a policy for the acquisition of private papers (Robert H. Bahmer to H. G. Jones, September 6, 1967).

48. Such a conversion, of course, would not necessarily involve the destruction of the originals. Indeed, the peculiar nature of the archivist would bar the destruction of documents that have an intrinsic value. On the other hand, huge quantities of 20th-century records, in particular, are now preserved only for their statistical or factual data, and the conversion of these data to a machine-readable form and the disposal of the originals would do no harm to—in fact, would facilitate—the archivist's responsibility.

of compiling in minutes data that previously might have taken the statistician months to produce, has already become a familiar fixture in not only large public agencies but also in research institutions themselves. These new systems are as numerous as there are manufacturers, and there has been little effort to standardize data formats, coding procedures, and storage and maintenance methods. The prospects of this diversity—and its consequent danger of requiring many different and expensive retrieval devices in the repositories established to house the data—are frightening. The only solution to this dilemma lies in the continued close relationship of the records management officials who design and oversee the recording equipment and the archivists in whose hands the data will have continuing usefulness.

Though little attention was given to the new technology until recent years, scholars in particular have awakened to the need for establishment of a federal centralized "data bank," "magnetic tape library," or "social science tape archives." [49] Organizations such as the Social Science Research Council have taken the lead in exploring these needs, and recommendations have been made for meeting them. Some recommendations envision a "Federal Data Center" that would (1) centrally house certain machine-readable records and (2) coordinate referrals, promote standards for collecting, coding, "formating," and preserving such data, and assist users in gaining access to the information. In the high-level discussions thus far conducted too little thought has been given to the one and only logical location of such an archives of machine-readable records—the National Archives and Records Service.

The need for an archives of machine-readable federal records is urgent. The computer is not only changing the records creating process but it is changing the nature of records themselves. Computers are forcing archivists to reconsider what to keep. Large groups of records previously destroyed because their sheer bulk made them unmanageable, when reduced to a small volume of magnetic tape and searchable by machine, are worth

49. A review of activities in the field will be found in Ralph L. Bisco, "Social Science Data Archives: A Review of Developments," *American Political Science Review*, LX (March 1966), 93–109.

keeping for broadening the research base. Already the federal government has several million reels of magnetic tape. A sizable number of these will be kept for long periods of time, especially those containing statistical data valuable to the American economy. These materials are federal records no less than are the millions of cubic feet of paper records and microfilm. They come under the statutory provisions for public records; and the responsibility for appraising, retaining, or approving disposal of all records lies in the National Archives and Records Service through delegation from the Administrator of General Services. The very thought of there being operated *two* National Archives within a few blocks of each other is bewildering. Of even more concern is the thought of having two agencies sharing the statute and common-law responsibilities for federal records. Thus the problem is twofold: (1) The need for a national archives of machine-readable records is evident; and (2) the centuries-old archival principle of accountability for the records of the people would be threatened if serious consideration were given to the establishment of such an archives outside the National Archives and Records Service.

The question of the organizational location of such an archives involves the fundamental nature of public records and their management. It also involves the training of technical personnel who must maintain close ties with the patrons of the archives. In NARS these several categories have been brought effectively into interplay: social scientists aware of informational needs, archivists knowledgeable in principles of archival science, and records managers trained in techniques of record-making and record-keeping. These three groups are now involved in recording, preserving, and retrieving information. Machine-readable records require those characteristics just as eye-readable records do. The new media, however, demand additional training in the recording of the data, its preservation, and its manipulation. The principles are the same; only the techniques are different.

Just as it has the basic though inadequate human resources, NARS has the physical facilities for the establishment of a national archives of machine-readable records. Its Records Center in Suitland furnishes vaults especially designed for the protection of magnetic tapes and other recording media.[50] Suitland not only offers the potential as the repository for the tapes, it can also serve as the generating point of an information network that can encompass the Regional Archives in the twelve other cities where they are to be located. Thus the researcher in Chicago or San Francisco or Fort Worth will be able to query the network and receive, through an advanced visual and perhaps print-out system, the information he needs. Leading libraries and research institutions outside the NARS network may be tied into the system, thus adding to its potential.

A truly national information network is in the offing. It has long been envisioned by farsighted officials within NARS, and several important steps have been taken that, if funds become available for the purpose, may lead to its implementation. An inventory of federal machine-readable records of possible archival significance was prepared for the Social Science Research Council; conferences and symposia have been conducted for NARS representatives, other government officials, and interested economists, historians, and other social scientists; a directive has been issued to all federal agencies on documenting automated data-processing operations, and NARS has helped a number of agencies prepare data-processing documentation; and a special committee, appointed by the Archivist in 1966, has drawn up a program for accessioning and managing archives in magnetic tape form. The most significant step, however, was the appointment on February 13, 1968, of a special assistant to the Archivist for the purpose of proposing plans for an archives of machine-readable archives.[51]

The hour is late, and further delay will lead to serious consequences not only to NARS but to the government as a whole and the public in general. It took the federal government a century and a half to establish a national archival program, a delay that

50. One of the most essential features of such facilities must always be protection. Magnetic tapes, for instance, may be rendered useless by heat, moisture, or errant electrical current. This type of record cannot safely be stored in areas not affording special protection.

51. The appointment of Everett O. Alldredge, a long-time proponent of an archives of machine-readable records, came less than two months after the Joint Committee on the Status of the National Archives released its report which strongly advocated the establishment of such an archives.

resulted in unnecessary expenditures and great losses of important records. The story of the struggle for an adequate repository for the preservation of the original records should be lesson enough to demonstrate that now is the time for the development, within the National Archives and Records Service, of an archives of machine-readable records.[52]

52. The proposed archives of machine-readable records should not be confused with a "data bank" advocated by social scientists. The former will be a repository for machine-readable records of the *federal government*, not a hodgepodge of statistics and other data collected from nonfederal sources. The same principles of access as have been adopted for paper records will apply. The invasion of privacy issue raised in Congress is no more relevant to the creation of the proposed archives of machine-readable records than it is to the administration of the present papers and film records in the National Archives and in the Federal Records Centers.

[5]

THE PUBLICATION OF DOCUMENTARY

SOURCES, 1934–1968

For more than a decade, the [National Historical Publications] Commission has done the most valuable work in stimulating publication from the documentary sources of American history. This work, now progressing with such momentum, must not be allowed to falter. I note with pleasure that our scholars are already speaking of these remarkable cooperative undertakings as achieving no less than a "bloodless revolution" in American historiography. —John Fitzgerald Kennedy, *1963*

THE PUBLICATION of official records of historical value by the federal government in the nineteenth century had been so haphazard in character, had proved so very costly, usually because of inexperience on the part of officials in charge, and had been carried out in detail so generally by government employees untrained in such specialized work that it was no wonder the results failed to meet the standards of historians of the more critical "scientific" school. The latter were becoming dominant toward the close of the century, and many of their leaders had been trained in European universities. As early as 1890, J. Franklin Jameson and others were calling for the establishment of a permanent commission for planning "a comprehensive and well arranged scheme of government publication" of historical documents. "A Commission consisting simply of government officials can never meet the requirements," Jameson said, adding that such a commission "should have power to edit and publish not only materials in the possession of the Government, but also those which are in private hands." He advocated in this connection the study of the experience and expenditures of foreign governments in making available the documents of their history, and he prepared an able report on the subject.[1]

1. Among recent reviews of documentary publication in the United States are Robert L. Brubaker, "The Publication of Historical Sources;

In the following years Jameson returned to this theme again and again. In 1906 he presented a paper before the American Historical Association, "Gaps in the Published Records of United States History." In 1907, as president of the Association, he appointed a national committee on the subject, and shortly afterward President Theodore Roosevelt, historian enough to understand such matters, found a way to give this committee official status and made Jameson its secretary. In this special committee's report to Congress the creation of a permanent commission was recommended.[2] Hearings were held in 1910, but the bill was not brought to a vote, and efforts to revive it in subsequent Congresses failed.

It was only when he was drafting the legislation establishing the National Archives that Jameson finally achieved the goal he had advocated 44 years earlier.[3] He incorporated in that act provision for a National Historical Publications Commission, with the Archivist as *ex officio* chairman, that "shall make plans, estimates, and recommendations for such historical works and collections of sources as it deems appropriate for printing or otherwise recording at the public expense."

The new Commission brought up to date the survey of the Jameson Committee of 1908 on historical publications by the United States government and began to make plans for new ones, its first proposal being the collection and publication of documents relative to the ratification of the Federal Constitution by the states of the Union. The 1934 legislation, however, required that each such proposal be approved by act of Congress before appropriations could be made available, and Congress failed to act on this and other recommendations before the advent of World War II. During the war the Commission

---

Recent Projects in the United States," *Library Quarterly*, XXXVII (April 1967), 193–225; L. H. Butterfield, "The Recent Past," and Julian P. Boyd, "The Next Stage," in L. H. Butterfield and Julian P. Boyd, *Historical Editing in the United States* (Worcester, Mass.: American Antiquarian Society, 1963); and Burl Noggle, "A Note on Historical Editing: The Wilson Papers in Perspective," *Louisiana History*, VIII (Summer 1967), 281–297.

2. 60th Cong., 2d Sess., S. Doc. 714.

3. Jameson's role in the establishment of the NHPC is described in Waldo Gifford Leland, "The Prehistory and Origins of the National Historical Publications Commission," *American Archivist*, XXVII (April 1964), 187–194.

lapsed into inactivity. Revised legislation seemed necessary to make it the effective body that had been envisioned by Jameson, and the opportunity came when the new Federal Records Act of 1950 was being drafted.

The new legislation enlarged the mandate of the Commission by directing that it also "cooperate with and encourage appropriate Federal, State, and local agencies and nongovernmental institutions, societies, and individuals in collecting and preserving and, when it deems such action to be desirable, in editing and publishing the papers of outstanding citizens of the United States and such other documents as may be important for an understanding and appreciation of the history of the United States." Absent was the impractical provision that each proposal first be approved by special act of Congress. Finally, the Commission's standing was benefited by an enlargement of the membership to include one representative from the judicial branch of the government to be appointed by the Chief Justice, one member from the Senate to be appointed by the President of the Senate, one member from the House to be appointed by the Speaker of the House, and two members "outstanding in the fields of the social or physical sciences to be appointed by the President of the United States." The Library of Congress, the Department of State, and the Department of Defense continued to be represented, as did the American Historical Association, the latter by two members appointed by its Council.

By this legislation also the National Historical Publications Commission was for the first time "authorized to appoint . . . an executive director and such editorial and clerical staff as the Commission may determine to be necessary." Previously it had had only a secretary who also held a full-time position as Director of Publications in the National Archives. The first Executive Director, Philip M. Hamer, and his two or three staff members were then assigned two separate rooms in the National Archives Building, and the Commission has continued since to have these as a headquarters of its own. The Commission in 1951 described itself as "a staff agency of the Federal Government, responsible for planning and recommending national programs for collecting, preserving, and publishing archival and other manuscript materials and for encouraging and facilitating the execution of these programs by appropriate public and private institutions." [4]

The times had been unfavorable for the publication of historical documents by the federal government or by state agencies, private historical societies and libraries, or other scholarly institutions. The long economic depression and then an exhausting world war had brought all these programs and undertakings one by one to a halt. But once the war was over and Americans realized that their nation faced new responsibilities in the world and at home, a wave of renewed interest in American history appeared to sweep over the land. It was manifested by a concern with historic sites and restorations, increased enrollments in history courses in institutions of higher learning, and the greatly accelerated publication of volumes of history and of history magazines, both scholarly and popular. New legislation, a staff of its own, and this wave of interest in history would in themselves, doubtless, have given the Commission new life, but the important thrust forward came in a directive from President Truman.

On May 17, 1950, the President had been presented with the first volume of the *Papers of Thomas Jefferson*, planned to be a scholarly edition of all Jefferson's papers, prepared and published at Princeton University, with Julian P. Boyd as Chief Editor. Truman praised the enterprise and expressed the hope that the papers of other American leaders might be made accessible in similar fashion. He then directed the National Historical Publications Commission to report a plan for making available "the writings of men whose contributions to our history are now inadequately represented by published works."

In its final form the requested report, entitled *A National Program for the Publication of Historical Documents*,[5] was presented to President Eisenhower, who wrote that the plan presented "a challenge to all of us who are privileged to participate in it, for its fulfillment will be of lasting benefit to all Americans." [6] Both houses of Congress by a concurrent resolution of August 22, 1957, endorsed the Commission's program

4. *Annual Report of the Administrator of General Services for the Fiscal Year Ending June 30, 1951*, pp. 29–30.
5. Washington: Government Printing Office, 1954.
6. President Eisenhower to members of the Commission, November 22, 1954.

and urged "the governors and legislatures of the several States and the State historical commissions and archival agencies, as well as appropriate libraries, historical societies, colleges and universities, business corporations, foundations, civic and other nonprofit organizations, and individuals to cooperate with the National Historical Publications Commission in the fulfillment of the said program." [7]

In this report the Commission had recommended two approaches: (1) the publication of the papers of individual leaders in different fields of activity and (2) the publication of documents selected because of their relationship to important events and developments. With respect to the first, the report listed the names of 361 persons whose papers had been suggested by various scholars as deserving of consideration for publication and presented additional information about the papers of 120 of these. It recommended "comprehensive" publication of the papers of Benjamin Franklin, John and John Quincy Adams, James Madison, and Alexander Hamilton in addition to, and in the manner of, those of Thomas Jefferson, already in progress. With respect to projects documenting important events and developments, priority was given to documentary histories of (1) the ratification of the Federal Constitution and Bill of Rights and (2) the work of the first Federal Congress. The two latter were to be sponsored by the Commission itself, and they, together with the proposals for publishing the papers of the six leaders listed, are often referred to as the Commission's "priority" projects. Within a few years all were under way, the Franklin papers at Yale and the American Philosophical Society, the papers of the Adamses at the Massachusetts Historical Society and at Harvard, the Hamilton papers at Columbia University, and the Madison papers at the University of Chicago and the University of Virginia, joint sponsors. The Commission's report also announced plans to compile and publish a one-volume guide to repositories of archives and manuscripts and their holdings of unpublished source materials.[8]

The Commission in these years assisted with information and advice in organizing a number of other projects besides the "priority" ones—for example, the Calhoun papers at the South

7. 71 Stat. B 41.   8. See p. 128.

Carolina Department of Archives and History, the Clay papers at the University of Kentucky, and the Andrew Johnson papers at the University of Tennessee. It provided an important searching service in the National Archives and the Library of Congress for all these projects and others. The prestige given by the Commission's endorsement of a project helped that project in its canvass of other repositories for photocopies of the documents needed for a soundly based edition. The Commission also tried, with some success, to assist and support approved projects in their search for financial support.

But the Commission had no funds of its own to hand out to deserving documentary publication projects. It could not get started what it felt were some of the most important projects because it had no carrot with which to draw forth matching support from private sources. Furthermore, it could do nothing to assure the continuity to completion of important long-term undertakings it had helped to start. Even certain of the "priority" projects were reaching the end of their resources. They had assembled the basic documentation and put it under control, but now had no funds to continue the preparation of the editor's copy for the printer. The law stated that the Commission "shall . . . encourage," but the Commission hesitated to encourage new projects if it was but leading the well-intentioned into trouble. The whole program was in jeopardy if funds could not be found to shore up and stabilize existing projects. The government had not even appropriated funds to finance the Commission's own projects, the documentary histories of the ratification of the Constitution and the first Federal Congress; and funds had to be sought from the Ford Foundation to support them—sought successfully, fortunately—but even they were running out.

Yet the program the Commission had encouraged was beginning by the early 1960s to have an impact. As early as 1958 President Eisenhower had commented on the Commission's "splendid progress toward enlarging the basic stock of source materials of American history" and had spoken of the "essential need of a broad and incorruptible supply" of such sources.[9] The new standards of editorial treatment were winning acclaim in

9. *Congressional Record*, CIV, July 29, 1958, 15502.

review after review as the volumes appeared in increasing numbers. It was unthinkable that in a country like the United States this movement should be brought to a halt for lack of adequate funds. Surely a nation spending billions for research in science could spare $500,000 a year for encouraging needed projects in American history. Government records were involved in these projects; they were being edited by professional scholars with a completeness and accuracy never before known and were being published and distributed by university presses in volumes rarely equaled for durability and attractiveness, without any cost whatsoever to the government.

It was in this crisis that the Commission in 1963 prepared and submitted to President Kennedy an impressive but bewilderingly titled *Report to the President Containing a Proposal by the National Historical Publications Commission to Meet Existing and Anticipated Needs Over the Next Ten Years Under a National Program for the Collection, Preservation, and Publication, or Dissemination by Other Means of the Documentary Sources of American History.*[10] The importance to the American people of the kind of work the Commission had been promoting was presented in that report in language more eloquent and convincing than any that can be offered here. To insure its continuance and expansion the Commission called for support totaling not less than $1,000,000 annually, to be provided by private philanthrophy and the government in approximately equal amounts. It asked, therefore, that a half million dollars be made available in appropriations each year by the government to be used for a grant program for which it also requested authorizing legislation. The report stated:

> [The Commission] does not directly promote the study of history or concern itself with the writing of history, though documentary sources with which it deals are the foundation on which all efforts to study, interpret, or recreate the past must rest. Nor does its obligation to develop a national program imply that it has any authoritarian or proprietary jurisdiction over related activities initiated under other auspices. On the contrary, its legislative directive obliges it to cooperate with Federal, State, and local agencies and non-

10. Washington: Government Printing Office, 1963.

governmental institutions, societies, and individuals in collecting, preserving, and publishing documents that are important for an understanding of the history of the United
States. If governmental and privately initiated enterprises
in this area are not to be stimulated to increased activity by
its program, the Commission will fail in its primary obligation. Its duty is to assist, not to interfere; to coordinate, not
to command; to see that a broad national program is promoted, not to emphasize one segment or period of history to
the neglect of others.[11]

President Kennedy supported the request with enthusiasm:
"If the Commission is to plan a balanced national program of
editing and publication for the next ten years, with collecting
and microfilming activities to support and supplement letterpress publication, it must have resources on which it can depend." He characterized the program as "this great effort to
enable the American people to repossess its historical heritage"
and added, "Documents are the primary sources of history; they
are the means by which later generations draw close to historical
events and enter into the thoughts, fears and hopes of the
past." [12]

With support also from President Johnson after President
Kennedy's tragic death, the proposed legislation was passed by
the Congress and signed into law on July 28, 1964.[13] The new
language authorized the Administrator of General Services
"within the limits of appropriated and donated funds available
therefor, to make allocations to Federal agencies, and grants to
State and local agencies and to nonprofit organizations and institutions, for the collecting, describing, preserving and compiling,
and publishing (including microfilming and other forms of reproduction) of documentary sources significant to the history of
the United States." The next sentence specified that prior to
making such allocations and grants, the Administrator should
"seek the advice and recommendations of the National Historical Publications Commission." The act authorized appropria-

11. *A Report to the President* . . . , p. 26
12. The President's letter, dated January 19, 1963, is reproduced in
A Report to the President . . . , pp. iv–v, and is printed in Julian P.
Boyd, *Remarks at a White House Luncheon* (Princeton: Princeton University Press, 1963), pp. 6–7. See also epigraph, p. 117.
13. P.L. 88–383.

tions "for the fiscal year ending June 30, 1965, and each of the four succeeding fiscal years, an amount not to exceed $500,000 each year for the purposes specified" (that is, grants). The unexpected five-year limitation was inserted by the House committee in charge of the bill. Unless the authorization is extended shortly, the grant program will end with the appropriation for the fiscal year beginning July 1, 1968. The appropriation for the first fiscal year, ending June 30, 1966, was for $350,000 only, probably so curtailed because part of the year was already gone. The greater disappointment, however, was that the appropriation for the second fiscal year was likewise cut to $350,000 in its passage through Congress and that, for the third year, the Administration requested only $350,000.

For the fourth year the request was for $500,000, but despite Senate support for the higher amount, the appropriation remained at the $350,000 recommended by the House Appropriations Committee. For the fifth year the Administration, facing an even tighter financial squeeze, cut its request back to $350,000. The program has thus never been funded at its intended level.

With the passage of Public Law 88–383, however, despite the limitations mentioned, the Commission entered upon a third and still more productive period of its existence. As of May, 1968, the Commission was able to cite an impressive list of projects that it had assisted or was then assisting. Once Congress passed the grant legislation, the Ford Foundation, which had been withholding additional support until the federal government assumed a larger share, granted $2,000,000 to the Commission and designated it for the support of the Adams, Franklin, Hamilton, Jefferson, and Madison projects, the annual allocations to these projects to be determined by the Commission. Federal grant funds are used, however, to support continuation of the documentary histories of the ratification of the Constitution and the work of the first Congress, to which has been added a documentary history of the first federal elections, being sponsored by the University of Wisconsin. Grants have been made available to assist 14 additional projects involving publication by printing in the conventional manner. Some 15 others have been endorsed and assisted professionally, but not with funds.

With grant funds the Commission has also inaugurated a program of documentary publication on microfilm, the impressive results of which are just now becoming known. Grants have been made since 1964 to 23 participating repositories, which have agreed to place treasured original sources at the service of scholarship generally by arranging them in a usable order, filming them, and preparing a guide to the film. From the master negative the cooperating institution agrees to provide positive prints at "reasonable cost" to any person or institution ordering them, or to honor requests for interlibrary loans. A "Catalog of Microfilm Publications," issued by NHPC in July 1968, lists 72 microfilm publications totaling 1,324 rolls of film which are available for purchase or loan. Many others were in various stages of production and will soon be available.

Publication by microfilm, in this manner, of documentary materials that are important but not quite important enough to justify expensive editorial annotation and letterpress publication is an area that the Commission feels needs as much encouragement as the traditional publication of source materials by letterpress; and it is an area of just as great dimensions. Such microfilming projects can be considered important supporting activities to existing and future letterpress publication, which is intended for a wider public, but they also serve in the training of historians at the graduate level and below. It is felt by many that one of the great needs of the nation's expanding educational systems, insofar as the teaching of history and the methods of historical research are concerned, is to have more widely available research material of this nature and degree of importance.

The surprising response to the microfilm publication program of the National Archives and to the filming of the presidential papers in the Library of Congress appears to support this view. It suggests that what is needed is an extension of this kind of operation to many other manuscript repositories and libraries in order to make their rich holdings generally available upon order at a number of research centers throughout the country, and available even to individual scholars. Besides the benefits to scholars and scholarship, this in the end should save the time of the holding institutions in servicing their manuscripts, and should help preserve the manuscripts themselves, since the originals would have to be consulted less and would not have to be

126

photographed again and again in response to the needs of individual scholars.[14]

The Commission has taken no formal position in a debate that goes on among historians as to which is the more deserving of encouragement, microfilm publication or letterpress publication. It feels that each has its place, each supplements the other, and together they comprise the whole of what is needed in documentary publication at the present time. It has so far tried to divide the grant funds available under P.L. 88–383 about evenly between the two types of publication, which has meant about $175,000 per year for each since the 1965 appropriation. It hopes that it will not be necessary to support one program at the expense of the other, and that additional funds may become available for both. If these funds are provided, it is not too much to anticipate the eventual dissemination (and hence security against loss) of all unpublished documentation—wherever it happens to be, throughout the land—that is considered significant for the history of the United States. Ernst Posner has referred to microfilm publication as "basically a final break with the archivist's proprietary attitude toward his records." [15] It may be added that the example set by the United States in this respect is already influencing other countries toward assuming a more liberal attitude toward microfilming their records, which include many of great importance for our own history.

In its 1963 *Report* the Commission expressed an intention to "give increased attention to encouraging on a national scale programs for the collection and preservation of historical manuscripts and for making these sources of history more readily available to scholars by the development of union catalogs, guides, indexes, and other tools to facilitate their use." [16] But this still remains a major lacuna in its program. To encourage

14. The objectives of this program are well stated in an article by the former Archivist, Wayne C. Grover, entitled "Toward Equal Opportunities for Scholarship," in the *Journal of American History*, LII (March 1966), 715–724.

15. Posner, "The National Archives and the Archival Theorist," *American Archivist*, XVIII (July 1955), 211.

16. The various publication projects also serve as a magnet for drawing from their hiding places papers in out-of-the-way repositories and private hands. The papers of Jefferson, for instance, are scattered among more than 600 repositories and individuals throughout the world; yet copies of all of the known manuscripts have been brought together in one place.

collecting has not been so necessary, because historical agencies and university libraries have become active in this field in recent years on a scale never before known. What is necessary is to encourage the preparation of guides to the holdings of institutions, because all too often the accessioning repositories do not have the funds to arrange and describe the material they receive into their custody. Collections and their contents remain known only to the custodians, if even to them. Yet to make known the existence of something to a creative user is as important as preserving it. Most of the proposals made to the Commission have involved indexes or calendars to individual pieces in specific collections, but the Commission feels that priority should be given to general guides to the holdings of collecting institutions. It does not feel it should pay the whole cost, because the provision of such finding aids is part of the normal responsibility of any manuscript repository. But if it had more funds available it could encourage action by offers to pay part of the costs, especially to institutions that have rich holdings and heavy reference loads and, consequently, are never likely to have resources to prepare and publish guides on their own.

In this connection one of the great accomplishments of the century for American history was the publication in 1961 of the *Guide to Archives and Manuscripts in the United States*, compiled by the Commission's own staff under the direction of the former Executive Director, Philip M. Hamer. No such general guide had ever existed before. Its compilation was motivated in part by the need to inform and serve Commission-sponsored editorial projects, existing and prospective, but it rapidly became a basic reference tool for libraries and scholars all over the country. There have been many demands for an updated edition, but in the ten years since the information in the first edition was assembled, manuscript-collecting institutions have so increased in number (perhaps one-third more), and their holdings so increased in volume and variety (perhaps a 50 percent increase in volume), that the preparation of a new edition would be an undertaking hardly less costly in time and personnel than was the original task. Yet it is generally agreed that this would be the most useful expenditure of funds for guides at the present time. The entire situation with respect to this important aspect of the Commission's program emphasizes the need for additional financial support, for the Commission cannot now enter upon this undertaking without withdrawing support from existing projects to which it is committed.

The Commission has also since 1952 had responsibility for compiling the annual volumes of *Writings on American History*. This is the standard bibliographical reference series that since its beginning in 1902 has been consulted by everyone concerned with any aspect of the history of the United States. Eleven volumes covering the years 1948–58 have now been compiled by the Commission and published. The two for 1959 and 1960 are at the Government Printing Office. Work on the manuscript of the volume for 1961 is nearing completion. The "explosion" in the publishing of books and articles in this immense field has, however, created a serious problem, and the two staff employees the Commission has had available for this basic professional service can no longer keep up year for year. Entries in the volume for 1948 numbered 5,708; in that for 1961 there will be more than 15,000. The Commission has made the situation known to the American Historical Association and to the Organization of American Historians and is represented on a "Joint Committee on Bibliographical Services to History," which has been established to study the problem. The answer probably lies in converting to a computerized system similar to that used by the National Library of Medicine for its *Index Medicus*, but in any case funds for additional personnel will be required if this important task remains with the Commission. Sufficient funds should have been provided some years ago to keep these volumes reasonably current and also to fill a still existing gap for the years 1941–47. Otherwise the history profession has high praise for the Commission's performance in this area.

A few words should be said about the Commission's inconspicuous but vital function as a clearinghouse of information concerning not only the location of particular collections of records but the existing and proposed documentary publication projects throughout the country. The Commission has not intended its office to serve as a central place to register such undertakings, but hardly a week goes by without some scholar writing to announce that he is engaged in preparing for publication the letters of so-and-so. He may ask for advice and suggestions, or he may ask about prospects for financial assistance, but he may also be announcing his undertaking just to find out if someone else has already had the same idea or in the hope that he can protect this particular domain from trespass by others. Of course the Commission reserves no particular project for anyone, but it has informed inquirers of competing or overlapping projects, for competition in this area is wasteful of funds and talent. Planning and coordination are badly needed in the field of documentary publication just because these projects are so expensive, whereas in the writing of history overlapping is to be expected if not encouraged.

With funds provided by the Ford Foundation, during the past two years the Commission has been carrying out an important nationwide "Survey on the Use of Original Sources in Graduate History Training." Reliance has been chiefly on personal interviews. Seventy universities offering the Ph.D. in American history were visited, and professors, graduate students, and librarians were interviewed. In addition some 40 private libraries, historical societies, state archives, Federal Records Centers, and other manuscript repositories concerned with graduate students' investigations were visited and their directors and staff members interviewed. Other institutions were covered by questionnaires. The survey has sought to assemble information on the content of courses in research methodology, the degree to which original sources are expected to be used and are actually used in connection with seminar papers and dissertations, the nature and sufficiency of such source materials in the different institutions, the availability of adequate guides and other finding aids, the availability and use of photocopies (especially microfilm publications), relations between the custodians of sources and the professors and students, and preferences in spending money on original sources. This is the first such large-scale survey ever to be made, and it is expected that the results will be useful not only to the Commission in planning its future programs but to foundations giving funds to universities and libraries, to publishers—especially those involved in documentary publication enterprises—and to this generation of history professors.

Finally, mention should be made of a program for the training of editors upon which the Commission has embarked, also chiefly with the use of Ford Foundation funds. It has done much over the years merely by bringing editors of letterpress projects together at luncheons and on other occasions so that they may exchange information and experiences. In recent years it has likewise brought directors of microfilm publication projects together for conferences of a day or two. This was especially necessary in so new a program, where techniques were so important and standards had to be explained and demonstrated. The success of the program has resulted in no small degree from these conferences. In 1967–68 for the first time the NHPC, after announcement in professional journals, reviewed applications and, with the help of the editors, chose five "Fellows in Advanced Historical Editing" to serve one year each with one of the Commission-supported documentary publication projects, paying them from $6,500 to $9,000 each. A similar program has been announced for 1968–69, and three more fellows have been selected. It is hoped this program may be continued in subsequent years so that more young Ph.D.s may become interested in this kind of work. Plans are also being made to hold a two-week summer institute in the editing of documentary materials.

For several years the staff actually administering this entire Commission program has numbered just four persons: the Executive Director, the Assistant to the Executive Director, and their two secretaries. Their combined salary is $45,538 per annum. Two other employees, at a cost of $22,960 in salaries, have compiled the *Writings*; but that is more properly considered a project, and they do not have time even to read proof and see the annual volumes through the press. Three other employees, with salaries totaling $22,947, are engaged in what may be called a "central searching service" for all the Commission's projects, locating and making available photocopies of relevant documents in the National Archives, the Library of Congress, and other Washington repositories. They do not assist otherwise in administering the general program. Finally, four persons whose salaries are paid from grant funds are under the Commission administratively but work on the documentary history of the ratification of the Constitution and Bill of Rights. However, that, too, is only one of the Commission's projects and adds to but does not help with administration. In other words, the NHPC has operated for years on a budget varying between

$100,000 and $130,000 for personal services, but less than half of that has been used for actual administration. Funds appropriated for the grant program are used in their entirety for grants. Nothing is taken out for administration. An additional administrative burden has been placed upon the Commission's staff by making it responsible for distribution to the five designated projects of needed annual support from the Ford Foundation grant of $2,000,000, to which has been added the responsibility for using the interest for training programs in documentary editing. Nothing has been said about the amount of work involved in investigating many formal applications for grants that are turned down for one reason or another, or in reviewing financial reports from projects to which grants are given, for, although some assistance is given by legal and fiscal officers in the General Services Administration, the burden of review and adjustments falls upon the Commission's tiny staff.

J. Franklin Jameson worked as long and persistently for a National Historical Publications Commission as he did for a National Archives, and his persistence has been vindicated. So has that of Wayne C. Grover, who led the successful movement to revive the NHPC in 1951. Its successes have been little short of phenomenal. Yet its work has only begun. Whether one considers the letterpress publication program, the microfilm publication program, the work that needs to be done with respect to finding aids, or the need for an informational and training center, he sees limitless horizons. But certainly there can be no further progress in any of these directions without an increase in staff. The half million dollars a year authorized is far too small a sum for those activities even when supplemented by a generous foundation. But only $350,000 has ever so far been appropriated. An all-out effort should be made to raise the authorization to $1,000,000 or more, a percentage of which should be allowed for the administrative expenses of the grant program. Without such an increase in authorization, to be followed by increased appropriations, the present momentum will be slowed and many badly needed projects discouraged. Such appropriations will increase the federal bureaucracy but little. It is noteworthy that most of the funds go to nonfederal agencies and institutions; thus the NHPC's program in no way conflicts with an American tradition of federal encouragement on the state and local level.

The work described has been so revolutionary as to comprise one of the most important archival developments of this century. Its beneficiaries are initially scholars and students; ultimately, if not immediately, the public will benefit from new and better histories and biographies that will spring forth from these sources. Indeed, in the future the educated American can depend not on such derivative writings but upon the sources themselves, and can thus arrive at his own conclusions as befits a citizen of a democracy. Increasingly, scholars and students of other lands will also be able to learn of America for themselves and not through intermediaries. The publication of his documents is the ultimate service of the archivist. He thus enhances their meaning, he thus insures their greater use by more and better qualified interpreters, and he thus enriches the cultural heritage of oncoming generations.

⌈6⌉

THE FEDERAL REGISTER SYSTEM OF

PUBLICATION, 1935–1968

Rules, regulations and other exercises of legislative power by executive and administrative officials should be made easily and readily available at some central office. —Special Committee on Administrative Law, American Bar Association, *1934*

Just as everyone is charged with knowledge of the United States Statutes at Large, Congress has provided that the appearance of the rules and regulations in the Federal Register gives legal notice of their contents.
—United States Supreme Court, *1947*

AMERICANS live under several strata of statutory law; they are also subject to a plethora of rules issued by scores of government agencies. This situation was born and nurtured as an almost unnoticed feature of the early twentieth-century expansion of the executive branch of government. By reason of the rapid advance toward the age of electronics and social security, Congress increasingly delegated the details of law-making to experts in the executive branch. Finally it became apparent that the main bulk of "legislation" was actually in the form of administrative rules. Statutes creating new agencies typically delegate to the agencies power to adopt rules for the implementation of the enabling legislation. These enforceable administrative rules form a web around every citizen, partnership, or corporate entity. Nonetheless, there was prior to 1936 no central compilation or publication of this "quasi legislation."

The need for making such administrative rules more readily available to the legal profession in particular and the public in general had long been recognized. In 1934 a special committee on administrative law of the American Bar Association proposed a central office for that purpose.[1] Later in the same year the

1. *Second Annual Report of the Archivist of the United States for the Fiscal Year Ending June 30, 1936*, p. 8. See epigraph, above.

Executive Committee of the National Emergency Council issued a report calling for the publication of an official periodical to be titled the "Federal Register." Based upon this report, the Interdepartmental Legal Committee, composed of the chief counsels of the major agencies of the government, drew up a bill for introduction in Congress. Three months later the government was embarrassed before the Supreme Court because it had prosecuted under a revoked executive order,[2] and the Federal Register Act was approved by Congress on July 26, 1935.

The act provided for the creation in the National Archives of a Division of the Federal Register for the receipt, custody, and publication in the daily *Federal Register* of every presidential proclamation, executive order, and generally applicable "order, regulation, rule, certificate, code of fair competition, license, notice, or similar instrument issued, prescribed, or promulgated by a Federal agency. . . ."[3] The Director of the Division, appointed by the President, was to be assisted by an Administrative Committee made up of the Archivist of the United States, the Public Printer, and a representative of the Attorney General, with the Archivist as chairman.

The Division of the Federal Register was made a combination archival, legal, and editorial office. It was to receive the original and two certified copies of each document required to be filed and published; the original was to be retained in the National Archives, one copy was to be filed in the Division, and the other was to be used for publication. A further provision, for the publication in a special issue of the *Federal Register* of all proclamations, orders, rules, and regulations having general applicability and promulgated prior to the effective date of the act, was replaced in 1937 by provisions for the *Code of Federal Regulations*.

Filing of documents commenced March 12, 1936, and the first issue of the *Federal Register* appeared two days later. Not surprisingly, the circulation of the publication grew rapidly. Within four months there were 600 paid subscriptions and 5,000 copies were being distributed free to federal officers and agencies.[4] For the first time legally enforceable administrative

2. *Panama Refining Company v. Ryan* (293 U.S. 388 [1935]).
3. 49 Stat. 500–503.
4. *Second Annual Report, 1935–36*, p. 63.

rules and regulations of the executive agencies were promulgated in a central publication. The United States Supreme Court accepts appearance of these rules and regulations as "legal notice." [5]

Congress in 1937 amended the act and placed in the Division the responsibility for preparing and publishing "a complete codification of all documents which . . . have general applicability and legal effect and which have been issued or promulgated" by the departments and agencies.[6] Accordingly, work began on the new *Code of Federal Regulations*, and the last of the fifteen volumes of the first edition appeared in 1941. The *Federal Register* is keyed to and is a daily supplement to the *Code*.

After 1941 came the war years and the postponement by statute of the authorized quinquennial recodification. As a result, the 1938 edition was supplemented by bulky, individual, annual volumes until 1948. The Administrative Committee terminated the wartime suspension on recodification effective December 31, 1948, and recommended that the President authorize a new edition of the *Code*. The new edition was authorized by Executive Order No. 9930 of February 4, 1948.

This new edition (1949) followed the general format of the original 1938 edition, with its basic division into 50 functional titles arranged in alphabetical order. The titles were subdivided into chapters generally designated by the names of the agencies administering the programs involved. For more convenient supplementation the hardback volumes were issued with a pocket to accommodate the annual cumulative supplements. Individual volumes were revised and reissued whenever the pocket supplement became too unwieldy or too complex for convenient use.

A further refinement was introduced in the early 1960s. As the revision of a hardback book became due, it was studied with the view of splitting it into convenient paperback handbooks that could be completely revised and reprinted annually or at more frequent intervals. This new method of supplementation proved to be so effective and so popular that the *Code* today consists almost entirely of the new paperback "use units." From 45 volumes (20,000 pages) in the 1949 edition, the *CFR* has

5. 332 U.S. 380 [1947]. See epigraph, p. 134.
6. P.L. 158, 75th Cong.

grown to 112 volumes (50,000 pages) as of January 1, 1968. This great expansion in the volume of administrative regulations overstrained the production capacity of the Government Printing Office. This led to the addition of offset reproduction to supplement conventional printing. This step, together with the later development of "use units," involved new editing techniques and new decisions as to the best way to produce a given book.

The growth of the *Code of Federal Regulations* demands that attention be given to future developments. The field of electronic printing and retrieval may contain the solution to problems of sheer volume. The Federal Register staff is already looking ahead to the day when the *Code* may be produced largely by electronic computer printing systems. Plans for a pilot project are already in the mill. The project would cover at least one book issued as of January 1, 1969.

The compilation and publication of the *United States Government Organization Manual*, formerly the responsibility of the discontinued Office of Government Reports, were transferred to the Division of the Federal Register in 1948. This popular annual is a potpourri of data on the federal government: [7] a description of the creation and authority, organization, and functions of each agency; charts showing the organization of the government; information on executive agencies and functions abolished, transferred, or terminated since March 4, 1933; information on quasi-official agencies and selected international organizations; selected lists of publications available from the government; and a comprehensive index. Few publications are more essential to any library or research institution.

Important additional responsibilities were placed upon the Federal Register system as a result of a reorganization plan in 1950.[8] The Division assumed the duties, previously assigned to the Department of State, for the receipt and publication of the laws of Congress, and immediately proceeded to make the published versions more useful for lawyers, historians, and the affected public. A photoelectric printing process was introduced

7. Nearly 18,000 copies of the 1948 edition—the first edited by the Division of the Federal Register—were sold within the year (*Fifteenth Annual Report, 1948–49*, pp. 36–37).

8. Reorganization Plan No. 20 of 1950.

in the printing of the laws, insuring speed and accuracy and eliminating the former backlog in the *United States Statutes at Large*. Slip laws are now usually available within 24 hours after the President transmits the original to the Federal Register. Marginal notes, which had previously appeared only in the bound volumes of the *United States Statutes at Large*,[9] were introduced in the slip laws, making citations and references available at the time they are needed most—in the first printing of the law.

Beginning in 1956, each individual volume of the *Statutes at Large* contains a table designated as the "Tables of Laws Affected" showing what prior laws are affected by the laws set out in that volume. There is also a separate five-year cumulative table covering the years 1956–60, and a separate ten-year cumulative table covering the years 1956–65. Further cumulation is planned over the years.

The identification and numbering of laws was changed to ensure precision and to eliminate confusion in identifying laws. Prior to 1957, in order to identify and cite a law precisely, it was necessary to state not only the public law number but to add a reference to the Congress that enacted it. In 1957 the Federal Register took steps to eliminate this source of confusion by inserting in the law number a designator identifying the Congress by which the law was enacted. For example, the first public law enacted by the 85th Congress was numbered "85–1," the second "85–2," and so forth.

In 1963 the Federal Register again performed a valuable service for lawyers and scholars by including in the slip laws and in the bound volumes of the *United States Statutes at Large* a guide to the legislative history of the public laws. Federal Register editors added to each slip law references to appropriate House and Senate committees, committee report numbers, and citations to dates of the *Congressional Record* containing pertinent debates. Not included at the present time are references to committee hearings. Hearings are omitted primarily because they are too difficult to identify. If Congress should adopt a uniform style of identification, hearings also will be added to the legislative history guide. Under the same reorganization plan

9. *Annual Report of the Administrator of General Services for the Fiscal Year Ending June 30, 1950*, pp. 66–67.

View of the National Archives Building from Constitution Avenue

P R O P O S A L S

For PRINTING by SUBSCRIPTION,

A COLLECTION OF STATE PAPERS,

INTENDED AS MATERIALS FOR

An HISTORY of the UNITED STATES of AMERICA.

By EBENEZER HAZARD, A. M.

IN this Collection will be contained the CHARTERS of the feveral States which now compofe the UNION,—the Records of the UNITED COLONIES of NEW ENGLAND;—Royal Inftructions to COLONIAL GOVERNORS;—EXTRACTS from PUBLIC RECORDS;—and other authentic Documents tending to elucidate our Hiftory.

The defign of this Compilation was intimated to Congrefs, and honored with their approbation.—On the 20th July, 1778, their Committee, to whom his memorial was referred, reported it as their "Opinion, that Mr. Hazard's undertaking is laudable and deferves the public Patronage and Encouragement, as being productive of public Utility:" Whereupon they "Refolved, That it be recommended to the Governors, Prefidents, and Executive Powers of the feveral States in the Union, to affift Mr. Hazard, and give facility to his Labors; and that for this purpofe he be admitted to an infpection of public Records, and be furnifhed without expence with Copies of fuch Papers as he may judge will conduce to the valuable End he hath in view.

He was, of confequence, admitted to the infpection and ufe both of public Records, and the Collections made by individuals, from whence this Compilation (much the largeft he has ever met with on the fubject, and, he flatters himfelf, the largeft ever made in America) was formed. It has fince met the approbation of many eminent Characters, and, even its Manufcript ftate, has facilitated the fettlement of fome important controverfies.

The Compiler cannot fupprefs the following Letter from the Honorable the Secretary of State, to whofe infpection part of the compilation was fubmitted, as it contains fo flattering and refpectable a teftimony in favor of the importance of the Work.

"*Philadelphia, February* 18, 1791.

SIR,
I return you the two volumes of Records, with thanks for the opportunity of looking into them:—they are curious Monuments of the Infancy of our Country. I learn with great fatisfaction that you are about committing to the Prefs the valuable Hiftorical and State Papers you have been fo long collecting. Time and accident are committing daily havoc on the originals depofited in our public offices: the late war has done the work of centuries in this bufinefs: the loft cannot be recovered; but let us fave what remains; not by vaults and locks, which fence them from the public eye and ufe in confinging them to the wafte of time, but by fuch a multiplication of Copies as fhall place them beyond the reach of accident: this being the tendency of your undertaking, be affured there is no one who wifhes it a more complete fuccefs than,

SIR,
Your moft obedient and moft humble Servant,

Mr. HAZARD.

Thomas Jefferfon."

C O N D I T I O N S.

I. The Work to be publifhed in numbers, each containing 160 pages, large quarto:—A number to be delivered every three months.

II. On delivery of the firft Number, payment to be made for the firft and fecond, and afterwards for each Number as delivered (except the laft) fo that the price of one Number will be conftantly in advance. The very great expence attending fo large a Work, at the fame time that it renders this condition abfolutely neceffary, will be a fufficient apology to the candid, for its infertion.

III. The price to Subfcribers will be *one Dollar* for each Number. It is fuppofed that the Work will probably be comprifed in eight Numbers, forming two handfome Volumes, in large quarto, printed on a neat Type and good Paper.

IV. To thofe who choofe to fubfcribe for the Work in *Volumes*, the price will be *Four Dollars and a Quarter of a Dollar*, for each Volume, in boards.

V. The collection will be put to the Prefs as foon as there fhall be a fufficient number of fubfcriptions to juftify an hope that the expences will be defrayed.

☞ *Thofe who receive Subfcriptions* will pleafe *tranfmit accounts of the numbers obtained* to Thomas Dobfon, No. 41, Second-ftreet, Philadelphia, by the firft of May next.

SUBSCRIPTIONS will be received in Portfmouth, (New-Hampfhire) by Jeremiah Libbey; Bofton, Thomas & Andrews; Worcefter, Ifaiah Thomas; Hartford, Thomas Hildrop; New-Haven, Ifaac Beers; New-London, Timothy Green; Newport, (R. I.) Jacob Richardfon; Providence, John Carter; New-York, Hodge, Allen & Campbell; Albany, Abraham G. Lanfing; Philadelphia, Thomas Dobfon, and Hazard & Addoms; Wilmington, (Delaware) Frederick Craig; Baltimore, I. Holmes; Alexandria, Jofhua Merriman; Norfolk, Mr. Lindfey; Frederickfburgh, Callender & Henderfon; Peterfburgh, John Grammer; Richmond, Auguftine Davis; Newbern, (N.C.) F. X. Martin; Wilmington, John Bradley; Charlefton, (S. C.) William P. Young.

SUBSCRIBERS NAMES.

SUBSCRIBERS NAMES.

G. Washington — 2 volumes handsomely bound

John Adams. In volumes neatly bound

Rufus King   do.

Ph. Schuyler   do.

Ralph Izard   do.

John Laurance 2 volumes to be neatly bound

Elias Boudinot do. do.

Robt. Bowson   do. do.

Theodore Sedgwick do. do.

Subscription list for Ebenezer Hazard's A Collection of State Papers. *The original document is the property of the Historical Society of Pennsylvania.*

Ralph Izard — do.

Benjamin Hawkins do
Saml Johnston — do
[Wm Few] — do
John Langdon — do
Oliv: Ellsworth — do
Richard Bassett do
Theodore Foster — do
Ch. Carroll of Carrollton
  in volumes neatly bound } do
Tristram Dalton — do
Caleb Strong — do
Robt Morris — do
Jno Henry — do
Jas Monroe — do
Richard Henry Lee — do
Joseph Stanton Jr — do
Pd Butler in Vol: neatly bound
James Gunn do
Paine Wingate
Samuel Livermore
George Thatcher. in vol: neatly bound
Jno W Muhlenberg do

P. Sylvester in Vol: neatly bound
B. Bourn, in Boards
Ad. Burke
Tho. Scott, in Vol: neatly bound
Richd Hall — do do
Wm Duer — do do
Th: Jefferson in volumes neatly bound
Edm: Randolph in volumes neatly bound
Lambert Cadwalader in Numbers
Jeremiah Smith in Vol

Theodore Sedgwick do. do.
Samuel Griffin do do
Jona Trumbull — do do
Wm B. Giles do do
George Gale do do
Lambt Cadwalader

Tho. Hartley do do
Jere Wadsworth one in volumes
  one in number
John Vining
John Beckley. one in Volumes
Thos Tud. Tucker
J Parker
Andrew Moore
Alex White
M. J. Stone in volumes bound
J. B. Ashe
W Smith S.C
Wm Floyd
P Muhlenberg
Jer Van Rensselaer
P Schureman in volumes bound
Abr Baldwin bound

Ben. Contee, in Boards.
John Hathorn, bound.
No Gilman, in Vol: neatly bound
Henry Wynkoop, in Vol: neatly bound
Andrew G. Fraunces
Daniel Heister
Nathl Niles

*A typical view of the stacks in the National Archives,
showing records shelved in cardboard boxes.*

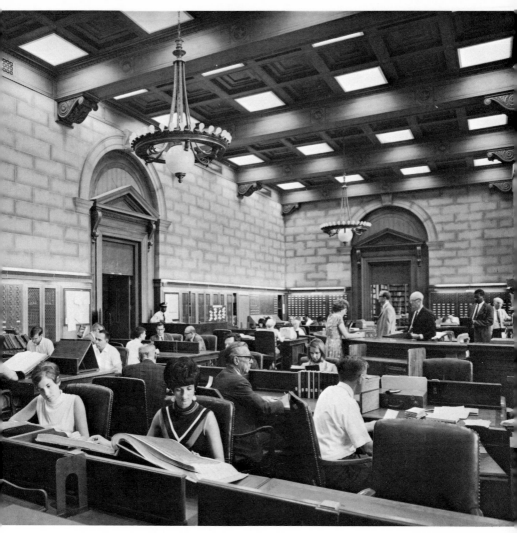

A view of the Central Search Room in the National Archives, showing charging desk and attendants at right. Additional study areas are located in adjacent rooms.

The entrance to the newest and largest Federal Records Center, located in Suitland, Maryland. Two floors covering ten acres each will house 3,800,000 cubic feet of records, including a Branch Archives.

View of the Rotunda in the Main Exhibition Hall, the National Archives, showing the display of the Declaration of Independence, the Constitution of the United States, and the Bill of Rights.

The Franklin Delano Roosevelt Library, Hyde Park, New York. Dedicated in 1941, this became the first of the presidential archival repositories administered by the [...] Each of these facilities serves as archives, library, and museum.

the Federal Register system was also required to receive and preserve original copies of Congressional bills, orders, resolutions, and votes; to certify, publish, and preserve amendments to the Constitution of the United States; and to receive and preserve certificates of the electoral votes for President and Vice President. Since 1955 the Division also has had the responsibility for receiving and preserving interstate compacts.[10]

Publication of the *Federal Register* and its companion *Code of Federal Regulations*, together with the related central filing of the documents involved, closed a gap that had existed since the creation of the first regulatory agency. The *United States Government Organization Manual* and the *United States Statutes at Large*, on the other hand, were not innovations but established publications that were transferred in the interest of efficiency and with a view to their further improvement.

In 1958 another gap was closed and another significant publication was added to the Federal Register system. In that year plans were completed for publishing a series of annual volumes containing the messages and other public papers of the President. The proceedings of Congress and the decisions of the United States Supreme Court had long been available in official series. However, no uniform and systematic compilation of presidential materials had been published since 1899, the terminal date of the ten volumes edited by James D. Richardson and published under Congressional authority.

The new series was entitled *Public Papers of the Presidents of the United States*. It was designed, the preface to the first volume stated, "to bring together material which hitherto has been scattered through the *Congressional Record* and the press generally, or which has existed only as White House mimeographed releases." [11] That volume covered 1957 and was published in the following year. Since that time volumes have been published for each year beginning with President Truman's taking of the oath of office on April 12, 1945. The volumes for the period of the Johnson Administration consist of two books for each year covered.

The series is intended to include only the *public* papers of the

10. Elizabeth H. Buck, "The National Archives and Records Service in the United States," *Archivum*, XI (1961), 126, 134–135.
11. *GSA Annual Report, 1956–57*, p. 16.

Presidents, as indicated by the title. It contains the President's speeches, his messages to the Congress, statements and public letters on a variety of subjects, records of his meetings with foreign leaders, the text of presidential awards and citations, and verbatim transcripts of the press conferences. Since proclamations and executive orders are fully treated in other Federal Register system publications, only a limited selection is included in the *Public Papers* series. However, all are listed in appended tabulations, as are reports submitted to the Congress and a record of White House press releases.

The series is also restricted in that it generally contains only materials that have been made public by the White House Press Office. Similar presidential papers, usually of a minor nature, are sometimes made public by the information offices of other government agencies and are even to be found at times in nongovernmental sources. To attempt to gather all such widely scattered materials would interfere with one of the avowed goals of all Federal Register productions—prompt publication. Accordingly, the Administrative Committee of the Federal Register, in authorizing the series following consultation with the National Historical Publications Commission, emphasized the need for limiting it to items emanating from the White House. The volumes are published as soon as practicable after the close of the year covered. Original source materials, where available, are used to protect against errors in transcription.

The annual volumes of the *Public Papers of the Presidents of the United States* with their detailed indexes and carefully reviewed text serve as an accurate and permanent record. They cannot, however, meet the needs of the current user. Accordingly the Federal Register system was again expanded in 1965, this time with the introduction of the *Weekly Compilation of Presidential Documents*.

Proposed as a means of keeping top officials posted on current presidential policies and statements (previously there had been only unorganized mimeograph releases), the new weekly soon exceeded the distribution of the annual volumes. Like the latter, the *Weekly Compilation* carries the President's speeches, his messages to Congress, his statements and public letters, and the news conferences. As in the case of the annual volumes, but only to the extent that a weekly deadline permits, the text is checked against tape recordings and other source data.

The *Weekly Compilation* is more inclusive than the annual volumes in that many nonpresidential items are published—for example, press briefings by other officials (if released by the White House), letters to the President so released, and various White House announcements. Carrying a Monday dateline, the weekly has a cut-off date of 5 p.m. on the preceding Friday. It contains an index of contents and a cumulative index that is separately published quarterly, semiannually, and annually.

The Office [12] of the Federal Register serves a training function in the government by instructing and assisting agency personnel in the preparation of rules, regulations, legal notices, and the like. With a staff experienced in legal publications, it is uniquely qualified to review drafts to insure their clarity and effectiveness. Over the years, assistance to the issuing agencies has grown in importance as it has tried to keep pace with the growing volume and complexity of agency documents and promulgation problems. Review of final documents before publication is now only the last step in the general process. Other steps include (1) advance personal consultation on specific problems; (2) a published handbook of instructions on the drafting of documents in general; [13] and (3) a formal program of illustrated lectures on the techniques of good drafting, good promulgation practices, and the use of special services in obtaining prints designed to meet agency program needs economically as well as effectively. This program was credited with an annual saving of $250,000 in reprint services alone as early as the fiscal year 1964. The value of clear, timely, and readily retrievable documents defies dollar evaluation. Nonetheless, the entire training program has been hampered by a shortage of staff. Publication deadlines must be met every day regardless of the long-range considerations of good government.

Akin to training agencies to produce clear documents is the matter of training all users of the Federal Register system in the techniques of retrieval. As all archivists and lawyers know, ready and dependable retrieval is second in importance only to the very existence and preservation of the documents them-

12. The designation "Office" replaced "Division" in 1958.
13. *Handbook on Document Drafting*, the latest edition of which was issued in January 1966.

selves. When the number of documents starts mounting into hundreds of thousands, with multiple sources, sizes, and subjects, the matter of retrieval becomes very important. In the case of the legislation and quasi legislation published in the Federal Register system two more factors are added: (1) frequent and unscheduled amendments, and (2) the need to know the precise language in effect on any given date in the past. Here retrieval is more than important—it is absolutely essential. Over the years the Federal Register has emphasized this essential aspect of its combined archival-legal-editorial function. The results of years of experience are reflected in the issue of the *Federal Register* dated December 17, 1965 (Vol. XXX, No. 243). Part II of this issue is entitled *Guide to Federal Register Finding Aids*. It covers the researching of agency, presidential, and statutory materials, and it includes a special information list that adds to the delight of the researcher. Item 17 of Table 1, for example, cites an annual publication entitled *Guide to Record Retention Requirements*. A copy of this Item 17 gives an index-digest of all the federal laws and administrative rules relating to the keeping of records by the public, with citations to the full text of every statute and every rule.[14]

The Office of the Federal Register operates on a budget of $568,000 per year and employs 55 persons including many editors and two attorneys. Though the size of the staff represents a fourfold increase since 1936, it has failed to keep pace with the increase in the work assigned the system. Not only have important new publications been added over the years, but the daily *Federal Register* has grown in size and complexity. Only through the adoption of new procedures and techniques—including photographic reproduction—has the Federal Register been able to maintain a minimum level of service. During fiscal 1967 an estimated 195,000 manuscript pages of laws, orders, regulations, and other legal documents were processed by the staff,[15] almost a 10 percent increase over the previous year. The growth of government and the increasing complexity of laws, orders, and regulations are likely to result in a higher annual "growth

14. The *Guide to Record Retention Requirements*, published each January, is available from the Government Printing Office for 40 cents.
15. The manuscript page is defined as letter size, typed double spaced, containing about 22 lines and 200 words.

trend" than the 5 percent officially estimated by NARS. Such a projection appears unrealistically low if the Office of the Federal Register is to "assure that all publications are as accurate, as current, and as usable as possible. . . ."

The projection of growth and related budgetary provisions have been too low for years. The Congress progressively has passed more and more acts requiring publication of specific matters other than those required by the Federal Register Act itself. Over 240 such acts have been passed since 1936. They range from ice patrols to seed standards, and from Indian tribes to outer space. The Federal Register Act required the publication of substantive regulations and notices of public hearings and similar actions. In addition to the 240 special acts that are superimposed on that act, the Congress enacted in 1946 the Administrative Procedure Act, which further enlarged general requirements to publish. Under the latter act agencies were required to publish descriptions of organization, delegations of final authority, procedural regulations, statements of policy, interpretations, statements of the general course and methods of agency activities, and notices of proposed rule-making. The over-all increase in the daily *Federal Register* has been from about 5,000 pages in 1940 to about 20,000 pages in 1966. The amendment of Section 3 of the Administrative Procedure Act (P.L. 90–23) effective July 4, 1967, emphasized the matter of the "public's right to know." It is already clear that this amendment will substantially accelerate the increase of materials submitted to the Federal Register by the agencies.

The responsibility of publishing the laws of the land, both statutory and administrative, is second to none in importance. Not only must the Office of the Federal Register have expert legal minds and meticulous publication specialists, it must also have sufficient manpower, for the work of the staff of the Federal Register, like that of appraisal archivists, cannot confidently be carried on with stop-watch precision. Its modest staff requirements must be met if it is to obviate the dangers inherent in pressure-driven work in which the public will be the loser when errors are made.

⌐7⌐

THE RECORDS OF THE PRESIDENCY,

1938–1968

*As President I accept this newest house in which the
people's record is preserved—public papers and collections which refer to one period in our history. This latest
addition to the archives of America is dedicated at a moment when government of the people by themselves is
everywhere attacked. It is therefore proof—if any proof
is needed—that our confidence in the future of democracy
has not diminished and will not diminish.*
                              —Franklin D. Roosevelt, *1941*

THE ANNALS of American presidential records—a chronicle
of chance marred by the dispersal and destruction of some
of the most important documentary sources of our history but
also distinguished by notable examples of care and preservation
—opened upon a remarkably different chapter just four years
after the creation of the National Archives in 1934. The new era
began with the establishment of the first presidential "library,"
an archival innovation inspired by a Chief Executive whose
administration was studded with bold and imaginative depar-
tures from precedent. No such institution had existed theretofore
in this or any other nation. The essential ingredients of its
character were present from the first, but its evolving progress
toward a not wholly predictable future has just begun. A proud
and fixed ornament in our cultural landscape, it also exhibits
some of the manifestations of immaturity and some of the hazards of undisciplined growth.

This landmark in the archival progress of the nation bears the
date of December 2, 1938. On that day President Franklin D.
Roosevelt dispatched a memorandum marked *personal and confidential* to a small group of citizens that included such leaders
of the historical profession as Charles A. Beard, Samuel E.
Morison, William E. Dodd, Randolph G. Adams, and Frederic

L. Paxson. The President asked those who received this document to weigh its proposal carefully and give him the benefit of their counsel at a luncheon to be held at the White House within a fortnight. The fact that on the day appointed the Washington press corps was alerted to receive an important presidential announcement after the meeting may be taken as proof of the assurance with which President Roosevelt contemplated the outcome. Such confidence was characteristic and on this occasion was fully justified.

At the luncheon the President guided the discussion with urbane mastery, working the magic of his personality and his high office upon the group of scholars, librarians, jurists, and political associates. He elaborated the plan and deftly anticipated such objections as might be raised against it. He was aware that his growing mass of personal and official papers were of interest to many institutions, including the Library of Congress and his own university. He pointed to past experience to illustrate the unwisdom of attempting to divide the documentary accumulations of a career that had been devoted to several public offices and to varied private interests. He even alluded to the possible dangers of modern warfare and counseled against the concentration of the nation's archival heritage in such a conspicuously vulnerable location as the national capital. Against the illogical and haphazard practices of the past and in the face of complex legal, financial, and other obstacles he urged the desirability of seeking new solutions, not merely to preserve historical records inviolate for future generations but also to release new potentialities. His argument reflected a deliberate and conscious break with the past. "It is my thought," he declared, "that an opportunity exists to set up for the first time in this country what might be called a source material collection relating to a specific period of our history, [to be housed in] a separate, modern, fireproof building . . . so designed that it would hold all of my own collections and also such other material relating to this period in our history as might be donated to the collection in future by other members of the present Administration." His first object was to keep intact what he described as "all of my Presidential papers from March 4, 1933," together with other business, legal, political, and official records accumulated during his career, and his own considerable library and collections of paintings, prints, and manuscripts.[1]

Then, with a disarming expression of deference to professional judgment, President Roosevelt asked for the individual and collective opinions of those assembled. No whisper of dissent was heard, only a unanimous and enthusiastic chorus of approbation followed by a discussion of ways and means for putting the plan into operation.

After adjourning the conference the President personally guided his guests through parts of the White House, regaled them with episodes of the safely remote politics of his years as a young senator at Albany, and showed them some of the gifts that the American people, out of exalted respect as well as undisciplined sentimentality, shower in embarrassing quantity and nature upon their chief magistrate. Then came a press conference at which the text of the historic memorandum, with only a few minor changes, served as the official news release. The journalists who had waited outside during the lengthy session, wondering what affairs of state could have caused them to be summoned to the White House during a quiet Saturday afternoon in a winter of relative calm, were amazed to find in the President's heralded announcement nothing more momentous than a plan for disposing of his personal papers and presidential records. Some, though not all, of the ensuing comments in editorials and cartoons echoed their somewhat derisive skepticism and looked for such significance as this announcement might have in its obvious relevance to the 1940 presidential election.[2] The calling together of a group of scholars and the dramatic timing of the announcement to the press were only elements of the stage-setting that had been arranged by a master of the art in order to make manifest to the American people the importance of their public records. The decision, long maturing, had in fact already been taken when the private and confidential memorandum was dispatched to those who so eagerly embraced its proposal.

*   *   *

1. Undated memorandum enclosed in President Roosevelt's letter of invitation to those who attended the luncheon at the White House on December 10, 1938; partially quoted in *The New York Times*, December 11, 1938.

2. See, e.g., the cartoons of Doyle in the *Philadelphia Record* and Lewis in the *Milwaukee Journal*.

Thus was unveiled the concept of the presidential archives, one of the most important and promising developments in all archival history. This dramatic and uniquely American departure from previous practice was bound to set an irreversible pattern for the future. The Adamses had added to their incomparably rich family archives the presidential records of John Adams and John Quincy Adams but had closed them to all save a few historical investigators. The heirs of Rutherford B. Hayes, in collaboration with the state of Ohio, had founded the Hayes Memorial Library at Fremont, in which Hayes's papers as President formed the most important resource and were accessible to the scholarly public. Herbert Hoover had placed his presidential records in the Hoover Library of War and Peace at Stanford. But nowhere in past experience could there be found a logical pattern or practical solution to the complex problem of what disposition to make of the papers of an outgoing President. Roosevelt's predecessors in office from George Washington on, like the prime ministers of England, had acted upon the assumption that the records of the presidential office were personal property, and the results had been varied and at times disastrous. While joining his predecessors in this assumption, Roosevelt made his most significant departure from their example by recognizing the paramount right of the public and by subordinating this private claim to public custody, support, and management under the direction of civil servants governed by professional standards. This, as will be indicated, fell short of the natural and logical goal. But it was a long, unprecedented step forward that no President thenceforth would be likely to disregard.

There can be no doubt that this pivotal decision was inspired primarily by Roosevelt's deep interest in the American past and by his consciousness of his own role in history. He had been an avid reader of history from youth, particularly of that part concerning his own region, and he had formed important collections of manuscripts, prints, pamphlets, and books, with special emphasis on local, naval, and maritime history. He had carefully preserved his own personal, business, legal, and political correspondence from the time he first entered public life, and he had been equally zealous in caring for the records of his family and of the locality in which he lived. It is symbolic of his deep concern for the sources of history that he continued as official historian of the town of Hyde Park while occupying the office of President of the United States.[3]

Another factor was the simple one of mass. Roosevelt's papers and collections were already of formidable size when he became President, but he was scarcely prepared for the overwhelming flood of documents that poured in upon him after March 4, 1933. The sense of an immediate relationship between the electorate and their President had caused untold numbers of individuals to address letters, petitions, and counsels to every incumbent of the office from the moment George Washington was inaugurated to the present. But with Roosevelt, for a variety of reasons, this manifestation of the democratic impulse assumed such massive proportions as to dwarf all previous experience. He himself estimated that the volume of communications coming to his office was tenfold that received by his immediate predecessor. This estimate was exaggerated, but the total of his presidential records ultimately amounted to 4,000 cubic feet, or some 5,000,000 sheets of paper in about 500 five-drawer filing cabinets. This order of mass documentation clearly ruled out for Roosevelt and his successors any solution dependent upon the claim of private-property rights except as a useful legal fiction. Warehousing and custodial costs, to say nothing of the prospect of enormous estate taxes levied upon such assets, combined with other factors to render previous practices of the Presidents and their heirs quite obviously obsolete.[4] The situation was further complicated by an equally unprecedented flood of gifts, some of them having great intrinsic value, that could not be kept with propriety as private property or returned without diplomatic embarrassment, since they were donated by heads of foreign states. It is thus not surprising that these intractable realities and his own historical instincts should have led Roosevelt gradually to the "realization of the need for a new and special kind of institution." Its nature would necessarily combine the features

3. Alexander C. Flick, State Historian of New York, was one of those present at the luncheon on December 10, 1938, and thus in one sense was the superior officer of his host.

4. For some comment on the legal and other difficulties imposed on an outgoing President by the growing mass of papers, see David D. Lloyd, "The Harry S Truman Library," *American Archivist*, XVIII (April 1955), 99–110.

of an archives, a library, and a museum.[5]

The process of realization was unquestionably quickened by the culmination in 1934 of the historians' long efforts to create a national archival establishment and by Roosevelt's appointment of R. D. W. Connor as the first Archivist of the United States. Connor was a Southern historian whom Roosevelt respected as a professional archivist and as a man of wise humanity whom he cherished as a friend. Out of this relationship, marked by mutual trust and respect, the vague concept of the new institution began to assume form and reality. The effect of this collaboration is implicit in a key paragraph of Roosevelt's memorandum:

It is my thought that if a building such as I suggest is erected and the material—not only my own but that of others who would contribute their own material—is placed there, the title to the building and all the material would be vested in the United States Government and placed under the primary responsibility of the Archivist of the United States. This would insure permanent care and the provision of adequate facilities for its use.

But more was at stake than mere preservation and provision of adequate facilities for use. Beyond this the President anticipated other needs, undefined but implied in words suggesting the careful thought that he and the Archivist had given to some of the inherent problems. The memorandum continued:

At the same time, being somewhat familiar with historical material, its preservation and its availability for students and scholars, I should much like to have the assistance of recognized scholars in American History and Government, past and present. That is why I believe that a collection of this kind should be under the supervision of a committee of historians working in cooperation with the Archivist and the Librarian of Congress.

Clearly, it was expected that the new institution would assume an active program of its own and not be merely a passive aggregation of historical resources. It would of course seek to

5. Herman Kahn, "The Presidential Library—A New Institution," *Special Libraries*, L (March 1959), 107.

acquire additional and related collections of documents. As an integral part of the National Archives Establishment, it would also bear a comparable responsibility for the preparation of guides, indexes, and calendars and for publishing such parts of the documentary record as might be deemed useful and desirable. Roosevelt believed that in carrying out its responsibilities in these and other areas the new institution would require the advice and assistance of both professional scholars and professional archivists. Their cooperation would help to insure the success of the venture, and he declared himself ready and eager after retirement to lend his own assistance to the effort.

The plan thus outlined was put in operation with remarkable speed, giving support to the conjecture that Roosevelt intended to retire at the end of his second term.[6] A National Advisory Committee to lend moral support to the enterprise was formed by expanding the original group of historians and other scholars to the number of thirty, each of whom was personally invited by the President to serve. The effective operating agency, however, came into being within two weeks when the Franklin D. Roosevelt Library, Incorporated, was formed. This private corporation was empowered to raise funds and to construct and equip a building to house the records and collections. It is worth noting that it had authority to erect this structure either at Hyde Park or elsewhere. It could also retain custody, control, and maintenance itself, or it could ultimately transfer these responsibilities to the United States, provided only that legislation should be enacted enabling the government to accept such property and support it in perpetuity. This private agency, declared Waldo G. Leland,

> was thus not only an operating agency for obtaining funds and constructing and equipping a building, but it was also a hedge against the failure of Congress (most unlikely in 1939) to enact the necessary enabling legislation. In the event of such failure, however, the corporation would have

6. It was only two days after the luncheon conference that Connor, at the request of the President, asked Waldo Gifford Leland to act as chairman of a small executive committee. See Leland, "The Creation of the Franklin D. Roosevelt Library: A Personal Narrative," *American Archivist*, XVIII (January 1955), 11–29—cited hereafter as Leland, "The Roosevelt Library."

been obliged to seek endowment or other permanent funds for the perpetual maintenance of the establishment.[7]

A tentative draft of the necessary legislation and architectural plans were far advanced even before the campaign for funds was opened early in 1939. By mid-year a joint resolution had been adopted authorizing the Archivist of the United States: to accept title to the land on which the library would be situated; to permit the corporation to construct the Franklin D. Roosevelt Library on the site; to accept as a gift the historical resources to be donated by Roosevelt; and to acquire other contemporary or relevant materials by gift, purchase, or loan.[8] The legislation also provided for a board of trustees, of which the Archivist of the United States was to be chairman. A clause of fundamental importance contained the pledged faith of the United States to provide such funds as might be necessary for the maintenance, operation, and administration of the Library and for the care and preservation of its historical resources "so that the . . . Library shall be at all times properly maintained." [9] The raising of funds presented no problem. A small group of wealthy individuals had already guaranteed the sum needed, and in the quiet campaign that followed, some 28,000 individuals contributed a total of $400,000 to the building fund. It was just a year and a half after Roosevelt had dispatched his memorandum to the original group that title to the completed building was transferred to the government.

In its essentials, but with natural variations, this was the pattern that would be followed in the next quarter of a century in the establishment of the Harry S Truman Library at Independence, Missouri; the Dwight D. Eisenhower Library at Abilene, Kansas; the Herbert Hoover Library at West Branch, Iowa; the John F. Kennedy Library at or near Boston, Massachusetts; and the Lyndon B. Johnson Library at Austin, Texas. In one fundamentally important respect, however, this first presidential archives set a standard that probably has not been

7. Leland, "The Roosevelt Library," p. 18.
8. Roosevelt himself suggested the desirability of accepting materials on loan.
9. Leland, "The Roosevelt Library," pp. 26–27; S. J. Res. 118; H. J. Res. 268, approved (as Public Resolution 30, 76th Cong.) on July 18, 1939. The debate in the House was lively, and the resolution passed by a partisan vote of 231 to 124.

equaled and certainly has not been surpassed by any of its successors. This involved the crucial question of control and accessibility, and its successful resolution derived in part from the fact that Roosevelt did not live to realize his cherished dream of aiding in retirement the development of an institution of which he was the creator and of which every detail of planning from architectural form to enabling legislation had engaged his enthusiastic interest. Had he done so, he could undoubtedly have contributed much toward the illumination of the records pertaining to his administrations and toward the development of a vigorous program for the Library. But such is the complexity and difficulty of the problem of establishing prudent controls over contemporaneous documents involving personal and state affairs of great importance, it is unlikely that Roosevelt's contributions in retirement could have caused the resources of the Franklin D. Roosevelt Library to have had such an immediate and such a spectacular impact on American historiography as they did have. To say this is not to suggest that his canons of accessibility would have been ungenerous or illiberal; it is merely to say that principles formulated and applied by professional archivists would quite naturally be different and less subjective than those devised by an individual for a great mass of records reflecting, often in highly classified and confidential detail, every aspect of his own personal and public life over a period of several decades.

On the simplest phase of this problem of control and accessibility—that posed by the sheer mass of materials—Roosevelt had declared his intent early in 1939:

> I have destroyed practically nothing. As a result, we have a mine for which future historians will curse me as well as praise me. It is a mine which will need to have the dross sifted from the gold. *I would like to do it, but the historians tell me I am not capable of doing it* [emphasis supplied].[10]

The historians meant no reflection upon the competence of the President. Knowing from long experience how difficult it is for

10. Quoted in Leland, "The Roosevelt Library," p. 25.

even the most conscientious scholar to distinguish the dross from the gold, they were merely suggesting that the task was one for objective, professional judgment. Four years later, despite this counsel, Roosevelt repeated his intention more emphatically. His purpose was not and perhaps never had been to go through the great mass of records in order to separate the trivial from the significant. It was rather to address himself to the problem of identifying those categories that should not be given to the Library at all or should be given only under restrictions as to use. In a memorandum to the Director of the Library dated July 16, 1943, Roosevelt stated "his intention of going through his personal or confidential files in order to select those which should never be made public, or which should be sealed for a prescribed period, or which dealt only with family matters and should be retained by the family." [11] He further declared that, if he should be unable to do this himself, three of his trusted associates should have authority to do it for him. It was Roosevelt's fate to be denied his dream, and thus, subject to the general authority given to the associates, it was under the direction of the Archivist of the United States and the staff of the Library that the categories of restricted materials were identified and segregated.

The principles determining access to the records of President Roosevelt followed the official regulations governing the Archivist of the United States concerning the availability of historical materials.[12] The restricted categories included such items as investigative reports on individuals; applications and recommendations for positions; documents containing derogatory remarks concerning the character, loyalty, integrity, or ability of particular persons; and records that would be prejudicial to national security or to the maintenance of amicable relations with foreign nations if released. These requirements for guarding against violation of private right and public security were prudent and necessary. The passage of time would ultimately render them obsolete. Meanwhile the segregation of classes of material that Roosevelt had stipulated was subject to periodic review by a staff of professional archivists.

The task of applying these principles was a truly formidable

11. *Ibid.*, p. 28.
12. *Code of Federal Regulations*, Title 44, Pt. 31, Secs. 31.3 and 31.4.

one, particularly in view of the fact that the war years caused simultaneously an augmentation in the mass of papers and a reduction of the staff available to cope with the problem. Furthermore, despite all of Roosevelt's efforts to ensure that his papers would be kept intact in their entirety, it was assumed at his death that those files at the White House offices that had not been transferred were a part of his estate.[13] Roosevelt had made no provision in his will against such a contingency, and it became necessary to obtain a judicial ruling before some 2,500 cubic feet of his presidential records could be transferred to government ownership. These represented more than half of the total, and they were not acquired by the Library until 1947. But the astonishing fact is that by the time the Roosevelt papers were formally opened to research on March 17, 1950, no less than 85% of them were accessible.[14] These included much that was important for the presidential years and also the remarkably full documentary record of Roosevelt's personal and public life before he became President.

The significance of this prompt availability of several million documents pertaining to one of the principal architects of social and political change in an era of revolution can best be appreciated in terms of its contrast with previous experience. The formal opening of the Roosevelt papers took place only a few months after the seal had been removed from the long-closed remnant of the papers of Abraham Lincoln. It came several years before the presidential records of John Adams and John Quincy Adams would be made accessible to historians. The beneficial effect of this event upon public knowledge of contemporary affairs was incalculable, but its impact upon historical scholarship is demonstrable. "This," wrote one grateful scholar, "is the largest collection of materials relating to one man to be found in the United States, and all but a small portion is open to examination. The size and range of the collection, and its availability to scholars so soon after the donor's death, are without

13. The same assumption was acted upon immediately after President Kennedy was assassinated. See William Manchester, *The Death of a President* (New York: Harper & Row, 1967), p. 403.

14. *Tenth Annual Report of the Archivist of the United States on the Franklin D. Roosevelt Library* (Washington: Government Printing Office, 1950), pp. 5–7; GSA-37 news release, March 5, 1950; *Archivum*, III (1953), 204.

precedent in American historiography." [15]

Within the next decade an impressive array of books and articles based on the Roosevelt and other collections at Hyde Park appeared over the names of such historians as Arthur M. Schlesinger, Jr., Frank Freidel, James MacGregor Burns, Sidney Fine, Edgar Nixon, John Blum, Wayne Cole, and others. One scholar, stating the obvious truth that Freidel's multivolume biography of Roosevelt could not have been written if the Roosevelt papers had not been available, declared it to be "the greatest monument to the presidential libraries." [16] These results show that Roosevelt had not merely created a new kind of institution but had been the first to demonstrate that presidential papers are indeed "the people's record" and the people's claim upon them is paramount. He had shown that the prerogative assumed by his predecessors in asserting private title was in fact only a lingering vestige of the attributes of monarchy, not an appropriate or compatible concept of archival policy for the head of a democratic state to adopt. He did not perhaps grasp all of the implications of this bold departure from precedent; his 1943 memorandum revealed in its opinion that some parts of the record should never be disclosed to public view. But he had made the break with the past, professional archivists had had the opportunity to apply objective rules of accessibility, and historians had made the most of the opportunity. This exemplified the manner in which the sources of history should be treated and the writing of history undertaken in a free society. Roosevelt's pragmatic and in part fortuitous demonstration of the truth may indeed prove in the long view that his finest monument lies in the opportunity he gave historians to carry on their impartial investigations so soon after the events.

President Harry S Truman, who also had a deep interest in American history, followed the precedent and authorized the establishment of a corporation to create his own distinctive kind of presidential archives in the heart of the nation. President Eisenhower announced his intention of doing the same. Both the

15. Thomas H. Greer, *What Roosevelt Thought: The Social and Political Ideas of Franklin D. Roosevelt*, p. 229, quoted in Richard S. Kirkendall, "Presidential Libraries—One Researcher's Point of View," *American Archivist*, XXV (October 1962), 447.

16. Kirkendall, "Presidential Libraries," p. 446.

experience of the Roosevelt Library and the prospect of a dozen or more presidential archival establishments in the next century indicated the need of a comprehensive plan for their administration. Accordingly, the Presidential Libraries Act of 1955 amended the Federal Property and Administrative Services Act of 1949 by authorizing the Administrator of General Services

> to accept for deposit . . . the papers and other historical materials of any President or former President of the United States, or of any other official or former official of the Government, and other papers relating to and contemporary with any President or former President of the United States, subject to restrictions agreeable to the Administrator as to their use; and . . . to accept for . . . the United States, any land, buildings, and equipment offered as a gift to the United States for the purposes of creating a Presidential archival depository, and to take title to such land, buildings, and equipment on behalf of the United States, and to maintain, operate, and protect them as Presidential archival property.[17]

The act also permitted the Administrator to enter into agreements with any state, political subdivision, foundation, or institution "to utilize as a Presidential archival depository land, buildings, and equipment . . . to be made available . . . without transfer of title to the United States, and to maintain, operate, and protect such depository as a part of the national archives system." Plans for any such proposed repository were required to be laid before Congress for sixty days, after which, in the absence of Congressional action, the Administrator could proceed to take title to the property or agree to administer it.

The joint resolution of 1939 had applied only to the Franklin D. Roosevelt Library, but the Act of 1955 was general legislation applicable to all such repositories. At a public hearing before a Special Subcommittee of the House Committee on Government Operations, testimony in support of the measure argued that it provided "a system for the preservation and use of Presidential papers that accords with our Constitution and traditions"; that it would enable the government to acquire as gifts

17. 84th Cong., 1st. Sess., P.L. 373.

expensive buildings and equipment that might be used both for such papers and for federal records accumulated outside of Washington; that the decentralization of such collections would stimulate interest in American history and government on the part of local scholars; and that the existence of nuclear weapons made it prudent to take into account "the growing need for the dispersion of research facilities." [18] The Administrator of General Services hailed the measure as a historic event and as laying "a foundation for the systematic preservation and use of the papers of the American Presidency." It would, he declared, establish in law "a system whereby Presidential papers, in their entirety, may become a part of the National Archives, by gift or by agreement." [19]

Both the provisions of the legislation and the testimony in support of it reveal its cautious approach. The appeal to motives of economy and to the value of decentralized cultural resources betrayed a sensitivity to criticism of the concepts of presidential archival repositories that had been both vigorous and widespread. The new measure was less restrictive than that of 1939 in some important respects. The records of a President, for example, could be accepted as a deposit without having title to them pass to the United States. Either as gift or deposit, they could also be received and given maintenance and support through public funds on land and in buildings not owned by the government but belonging to a private institution or to a state or a local unit of government. Only time could test the wisdom of permitting this degree of latitude in the disposition of records of the Presidency—a tolerance in the disposition of archival materials not granted in law to other offices in the executive department or to the legislative and judicial branches of government.

Presidential papers, so Roosevelt had declared, were "the people's record." But in 1955 the representatives of the people did not pursue the implications of this assertion. They and those who testified in support of this legislation were indeed careful to disavow any intention of doing so. The Act, being essentially a

18. Statement by House Majority Leader John W. McCormack, *Hearing . . . on . . . Bills to Provide for the Acceptance and Maintenance of Presidential Libraries, June 13, 1955*, p. 58; cited below as *Hearing;* quoted also in Elizabeth Hawthorn Buck, "General Legislation for Presidential Libraries," *American Archivist*, XVIII (October 1955), 339.

19. *Hearing*, p. 14.

compromise permitting the general application of the pattern of 1939, did not therefore represent any significant advance over the path-breaking precedent set by Roosevelt. The next step was clearly indicated, but the proponents of the legislation failed to come to grips with the expedient, though now potentially dangerous, legal fiction that a President or his heirs possessed a private right to the records accumulated during his tenure in office. The determined avoidance of any challenge to tradition on this crucial point was made explicit in the testimony of the Administrator of General Services:

> As a matter of ordinary practice, the President has removed his papers from the White House at the end of his term. This has been in keeping with the tradition and the fact that the papers are the personal property of the retiring Presidents. One unfortunate consequence has been that important bodies of Presidential documents have been dispersed and destroyed, particularly prior to the 20th Century.
>
> All this is recognized in this legislation; there is nothing mandatory in the proposal. It is not an ill-conceived attempt to bind any future President of the United States. Instead, it will provide the vehicle by which the President is assured the integrity of his papers, their proper and orderly arrangement, and their eventual availability to the people as the historical record of his administration. . . . In every case, the decision to make the gift will continue to rest with the former President and his heirs and friends.[20]

But what was thus stated to be a fact was only an assumption supported by a long tradition of acquiescence in the practices flowing from it. The allusion to the unfortunate consequences of this tradition was accurate enough, but it ignored the simple fact that this legislation did nothing at all to prevent such consequences in the future. The twentieth century, in fact, was not without its own example of the destruction of presidential papers, and as the representative of the Harry S Truman Library declared in an article that was printed in full in the testimony:

> . . . with all deference to the convenience of scholars, we must satisfy the wishes of the owner first, because if we do

20. *Hearing*, p. 14.

not the papers may never get to the scholars at all. The owner, after all, can always destroy them, and some Presidents, or Presidents' families have done—or tried to do— just that. . . . I do not say that all future Presidents will want to place their papers in Government ownership. We cannot now foresee what compelling reasons may rise against it.[21]

But the convenience of scholars was not the most immediate or indeed the most urgent reason for examining the assumption that had produced such loss in the past. The testimony and the Act of 1955 also overlooked the incongruity involved in assuming a President to have the right to determine conditions under which his presidential records should be used and, at the same time, in granting to the head of an agency appointed by him, or by his successor, the right to veto those conditions. The Federal Property and Administrative Services Act of 1949 underscored the incongruity by vesting the ultimate decision not in the Archivist of the United States, who with his trained staff had set such a notable example in making the Roosevelt papers promptly available under reasonable and judicious restrictions, but in an official who is, quite properly, appointed for qualifications other than professional competence in archival administration. This issue and its implications have not, in fact, been seriously explored in the growing literature on presidential archives except in allusive terms and as a part of the general response to criticism of such institutions.

The Archivist, R. D. W. Connor, who assisted Roosevelt in planning the library at Hyde Park, thought that Grover Cleveland had apparently been the first President to declare the papers of his office to be private property. Cleveland did this in an unequivocally expressed message to the Senate in 1886:

I regard the papers and documents . . . addressed to me or intended for my use and action purely unofficial and private, not infrequently confidential, and having reference to the performance of a duty exclusively mine. . . . They consist of letters and representations addressed to the Executive or intended for his inspection; they are voluntarily

21. David D. Lloyd, "The Harry S Truman Library," *American Archivist*, XVIII (April 1955), 105, 107–108.

written and presented by private citizens who are not in the least instigated thereto by any official invitation or at all subject to official control. . . .

The papers and documents which have been described derive no official character from any constitutional, statutory, or other requirement making them necessary to the performance of the official duty of the Executive.[22]

In citing this declaration, the Archivist accepted the view that the "papers of Presidents are not official," though he went on to declare that this fact did not lessen the moral if not the legal obligation of their owners to preserve them "for the benefit of posterity." Herman Kahn, as Director of the Franklin D. Roosevelt Library, gave to the traditional assumption the status of fact derived from fundamental law:

The office of the President is a constitutional office. . . . It is for this reason that, alone among all officials in the Executive Branch, a President's office files . . . are his private property. They are his to dispose of as he wishes. They are his private property while he is in the White House, and they are his private property after he has left the White House.[23]

David D. Lloyd, as a lawyer and as Director of the Harry S Truman Library, Incorporated, had elaborated the argument earlier:

The Presidency is a constitutional office and as such has an independence like that of the other two branches of the Government. One of the aspects of this constitutional independence is the treatment accorded to presidential papers. The national legislature cannot subpoena presidential papers while the President is in office. It cannot force a President to make his communications public. Over the executive departments, which are established by statute, the Congress exercises a degree of supervision which we need not define here—but when it comes to the acts of the

22. Quoted in R. D. W. Connor, "The Franklin D. Roosevelt Library," *American Archivist*, III (April 1940), 83.
23. Herman Kahn, "The Presidential Library—A New Institution," *Special Libraries*, L (March 1959), 106. Kahn was until 1968 Assistant Archivist for Presidential Libraries.

President himself the power of Congress stops, except in cases of impeachment.

This principle would, however, be overridden if after the end of a President's term in office his papers were assimilated to those of an executive department and subjected to the control of the succeeding administration and the legislative branch. Obviously, if presidential papers could be thrown open to public scrutiny as soon as a President left office, there would not be much privacy about them while he was in office. Few would write to a President in confidence and few Presidents would put their private thoughts on paper if the expiration of the presidential term were to be a signal for disclosure. And as a consequence the ability of the President to function as an independent officer of the Government would be curtailed, if not crippled, and our constitutional framework would be damaged.

These . . . are the fundamental constitutional and political reasons that justify the rule that our Presidents own their papers. And if we wish to mitigate the burden this imposes on ex-Presidents we should provide the sort of depository for their files over which they will have as much control as if they had personal possession.[24]

It is clear that the national legislature cannot regulate the actions of the constitutionally independent Chief Executive in respect to the records of his office. Nor can any prudent person deny that such records must of necessity be protected against premature or politically motivated disclosure.

But it is precisely because of these facts that the traditional assumption can no longer be viewed with uncritical equanimity. To recognize the constitutional independence of the Presidency is not to establish a sound premise for the conclusion that presidential records are the private property of the incumbent, whether in or out of office. On the contrary, it would seem that if any proposition collides with constitutional principles it is that the President should be exempted from the legal obligation that rests upon all other officials in government to protect and refrain

24. David D. Lloyd, "The Harry S Truman Library," *American Archivist*, XVIII (April 1955), 101–102.

from appropriating to personal use records produced or received into custody by virtue of the exercise of a public office. To assume otherwise would be to vest in the highest officer of the land, or in his heirs or descendants, the right to sell, to destroy, to disclose, to refuse to disclose, or otherwise to dispose of documents of the highest official nature involving information that, if improperly, prematurely, or irresponsibly revealed, could not only wreck private lives but also vitally endanger the security of the nation. For these documents, as Lloyd himself declared, are both official and personal—with the two characteristics being at times so intermingled as to make it extremely difficult if not impossible to draw a distinction between them.[25] To the extent that they are official they are indubitably public property, as in the case of any other public office. Grover Cleveland, following a precedent first set by George Washington, was only exercising his constitutional prerogative in refusing to make public certain papers. But his assumption that this right rested on private ownership of them placed him on extremely dubious ground both in logic and in law. For, as John Quincy Adams once declared, the right of withholding information pertains to the office and not to the man. Like all other presidential powers, it can always be used and may only be used by the individual who for the time being occupies the office of President.

The idea that this power of the President to disclose or not disclose information in the presidential records should follow the individual "into his retirement as a personal right to be exercised by him for the duration of his natural life and then to be descendable to his executors and heirs" is surely not justified under any constitutional principle, however much it may have been practiced in the past.[26] The assumption that the papers of the Presidency are private property leads those who support it into the illogical and quite unconstitutional proposition that a private citizen—perhaps one who never had exercised the office

25. President Hoover declared that he left all "official" papers in the White House, removing only those of a "personal" nature. President Truman, in a statement before a committee of the House of Representatives in 1957, voiced the opinion that almost every scrap of presidential paper was official in character.

26. Julian P. Boyd and Lucius Wilmerding, Jr., letter to the editor, *The New York Times*, May 1, 1960.

of President or could even be eligible to do so—could decide what papers of the Presidency a subsequent holder of its powers might or might not see. The right of a private citizen to make such a determination is clearly unauthorized by reason or by law.

The point needs to be elaborated not because of the convenience of historians or because of the claims of posterity, though these must be considered, but because American principles of government and the national interest require it. In a world in upheaval, continued acquiescence in the time-honored assumption that presidential records are private property may be the least effective way of ensuring that the public interest, the just claims of former Presidents, and the rights of posterity are given adequate protection. The dangers to the public safety in continuing to countenance the proposition that presidential records are private property are too obvious to be detailed.[27] To suggest that the ability of the President to function as an independent officer of government would be curtailed or that the framework of our federal system would be damaged if the concept of private property rights in such records were to be abandoned is to admit that no further progress is possible beyond the pioneering example set by Franklin D. Roosevelt. But one need only look to the experience of various states for examples to show by contrast the incompatibility of the traditional view with good archival policy, to say nothing of constitutional principles. In this, as in some other respects, state archival practices may profitably be examined when the final, logical, and necessary step is taken to make presidential archives what they should be—public institutions in every sense of the term.

The "libraries" constitute one of the six major archival achievements in the United States in the twentieth century, the others being the establishment of the National Archives, the development of a comprehensive records management program, the creation of a system of records centers, the rebirth of the National Historical Publications Commission, and the establish-

27. A single example may suffice. During a critical moment in World War II, Roosevelt's draft of a message to Stalin announcing the decision to launch the invasion of Western Europe was included by mistake in files being transferred to Hyde Park some time before the event. The document happened to come into the hands of two loyal archivists, who swore each other to secrecy. It could have been otherwise.

ment of the Federal Register system. They form an integral and inseparable part of a far-flung archival complex that is unprecedented in history. Approximately 92 staff members are assigned to the Office of Presidential Libraries, only two-thirds of whom are paid from direct appropriations amounting to about $690,000 annually. Other sources—endowments, contributions, admissions, and so on—increase funds available to nearly $1,000,000 per year. Each institution has, at its heart, the presidential records and papers donated or deposited by the President and by officials and friends associated with the President whose name the institution bears. Each also serves as a library and a museum. The 1967 holdings of the four operating libraries were as follows: [28] 72,000,000 manuscript pages, 229,000 photographs, 5,100 sound recordings, 1,300,000 feet of motion-picture film, 94,000 books, 112,000 other printed items, and 52,000 museum objects. Attendance in 1966 for the four institutions was 563,000.[29] Some idea of the increase in quantity of presidential papers may be gained from the fact that President Franklin D. Roosevelt received an average of 140,000 letters a year, President John F. Kennedy, 307,312 in one year, and President Lyndon B. Johnson, in 1965, 825,750.

But statistics do not reveal the importance or meaning of these institutions. Their true character is also hidden behind a misnomer. They are basically presidential archives, and they are in fact designated in law as "Presidential archival depositories." [30] They should therefore be redesignated as "Presidential Archives," in which archival as distinguished from library practices are followed. In the public usage, and even to most professionals, the word "library" refers to a book repository. Yet printed matter constitutes only a minor part of the holdings and functions of a presidential records repository.[31]

28. The Franklin D. Roosevelt Library at Hyde Park, New York (1940); the Harry S Truman Library at Independence, Missouri (1959); the Dwight D. Eisenhower Library at Abilene, Kansas (1962); and the Herbert Hoover Library in West Branch, Iowa (1962).
29. Roosevelt, 181,000; Truman, 193,000; Eisenhower (half-year), 93,496; and Hoover, 95,713.
30. 44 U.S.C. 397.
31. A *de*pository denotes a place of deposit and implies possible withdrawal; a *re*pository denotes an institution where materials remain. Consequently it appears that the term "repository" is more applicable to an archival institution.

Librarians cannot understand why a "presidential library" is not administered by a professional librarian; archivists object to an archival institution being misnamed a library; museum people can hardly conceive of a museum being a part of a library; and many historians are unacquainted with the basic differences between the policies and techniques used by archivists and those followed by librarians. These institutions exist because of the need to preserve and make available for use large masses of records of various sorts that are produced or that accumulate in the office of a modern President. They are therefore research institutions resorted to by scholars for the use of original historical sources. But they are also educational institutions. The hundreds of thousands of school children who visit Independence, gaze at a reproduction of the White House office of the President, and hear the voice of a former Chief Executive describe the responsibilities and meaning of the office, are being instructed in the forms and functions of representative government.

It is fortunate that the beginnings of these presidential archives, with their libraries, museums, and scholarly programs, witnessed their dispersal over the land in such a way that these and other local advantages promised by the advocates of the Act of 1955 have had an opportunity to materialize. But the fact remains that the dispersal has been up to now contingent upon the accidental factor of birth. This will perhaps remain so, but the decisions to associate the John F. Kennedy Library and the Lyndon B. Johnson Library with great university centers indicate a due regard for the fundamental archival nature of these institutions and for their great importance to students of history and government.

These presidential archives have met with challenge from the beginning, particularly from those in the academic community who regard decentralization of scholarly resources as objectionable and who perhaps have not sufficiently examined the very remarkable advantages they offer. Through all the literature concerning these institutions there is an undertone of response to criticism about the concept itself, about competitive acquisition policies,[32] about the sponsorship of research programs, and so

32. Presidential Archives should continue to restrict their acquisition policies to the records and papers of the Presidency and government officials closely associated with that office. They should not become

on. Some of the criticism has been uninformed and even irresponsible, some of it belated. This is not the place to evaluate all aspects of the discussion, but two points must be emphasized. First, among those scholars who have done research at Hyde Park or at Independence the chorus of opinion is emphatic in acclaiming the advantages of having professionally trained archivists in charge of highly specialized groups of records pertaining to one period of history. The benefits to be derived by scholars from the expert knowledge of the records possessed by the professional staffs of these institutions are obvious. Second, the doubts expressed by some responsible scholars about the different degrees of control and accessibility existing between one institution and another are clearly justified. In the case of the archives at Hyde Park, principles governing access were applied very early by trained archivists. In the case of the archives at Independence, this has been true only to the extent that the presidential records involved have been released from "private" to "public" custody. The contrasting results have been carefully appraised by a scholar whose findings merit serious consideration.[33]

Against these findings it is necessary to point out, first, the remarkable fact that the bulk, if not the most significant part, of every recent President's records has become available for research from five to eight years after his tenure of office—a fact unprecedented in American history and unique among the nations of the world. Second, it may be anticipated that the contrasts in experience between the first and second presidential archives will diminish if not be eliminated with the passage of time. Even so, the evolving progress of the presidential archives suggests the wisdom of looking forward to the next stage, not merely in order to provide for them, as for the whole of the archival system, a status more consonant with their character as cultural institutions but also in order to safeguard them against abuses to which they are peculiarly susceptible and to enable

---

general repositories for papers of persons not intimately connected with the Presidents. See James H. Rodabaugh (ed.), *The Present World of History* (Madison, Wis.: American Association for State and Local History, 1959), pp. 34–62.

33. Richard S. Kirkendall, "Presidential Libraries—One Researcher's Point of View," pp. 444–448, and also his "A Second Look at Presidential Libraries," *American Archivist*, XXIX (October 1966), 371–386.

them to realize their highest potentialities. That next stage is one that Franklin D. Roosevelt, as a bold pioneer, could not have been expected to envision at the outset, but it is one that now lies open and beckoning for a President prescient and generous enough to declare for himself and for his heirs that the claim of private right over the records of the office is both incongruous and obsolete even as a legal fiction. Such a decision would not merely carry to its proper conclusion the innovation begun by Franklin D. Roosevelt; it would be the best guarantee that the dangers of proprietary control over public resources would be averted and that the purpose for which these institutions were created would have the fairest chance of being fulfilled.

Thomas Jefferson once declared that the first requirement for a President who wished to gain the confidence of the people was to convince them of his own personal disinterestedness in the conduct of their affairs. The principle, instinct with the meaning of a free society, is applicable also to the manner in which a President regards the records of his office. These are in part unquestionably public and official documents, and even the great bulk of them, consisting of letters and documents addressed by the people to the incumbent of the Presidency, take on the character if not the legal status of—to use Roosevelt's phrase—"the people's record." Buildings to house them, professional staffs to manage and make them available, prudent controls established by law to guard them—these are all public responsibilities. They should be sustained by public funds. One of the consequences of the fiction of private ownership is that no incumbent of the office could demean himself or his station by asking the Congress to appropriate funds for the housing and maintenance of his private assets. In consequence, those who have followed the lead of Franklin D. Roosevelt have been obliged to resort to private solicitation of funds, a device scarcely less demeaning to the office and obviously more susceptible of abuse.

The complexity and the delicacy of the problem must be conceded. No solution would be acceptable that failed to encourage the creation of the fullest possible documentation in the White House, or interfered with its systematic preservation, or did not provide means of making it accessible as promptly for scholarly use as would be consistent with private right and the national interest. Yet the question is surely one of such moment that it should be brought into the open and examined with detachment. Indeed, the very success of the system of presidential archives is such as to call for reassessment of its underlying theory as set forth in the Act of 1955. It is no discredit to the successive Archivists of the United States who have helped to develop and administer this unique system to say that one could scarcely expect such a reexamination to arise from within the establishment. The delicacy of their situation is underscored not merely by their notable success in the case of the Franklin D. Roosevelt Library, where their professional approach became fully applicable at once, but also by the subordinate status they have occupied since 1949, which has had as one of its most unfortunate results the virtual abandonment of discussions of fundamental matters of policy in their annual reports. The fact is that the conventional responses to the problem that abound in the professional literature have never been challenged. The failure to raise questions about this problem in the face of conditions under which the institution of the Presidency operates in the twentieth century may, on some easily imagined occasion, pose threats to the national security that would take precedence over any of the claims of scholarship.

Various approaches to the next stage in the evolution of the system of presidential archives could be suggested. One might be the appointment of a presidential commission to conduct an impartial investigation of this important and complex problem in all of its many aspects. Another might be for the President to take another pioneering step forward, comparable to that of Franklin D. Roosevelt—that is, by issuing an executive order calculated to establish a similar precedent. Such a presidential act might declare at the outset of an administration that the documentation received and accumulated by virtue of occupancy of the office—those records and papers extending far beyond the statutes, executive orders, proclamations, messages to Congress, directives to agencies, and other documents immediately recognizable as official—would during that administration be deemed public property, forming an integral and inseparable part of the records of the nation. Such an order might emulate the practice of some of the states by directing the Archivist of the United

States to assist in devising plans for distinguishing private papers from public records. It might declare that experience had proved the inadequacy, the impropriety, and even the danger of relying upon a private individual of unforeseeable status—whether citizen or alien, whether friendly or hostile to the national security—to exercise control over records accumulated in the presidency and that, on the contrary, experience in the states and with the first of the presidential archives had indicated the wisdom of leaving to professional archivists the duty of applying objectively determined rules of access. Such a declaration of intent would be an act of statesmanship taken in the public interest. It would provide ample flexibility for meeting the changing needs of the system of presidential archives. Above all, it would erect a bulwark against the recurrent danger that these institutions, which by their very nature have a magnetic appeal lacking in other parts of the archival establishment, might be separated from that centralized administrative control that gives coherence and direction to the whole. No executive order, of course, could be binding on successors. But such a precedent, deliberately created and yielding claims of private right in favor of a paramount public interest, would be very difficult indeed for any successor in office to violate.

It would, moreover, clearly define the public responsibility for providing for records thus declared to be public. Accepting the evolving pattern of a system of presidential archives, the Congress, in an equally prudent and generous response, would not only provide for lands, buildings, and management but would also permit each President a voice in determining the location of the institution to house the records of his tenure in office.

Such is only one approach to a problem that has not as yet been critically examined. In recognizing that presidential records are best administered in the presidential archives when under the full and unhampered protection of professional archivists, such a solution would increase the opportunity for scholars to examine these sources on a basis of equality, without discrimination or favoritism and under necessary controls to safeguard confidential communications, private right, and public security. To the extent that the result would be determined by professional standards and left in the hands of archivists—to the extent, that is, that these public records are thought to be free

169

from all suspicion of tampering, manipulation, or improper private control—posterity could be depended upon to recognize and acclaim such an act as an example of disinterested conduct worthy of confidence.

In brief, one of the most powerful arguments that can be offered in support of independence for the entire archival establishment is the protection that it could give to this important new cultural institution, the presidential archives. For in meeting his sworn duty to give to the records of all branches of government an equal, objective, and professional care, the Archivist of the United States must rely in the final analysis upon his own and his institution's repute as impartial instruments of public policy. With the single exception of the presidential archives, the National Archives and Records Service has achieved such a reputation, not merely with honor but with distinction. As administrations come and go and political climates change, this quality of performance will provide the most effective bulwark against improper influences brought to bear from any quarter. But it is a matter for grave concern that the one exception relates to the system of presidential archives. Already one meets with responsible criticism alleging that archivists have shown partiality and subservience in administering presidential records. For example, Herbert Feis has this to say:

> These repositories of most important records are under direct executive control. They are run by the General Service Administration through the Archivist of the United States, with members of his staff working in Washington and in each of the libraries. Thus all the papers that may be collected by the magnetism of reputation or association are in the custody of officials who are well stitched into the executive webbing and subject to orders. In decisions about throwing open to general inspection records in the upper realm of historical interest, these archivists neither can nor will exercise independent judgment. They can hardly be expected to risk their careers in espousing the cause of the historians against the heads of executive departments or library trustees.
>
> The records of the recent past now in the custody of these libraries are fenced in with stakes as high and strong

as those around the White House grounds. The noted public figures for whom the libraries are named, or persons acting for them, determine in the first place which of the records they have collected will be put in these repositories, and which they or their families will retain. This right is theirs even after the papers have been mined and milled for published memoirs. President Truman has made no secret of the fact that he has kept several filing cabinets of his records out of the custody of the Truman Library—to make sure no one will see them until after he is dead and safe from the barbs of history. No outsider knows what records are or will be placed in the Eisenhower Library and which kept out. The papers of Kennedy are still being garnered; it is to be hoped that those who possess them will not screen them before placing them in public custody.

The donors of the records also retain the right to determine when and under what conditions the independent student may be allowed to acquaint himself with them. They can grant permission to study them to some students but not to others equally qualified. Lastly, they can rule that notes or manuscripts based on the records be submitted for approval of either the staff of the library or other designated scrutineers. Moreover, the officials and trustees who are guardians of these collections may regard themselves also as guardians of the reputation of the memorialized individual. They may be loath to expose that reputation to sting or stain as long as living persons care deeply.[34]

But the fault lies not in the administration of the system so much as in its underlying theory. Continued acquiescence in the concept of a private property right in the records of the presidency is surely not the way to eliminate such criticism. Nor is it a safe reliance to continue to place the responsibilities of the Archivist of the United States in the hands of an official and an agency whose primary duties and concerns, however important, are not archival in character.

34. Herbert Feis, "The Shackled Historian," *Foreign Affairs*, XLV (January 1967), 339–340.

[8]

THE FEDERAL RECORDS CENTERS, 1950–1968

The annex [Records Center] might well serve . . . as a temporary storage space for noncurrent records scheduled for destruction at a fixed time in the future, as a depository for records of doubtful value until the passage of time provides the answer to their ultimate fate, and perhaps as a permanent home for noncurrent records that are relatively inactive. —Solon J. Buck, *1941*

Significant savings are brought about by use of the records centers. Office and storage space are released for other use. The records are stored more economically. . . . They are so controlled that they will be disposed of at the earliest possible moment, and reference service on the records is being provided efficiently and economically. . . . —Wayne C. Grover, *1951*

Federal Records Centers are big money savers. The cost of Federal Records Center space is 21 cents per cubic foot of records; the cost of office space is $3.85 per cubic foot of records. The Federal Records Center program savings, plus the avoidance of expenditures which would otherwise have been incurred, may reasonably be estimated at $250 million for the 1951–66 period. —House Committee on Post Office and Civil Service, *1966*

B Y FAR the largest organizational unit within NARS is the Office of Federal Records Centers, which, with a staff of approximately 1,200 and an annual budget of about $10,500,000, administers twelve Federal Records Centers in the ten regions, the Washington National Records Center at Suitland, Maryland, and the National Personnel Records Center in St. Louis. Thus it is also the most far-flung activity and the one best known to federal employees. The records center program has the unique advantage of making sense alike to the scholar, the administrator, and the legislator. Not the least important characteristic is its contribution to economy. Thus it is

172

one government program that is not on the defensive; it demonstrates its usefulness to all. Someone—perhaps it was Tocqueville—said that in a democracy the people will always favor the useful over the beautiful. This prophecy seems to be borne out by the usually generous Congressional support given the Federal Records Centers as contrasted with the penurious support given the National Archives and other cultural phases of the NARS programs. Perhaps the lesson here is that the utility of the former is obvious while the public has never been convinced of the usefulness of the latter. Significantly enough, the Federal Records Centers serve both economy and scholarship.

The Federal Records Act of 1950 laid the statutory foundation for a comprehensive government-wide records program including the operation of records centers. Its provisions, while not inconsistent with proposals discussed earlier by archivists Buck and Grover, were more far-reaching. Essentially the Act provided for a decentralized program with primary responsibility resting upon the agencies, but with staff authority residing in the Administrator of General Services, who was authorized or required to:

> (a) . . . make provisions for the economical and efficient management of records . . . (1) by analyzing, developing, promoting, and coordinating standards, procedures, and techniques designed to improve the management of records, to insure the maintenance and security of records deemed appropriate for preservation, and to facilitate the segregation and disposal of records of temporary value, and (2) by promoting the efficient and economical utilization of space, equipment, and supplies needed for the purpose of creating, maintaining, storing, and servicing records.
>
> (b) . . . establish standards for the selective retention of records of continuing value. . . .
>
> (c) . . . inspect or survey personally or by deputy the records of any Federal agency. . . .
>
> (d) . . . establish, maintain, and operate records centers for the storage, processing, and servicing of records for Federal agencies pending their deposit with the National Archives of the United States or their disposition in

any other manner authorized by law. . . .

(e) . . . promulgate regulations governing the transfer of records. . . .

The immediate responsibility for records management was unmistakably placed upon each agency, the head of which was required to:

(a) . . . cause to be made and preserved records containing adequate and proper documentation of the organization, functions, policies, decisions, procedures, and essential transactions of the agency and designed to furnish the information necessary to protect the legal and financial rights of the Government and of persons directly affected by the agency's activities.

(b) . . . establish and maintain an active, continuing program for the economical and efficient management of the records of the agency. . . .

The Administrator of General Services delegated his archival and records management authority to the Archivist of the United States in September 1950.[1] NARS was now ready to proceed further into a field so ripe for reform that it has in recent years become known as the "paperwork jungle."[2] The magnitude of the challenge that it faced became clear even before passage of the Federal Records Act: A 1950 survey of the state of records management in some 80 agencies and bureaus revealed that there was "no consistent pattern as to what constitutes records management in Government agencies." Of eleven elements of records management surveyed, few agencies had developed programs extending beyond records retirement, files operations, records storage and centers, mail service, and microphotography; only seven maintained reports and adminis-

1. Herbert E. Angel, "Federal Records Management Since the Hoover Commission Report," *American Archivist*, XVI (January 1953), 14–15.
2. Arnold Olsen, "The Federal Paperwork Jungle—The Natives Are Becoming Restless," *American Archivist*, XXVII (July 1964), 363–370; 89th Cong., 1st Sess., *House Report No. 52* (Committee on Post Office and Civil Service), *The Federal Paperwork Jungle: A Report on the Paperwork Requirements Placed Upon Business, Industry, and the Public by the Federal Departments and Agencies.*

trative issuance controls; and only 15 included correspondence management. It was also learned that, in addition to the 104 "records centers" operated by various agencies, there were 204 other "substantial accumulations" of records. These 308 repositories occupied 6,212,000 square feet of space and employed 5,904 staff members at an annual cost of $15,000,000 for personnel and space.[3] These figures reinforced arguments for centrally operated records centers, a concept promoted by Solon Buck as early as 1941 and strongly recommended by the Leahy Report.[4] Accordingly, on May 1, 1950, the first officially designated Federal Records Center was opened by NARS in a government-owned building in Brooklyn, New York. Within two months after the start of this pilot project 45,000 cubic feet of records were being brought into the center at an estimated net annual saving of $57,000, based upon space, equipment, and personnel released for other purposes.[5] The Federal Records Center program, which within the next decade would dwarf the remainder of NARS, was under way.[6]

The phenomenal growth of the Federal Records Center program since 1950 can be understood only in relation to (1) the steady annual production of new federal records, (2) the economies made possible through comparatively lower-cost housing of these records, and (3) the pressure on agencies during the Korean War, which coincided with the early years of the program, to retire records and thus free space and filing equipment for reuse.

Two other important factors should likewise be kept in mind. The new Federal Records Centers in the National Archives and Records Service were administered by archivists who had directed successful records center programs during the war in the Army (Wayne C. Grover and Robert H. Bahmer) and the Navy (Herbert E. Angel and Everett O. Alldredge), and who not only retained excellent connections with their previous de-

3. *Annual Report of the Administrator of General Services for the Fiscal Year Ending June 30, 1950*, pp. 51–59.
4. See pp. 36 and 45.
5. *GSA Annual Report, 1949–50*, p. 59.
6. It must be noted that from the time of the creation of the Records Management Division (later Office) in 1949, until 1963, the Federal Records Center program operated therein; since 1964 there have been separate offices of Federal Records Centers and Records Management. For a discussion of the Records Management program, see Chapter 9.

partments but who also had the confidence of their records management colleagues in the other agencies of the government. Another plus factor for NARS was the Interagency Records Administration Conference (IRAC), an organization of agency records personnel that had met monthly since 1941 to discuss matters of mutual interest, first under the aegis of the Civil Service Commission and with the assistance of the National Archives, and then, after 1946, under the sponsorship of the National Archives. Thus important connections at the working level existed and were functioning when the new program was launched. These proved invaluable in the subsequent transfer of agency records and records centers to NARS.

During World War II the increase in records creation was considered a natural but temporary by-product of government during a national emergency, but the end of the war brought no slackening of the record-making machinery. The extension of federal assistance and regulation to hitherto untouched areas of American life resulted in a frightening increase in paperwork. The Korean conflict and subsequent international crises added to the ever-larger annual output of records. In 1950, federal records totaled about 20,000,000 cubic feet, fewer than half of which had been brought under any sort of inventory and schedule controls; and 3,000,000 cubic feet of new records were being created each year. Because only 37 executive agencies had schedule authorizations for destroying some of their records, officials of NARS looked optimistically to a concerted program of inventorying the records within the agencies and of establishing schedules allowing the orderly disposal of those of no further value. Even so, it was recognized that the existing holdings, plus new records being created annually, could not be expected to decrease noticeably. Accordingly, even the most favorable forecast—that of offsetting the quantity of new records by destruction of old ones—indicated that the government would continue to have on hand at least 20,000,000 cubic feet of records. That this figure was entirely too low is indicated in the following table showing graphically the federal records problem (figures are in cubic feet): [7]

7. These estimates, drawn from several sources, become progressively more reliable. Those for dates prior to 1943 are little more than guesses.

Year	New Records Created During the Year	Total Holdings on Hand	Housed in Federal Records Centers
1912	60,000	1,000,000	0
1930	200,000	3,531,000	0
1943	1,000,000	16,000,000	0
1950	3,000,000	20,000,000	45,000
1958	3,800,000	23,700,000	4,075,000
1968	4,500,000+	25,700,000	9,400,000

The mandate of the Federal Records Act of 1950 was a massive attack upon the mounting records problems. To carry out that mandate NARS sought to assist agencies in eliminating the creation of unnecessary records while providing facilities for

TABLE IV

*Regional Federal Records Center Statistics**

Fiscal Year	Reference Services	Total Holdings
1950	250	45,000
1951	71,467	603,221
1952	218,214	1,025,333
1953	384,306	1,563,803
1954	697,755	2,083,459
1955	899,514	2,472,495
1956	1,225,862	2,908,498
1957	1,662,748	3,186,186
1958	1,943,670	3,390,708
1959	2,621,195	4,677,387
1960	2,945,891	5,301,331
1961	2,972,133	5,362,236
1962	3,110,364	5,438,290
1963	3,125,472	5,784,140
1964	3,103,501	5,994,326
1965	3,166,499	6,129,357
1966	3,597,154	6,475,470
1967	3,477,211	6,673,728
1968	4,044,335	7,041,501

* The National Personnel Records Center, which holds approximately 2,300,000 cubic feet of personnel records and performs about 2,100,000 reference services per year, is not included in these statistics.

more economical and efficient housing of relatively inactive records not yet eligible for destruction or for transfer to the Archives.[8] The experience of agencies during wartime—notably the departments of War and Navy—proved the value of records centers. Even greater savings, however, were believed possible in NARS-operated Federal Records Centers, a prediction amply

8. The records management program will be discussed in Chapter 9.

demonstrated to be correct in each succeeding annual report of the Administrator of General Services.

Within a year after the first center was opened in Brooklyn, more than 550,000 cubic feet of records were transferred to that center and to three new Federal Records Centers—in Washington, Chicago, and San Francisco. The first year's savings were impressive: 245,000 square feet of office space and 275,000 square feet of storage space were released for other purposes at an annual saving of $905,000. In addition, 8,000 file cabinets with a replacement value of $400,000 were released for reuse.[9] These savings, however, were insignificant in comparison with those resulting from the transfer of vast quantities of records to the centers in later years.

Plans were laid for the establishment of at least one Federal Records Center in each of the ten GSA regions. These centers usually replaced a GSA records repository that had previously housed just the records of that agency and its predecessors. Only after a repository had been properly staffed and equipped to handle the records of other departments and agencies was it given the more exalted title of Federal Records Center. During fiscal 1952 such conversions took place in Atlanta, Dallas, and Denver, and an eighth center was established in St. Louis to accept personnel records of former civilian government employees. A center was opened in Boston the following year, and in fiscal 1954, GSA repositories in Kansas City and Seattle were converted into Federal Records Centers. At the same time an annex to the San Francisco center was established in Honolulu. Individual agency centers had by then been reduced to 78.[10] Thus within four years after the beginning of the NARS system of Federal Records Centers there were ten regional centers and one annex holding 2,439,000 cubic feet of records that were used 1,280,000 times during one year.

Meanwhile efforts were continued to encourage destruction of records of no further value. A GSA regulation in fiscal 1952 required agencies to compile control schedules for all major groups of records in their custody, and by June 30, 1954, agencies were able to report that 95 percent of their records

9. *GSA Annual Report, 1950–51*, pp. 12–13.
10. *GSA Annual Report, 1951–52*, pp. 65–66; *1952–53*, p. 7; *1953–54*, pp. 9–10.

were covered by such schedules. At that time the total of federal records had declined within a year from 25,300,000 to 24,700,000 cubic feet, and more were being destroyed than were being created.[11] This total, nevertheless, was still nearly 5,000,000 cubic feet above the figure for 1950.

The story of the Federal Records Centers since 1954 has been one of continued expansion and improved economies. New centers have been added, some eliminated, and some consolidated. Through more compactly arranged shelving and the use of buildings with higher ceilings, the ratio of cubic footage of records to square footage of floor space was increased from 2:1 in 1950 to 5:1 in 1967. Improved procedures have resulted in more efficient use of both space and personnel, and today approximately 35 percent of the nation's records are housed in Federal Records Centers.[12] But the proliferation of records shows no sign of tapering off. Ten years ago the federal government had on hand 23,700,000 cubic feet of records and was creating 3,800,000 additional cubic feet annually while destroying 3,300,000. In 1967 the holdings amounted to 25,700,000 cubic feet of records, while more than 4,500,000 feet were being created and 4,250,000 feet were being destroyed. Of the total, 6,700,000 cubic feet with an average life of seven years were in the 13 general-purpose Federal Records Centers, and about 2,000,000 feet were in the National Personnel Records Center in St. Louis. Whereas reference requests a decade ago totaled about 2,500,000 annually, they amounted to more than 5,750,000 in 1967, an indication of the transfer of more active records to the centers. Of the remaining nearly 17,000,000 cubic feet, 13,400,000 feet were in current use in the agencies, 490,000 feet were in the remaining 11 small agency-operated centers, 900,000 feet were in the National Archives, and the remainder was in other agency storage. The second Hoover Commission recommended that less than one-half of the total be retained in office space; NARS is now making headway toward that mark.[13]

11. *GSA Annual Report, 1951–52*, p. 59; Robert W. Krauskopf, "The Hoover Commissions and Federal Recordkeeping," *American Archivist*, XXI (October 1958), 385–386.

12. For statistics on Federal Records Centers, see Tables IV and V.

13. Among the factors accounting for increased accessions in the centers have been the President's moratorium on the purchase of new

TABLE V

Statistics on Federal Records Centers
June 30, 1968

Region		Holdings (cu. ft.)	Capacity Available for New Accessions (cu. ft.)	Annual References (Number)	Total Staff*
1		139,153	87,535	99,871	15
2	New York	639,529	117,367	407,495	40
	Philadelphia	395,797	35,063	267,048	25
	Mechanicsburg	999,071	268,465	636,220	49
4		473,091	115,984	427,693	35
5		544,116	20,801	369,882	31
6		377,880	166,381	214,974	26
7		342,288	88,847	165,924	26
8		357,874	66,655	102,810	13
9	San Francisco	310,409	134,288	211,347	23
	Los Angeles	229,111	108,145	164,437	22
10		146,483	98,569	81,039	12
Washington National Records Center		2,086,699	1,738,769	895,595	206
Subtotal		7,041,501	3,046,869	4,044,335	523
National Personnel Records Center					
Military		1,385,667	76,493	1,631,566	482
Civilian		939,713	242,275	489,202	200
Subtotal		2,325,380	318,768	2,120,768	682
GRAND TOTAL		9,366,881	3,365,637	6,165,103	1,205

* Staff figures include some employees paid from nonappropriated funds.

A Congressional Committee in 1966 reviewed the accomplishments of the Federal Records Centers.[14] In terms of expenditures that would have been necessary without the centers, the legislators estimated the savings to the government from 1951 to 1966 at $250,000,000—far more than the total spent for the operation of the entire National Archives and Records Service throughout its existence.[15]

---

filing equipment, effective January 1965, which reduced in 2½ years the government's purchase of cabinets by 158,000 at a saving of $7,925,000, and his order of September 1966 for a "cleanout" of records used infrequently.

14. 89th Cong., 2nd Sess., *House Report No. 2197* (Committee on Post Office and Civil Service), *How to Cut Paperwork* (Washington: Government Printing Office, 1966).

15. In computing savings, NARS currently uses the following figures: $3.76 per square foot for office space released; $1.06 per square foot for storage space freed for other purposes; and $50.00 for each 5-drawer file

The National Personnel Records Center in St. Louis, which accounts for more than half of the employees of the Office of Federal Records Centers and about half of its budget, is a one-of-a-kind operation. Its 2,300,000 cubic feet of records [16] are referred to 2,100,000 times a year. Because the records are of a specialized type, most of the employees are military personnel clerks or are in other clerical classifications. An automated records indexing system has been installed in the center—an essential in view of the increase in holdings resulting from the annual departure from federal service of 600,000 civilian employees and 800,000 members of the armed forces.

With the completion of the giant Federal Records Center in Suitland, which will provide shelving for 3,800,000 cubic feet of records on two floors of ten acres each, the most serious space problems will have been alleviated for a time. Even so, additional space will be needed in Denver and Fort Worth, and if present negotiations with the Internal Revenue Service result in acceptance by the centers of income tax returns directly from the IRS processing centers, more space will also be needed in several other regions. The Chicago center, now the only one in rented space, is expected to occupy a government-owned building by 1970.

Federal Records Centers are far more than money-saving storage buildings for records scheduled for destruction; they are also intermediate records repositories combined with regional archives. Their development, therefore, has been in line with the ideas of Buck, Grover, and other archivists, who had seen the need for additional space in the Washington area and in the parts of the country with a heavy concentration of federal offices long before the Leahy Report was written. As early as 1941 Buck had envisioned a building to serve "as a temporary storage space for noncurrent records scheduled for destruction at a fixed time in the future" and as a "permanent home" for noncurrent

---

cabinet released for reuse. Counting space and equipment, it is estimated that it costs $4.43 per cubic foot per year for records to be maintained in office space, whereas the same cubic foot of records can be housed in a Federal Records Center for only 29 cents per year. See epigraph, p. 172.

16. These include 60,000,000 records of former civilian employees and 43,000,000 records of individuals who have served in the armed forces. James Hughes, "The World's Largest Records Center," *Information and Records Management*, I (June–July 1967), 18–19.

records that are relatively inactive. He proposed "branches" throughout the country in which field records would be assembled.[17]

This broad concept of Federal Records Centers thus stemmed from an early recognition of the need for (1) additional space in Washington for records scheduled for transfer to the National Archives; (2) a screening and staging area for records ultimately destined for the National Archives; (3) a regional archives for the housing of records of permanent value but primarily of regional interest; and (4) a low-cost storage area for records scheduled for ultimate destruction and used infrequently enough to permit their removal from agency office and storage space.

The National Archives Building was filled to capacity within a decade after it was completed. President Roosevelt's serious suggestion that the Pentagon be converted into an Archives Annex after World War II [18] went the way of many other hopes of peace and normality and the high cost of land and buildings in the vicinity of the National Archives led archivists virtually to abandon hope for sufficient space near the present building. Attention, therefore, turned to a combined Archives Annex and Federal Records Center in the Washington area, the former to accommodate the overflow of records of national importance but of relatively infrequent use, as well as archival materials under long-term restrictions. Such a structure would allow the National Archives Building to be reserved for the most valuable and active national records. At last this facility has been provided in the huge Federal Records Center in Suitland, in which provision is made for 570,000 cubic feet of permanent records in addition to more than 3,200,000 cubic feet of records scheduled for destruction or other disposition. The movement of records into the center was completed in 1968. The building is constructed along functional rather than artistic lines, and researchers working there may covet the more ornate surroundings of the National Archives Building. Even so, this long-needed safety valve for the federal archives is an important step and one to be appreciated by scholars who have watched with

17. *Seventh Annual Report of the Archivist of the United States for the Fiscal Year Ending June 30, 1941*, pp. 5–6. See epigraph, p. 172.
18. See p. 36.

anxiety as the capacity of the main archives building was reached.

The Archives Branch of the Suitland FRC will provide less of a Regional Archives than a National Archives Annex. However, the problem of federal records of regional importance, as differentiated from those of national significance, has also been long recognized.[19] Included in this category are records relating to district courts, land, customs, and Indians. Since the establishment of the first centers these records have generally been retained in the regions, and as one scholar put it, "willy-nilly, the Records Centers gradually began to take on the character of junior archival institutions. . . ."[20] In reading the thoroughly documented papers by Professors White and Petrowski, one must be impressed with not only the sheer quantity of scholarly research carried on in the Regional Archives but also with the stature of the researchers and the wide spectrum of records and subject matter covered. In addition, certain specialized records are housed in selected regional centers, such as the World War I draft registration records in the Atlanta center. These records are often housed alongside temporary records in the centers, without atmospheric controls and without a specialized staff to service them.

To provide better for the archival materials in the various centers, the Regional Archives are now being systematically developed. In each Federal Records Center will be added the basic facilities for archival preservation and service.[21] The total cost of these additional facilities throughout the country, in terms of physical alterations and additions, is estimated at less than $500,000. The need for a modest increase in the number

19. See, i.e., Oliver W. Holmes, "The Problem of Federal Field Office Records," and Richard B. Morris, "The Need for Regional Depositories for Federal Records," *American Archivist*, VI (April 1943), 81–104 and 115–122, respectively.

20. Gerald T. White, "Government Archives Afield: The Federal Records Centers and the Historian," typescript of address delivered before the Organization of American Historians and the Society of American Archivists, Chicago, April 1967. Some of the centers have prepared useful finding aids of selected archival series, and one—the Federal Records Center in East Point, Georgia—has published a general leaflet, *Research Opportunities*, publicizing its holdings. See also William R. Petrowski, "Research, Anyone? A Look at the Federal Records Centers," *American Archivist*, XXX (October 1967), 581–592.

21. Such facilities are already provided in the Boston, Kansas City, Fort Worth, and Suitland centers.

of first-rate archivists will add to this figure. The potential dividends from the Regional Archives are great, and NARS should accelerate their establishment.[22]

The Federal Records Centers, as part of their archival activities, have also provided a secretariat and have often served as a meeting place for a series of archival symposia held during the last four years to advance the profession in numerous locations around the country. Since 1964 more than 25 symposia have been held in a score of such cities as Boston, Philadelphia, and Trenton in the East; Atlanta, Tallahassee, Nashville, Raleigh, Columbia, and Jackson in the South; Minneapolis, St. Louis, Kansas City, Austin, Fort Worth, and Denver in the mid-continent; and Los Angeles, San Francisco, Sacramento, Portland, Pullman, and Seattle on the West Coast. Besides being limited to one day, these symposia have many other things in common. All are sponsored primarily by the Society of American Archivists; by one or more archives, libraries, universities, or historical societies in the locality; and by the nearest regional office of the National Archives and Records Service, generally operating through the Federal Records Center. They meet in space provided by one of the sponsoring institutions. Speakers and panel members are drawn from the same sources.

Attendance at these symposia has ranged from 30 to 150, averaging about 70. Occupationally, the participants are mostly archivists, librarians, historians, and officials from colleges and universities, churches, hospitals, business organizations, and federal, state, and local governments. Most reside in the vicinity of the symposia, but nearby states are often represented. Six to eight papers or panel discussions are usually included in each symposium, with ample time for questions from the floor. Their subject matter is highly varied and depends on the wishes of

22. The National Archives and Records Service, however, is responsible only for federal records, and it should not go beyond that responsibility. The Regional Archives are indeed appropriate repositories for any federal records that may be placed in them, as well as microfilm copies of other federal materials, as outlined in Wayne C. Grover's article, "Toward Equal Opportunities for Scholarship," in *Journal of American History*, LII (March 1966), 715–724. Private papers are the responsibilities of the states, local governments, and academic and private institutions; and even where the responsibilities are not being carried out vigorously, NARS should remain clear of the field. NARS has sufficient responsibilities to demand all its resources and all the good will and support that it can get from the public. See pp. 109 ff.

those attending. The first symposium in a locality generally concentrates on such basic topics as the need for archival institutions; appraisal, accession, arrangement, description, preservation, storage, and use of archives and manuscripts; and training of archivists. Subsequent symposia move on to more varied topics, such as special classes of archives (including maps, photographs, taped interviews, and microfilm) and sophisticated records systems involving information retrieval and computers. Sponsoring institutions describe their holdings and techniques and frequently conduct a tour of their facilities. Understandably, the symposia have been well received, and successive meetings in the same locality have grown in size.

Ironically, Federal Records Centers, though comprising the largest and most dispersed of the NARS activities, are among the least understood of those activities. Because of their great appeal as money savers, they are often looked upon by government officials and scholars alike as little more than warehouses filled with records and file clerks. Such an impression is directly in conflict with the whole philosophy behind the federal records program. Though the Archives Building may figuratively be considered the "heaven" for permanent records, the Federal Records Centers were never conceived as their hell. They are, instead, something of a purgatory. The records, in other words, are not ready for their final disposition. They are still available for use. Many have not yet been diagnosed, and the Federal Records Center is the scene of this diagnosis by the doctor of records, the appraisal archivist. It is only the appraisal archivist who can pronounce the verdict: further protection or destruction. The records have been placed in the Federal Records Center simply because it is cheaper and more efficient to maintain them there than in the offices where they were created. It is in the records centers that appraisal archivists must (1) prepare appraisal recommendations for records not already evaluated; (2) apply provisions of records retention plans; (3) apply existing schedules to remove material of temporary value; (4) weed out nonrecord and duplicate materials; (5) apply sampling techniques in accordance with retention plans and schedules; (6) organize fragments into archival series; (7) merge blocks of splintered files; (8) resolve problems of confidential, privileged, and other classified records; (9) recommend records for incorporation in Regional Archives; and (10) box and label archival materials to be transferred to the National Archives or to be retained in the Regional Archives. In addition, the archivists at the centers monitor the effectiveness of schedules and retention plans in field activities and assist in preparing and installing schedules for field records.

Thus the notion that all work in a regional records center can be turned over to cheap labor is as foreign to the philosophy of archival and records management as would be the proposal to place records of temporary value in the National Archives Building. Of the approximately 500 staff members manning these thirteen regional centers, the largest number are subprofessional archives assistants, but their work is guided and controlled by archivists applying archival methods and principles.

Records centers, then, have developed in a manner different from that envisioned by the Leahy Report of 1949. Leahy viewed the centers as providing physical space for low-cost storage where the records could be handled by "clerical and administrative employees rather than professional, archival assistance." Actual experience in the establishment and operation of the centers soon dispelled this restricted view, and the potentials of an intermediate repository, archivally oriented but operated with emphases upon economy and efficiency, were soon recognized. It was at this point, early in the last decade, that the true value of records centers was realized. So obvious was the lesson that one state after another patterned programs after the NARS example, and a study of Ernst Posner's *American State Archives* is sufficient to reveal that the successful state programs have almost uniformly been those that learned from the federal example. Many governments in foreign countries too have modeled their programs after the United States experience. It is also significant that over half of the 500 largest corporations in the United States have corporate records centers. Finally, it must be observed that a large proportion of the state, municipal, and corporate records centers in this country follow the general pattern of the Federal Records Centers. This is not surprising, because the Federal Records Centers evolved from the Navy and Army records centers of World War II, and many of those responsible for records centers around the country today either have had Navy or Army FRC experience or were trained by others who did have such experience.

The Federal Records Centers are an integral part of the national archival system, inseverable both in theory and practice. There is a danger, however, that the formal designation of portions of each Federal Records Center as a "Regional Archives" may be interpreted by efficiency experts as indicating that the remainder of the functions of the centers are purely managerial and therefore subject to administrative separation from the Regional Archives. If such a danger arises, it must be resisted by those who recognize the great contributions that centers are making in the total federal records program.

GSA has assisted the Federal Records Centers measurably in providing increasingly adequate physical facilities. Located originally in whatever space could be found readily, often obsolete warehouses, old munitions plants, and similar structures, the centers are now much better situated. New buildings especially designed as records centers have been constructed in St. Louis, Boston, and Suitland, and Congress has just appropriated funds for plans for a similar building in Chicago. Modern warehouse buildings have been or are being converted into suitable records centers in Atlanta, Kansas City, Fort Worth, Denver, and Seattle. Undoubtedly the remaining buildings will be modernized in the course of time or will be replaced. As pointed out earlier, archival areas with temperature and humidity controls should be provided in all of these buildings that do not now have such areas. One cannot enter a Federal Records Center, however, without noticing a phenomenon that may be a result of economizing on the purchase and installation of raised or painted lettering, but that has the effect of denying to the National Archives and Records Service the public recognition it richly deserves. The typical front-entrance designation of the centers is:

FEDERAL RECORDS CENTER
General Services Administration

May there not be an intangible advantage for each Federal Records Center to be associated in the public mind with the National Archives and Records Service? Certainly NARS would benefit from such an association.

The development of the Federal Records Centers, envisioned

187

in miniature by archivists prior to World War II, experimented with by large agencies during and after the war, recommended by the first Hoover Commission, provided for in the Federal Records Act of 1950, and brought into existence in the National Archives and Records Service since 1950, ranks as one of the most successful examples of the merging of complementary emphases for the improvement of the functions of government. The tasks of the centers, however, far from being finished, are just beginning. A new era in information recording has arrived. More and more records are being created in nonpaper forms, and the centers are already receiving records in the form of microfilm, motion pictures, and analog and digital magnetic tape. Working in cooperation with other offices in NARS, the Office of Federal Records Centers must now turn much of its attention to these new media and develop programs of evaluating, preserving, and servicing materials that involve complex automated systems for the control of information and communications. Judging from the past performance of the center program, it will be equal to the new challenges.[23]

23. Herbert E. Angel, then Assistant Archivist for Federal Records Centers and immediate past president of the Society of American Archivists, comprehensively surveyed the history and status of records centers in his presidential address, "Archival Janus: The Records Center," published in *American Archivist*, XXXI (January 1968), 5–12.

[9]

THE RECORDS MANAGEMENT PROGRAM,

1950–1968

. . . The National Archives must inevitably be concerned with the creation, arrangement, and administration as well as with the appraisal, disposal, and preservation of Government records, and . . . in order to perform its functions satisfactorily it must have a knowledge of the records that can come only from continuous survey of them. —Solon J. Buck, *1941*

I can't imagine any agency head trying to establish a records management program without including techniques to control records creation. My belief is that requiring the agencies to do something about controlling records creation is one of the best features of the Federal Records Act. I get the impression that the Federal Government has to date done much better in the field of records disposal and records maintenance than in the matter of controlling records creation.
        —Representative Richard W. Bolling, *1951*

The records management program of the National Archives and Records Service . . . should be vigorously supported by the Congress and in the executive branch and should be expanded in the areas of paperwork simplification, standardization, and research. —House Committee on Post Office and Civil Service, *1965*

RECORDS ADMINISTRATION, promoted by the National Archives almost from its establishment, began to get outstanding results as "alumni" from the Archives organized records programs in the War and Navy departments and in other agencies during the war. These results were expressed in terms of office space and filing cabinets released for other use, cubic feet of records destroyed, copies of forms and reports eliminated, and other savings of vital importance to an agency administrator trying to keep his organization effective in a period of wartime expansion.

The Navy Department began putting a dollar value on these

189

computable benefits. So impressive were its figures that the first Hoover Commission in 1949 set as one of its goals the establishment of a "Navy type" records management program in every agency. This had not been accomplished by President Truman's executive order in 1946, for, though the order was given lip service in most agencies, there was no effective follow-through. Consequently, many records management programs existed on paper only. Convinced that the remedy for this situation required legislation, the Hoover Commission task force report provided the outlines of such a statute. The Congress, in the Federal Records Act of 1950, directed each agency and department to "establish and maintain an active continuing program for the economical and efficient management of the records of the agency." The same act required the Administrator of General Services to

> make provisions for the economical and efficient management of records of Federal agencies (1) by analyzing, developing, promoting, and coordinating standards, procedures, and techniques designed to improve the management of records, to insure the maintenance and security of records deemed appropriate for preservation, and to facilitate the segregation and disposal of records of temporary value, and (2) by promoting the efficient and economical utilization of space, equipment, and supplies needed for the purpose of creating, maintaining, storing, and servicing records.

He also was authorized to "inspect or survey personally or by deputy the records of any Federal agency, as well as to make surveys of records management and records disposal practices in such agencies," and was to be given the "full cooperation of officials and employees of agencies in such inspections and surveys. . . ." [1]

The act did not provide for a large central regulatory staff to direct agency management programs; instead, it placed primary responsibility for such programs in the agencies themselves. It gave to GSA powers only in "developing, promoting, and coordinating standards." Thus the federal program is one of decentralized responsibility but with surveillance and guidance from

1. 44 U.S.C. 395.

TABLE VI

Interrelationships Between Archives and Records Management

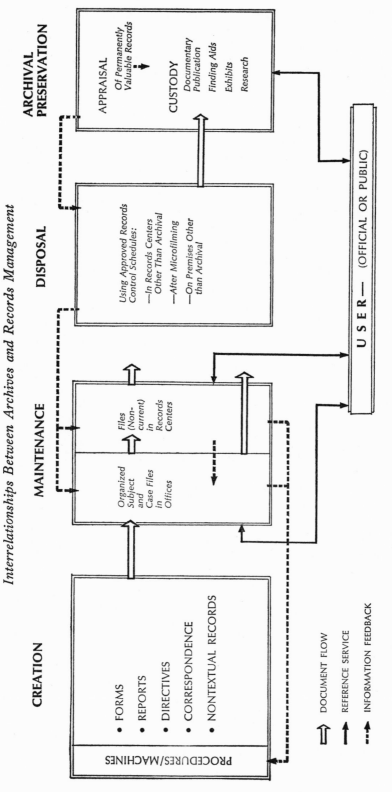

CREATION

- FORMS
- REPORTS
- DIRECTIVES
- CORRESPONDENCE
- NONTEXTUAL RECORDS

PROCEDURES/MACHINES

MAINTENANCE

Organized Subject and Case Files in Offices

Files (Noncurrent) in Records Centers

DISPOSAL

Using Approved Records Control Schedules:

—In Records Centers Other Than Archival

—After Microfilming

—On Premises Other than Archival

ARCHIVAL PRESERVATION

APPRAISAL
Of Permanently Valuable Records

CUSTODY
Documentary Publication
Finding Aids
Exhibits
Research

U S E R — (OFFICIAL OR PUBLIC)

⇧ DOCUMENT FLOW

↑ REFERENCE SERVICE

⇡ INFORMATION FEEDBACK

the central staff agency, which is, by delegation of authority from the GSA Administrator, the Office of Records Management of NARS. It has been, a NARS official writes, "a cardinal policy of the program that its real authority derives from its own competency to provide agencies with technical assistance and standards." [2]

Some state officials and business leaders, accustomed to highly centralized programs of records management, may suspect that there is too little centralization of authority in the federal program, but they overlook the size of the federal government and the complexity of its organizational traditions, which have produced monolithic entities virtually immune to any influence except salesmanship. NARS, therefore, has wisely followed the assumption that a good program will be accepted if properly promoted.

Previous experience during the 1940s in the more restricted areas of records administration was insufficient to permit NARS to staff a full-grown program of service in records creation problems during the 1950s. Happily, it found the answer: A number of its former staff members who had, during and after the war, gone off to establish effective records management programs in the larger agencies were willing to return home after the passage of the Federal Records Act of 1950 with their recently acquired store of experience and knowledge. Among the leaders of this group were Herbert E. Angel and Everett O. Alldredge, both of whom were "alumni" of the National Archives who had gained valuable records management experience with the Navy Department. Angel, who was Solon Buck's editorial chief before the war, had also served in 1948–49 on the Hoover Commission task force.[3]

The phenomenon of homing pigeons not only was a source of pride for NARS but a fortunate turn of events for the government's newest program. It proved a point that tireless exponents of archival participation in records management had argued all along: There is no logical breaking point between the management of records anywhere along the spectrum of creation, maintenance, and, eventually, disposition or preservation in the archival agency.

2. Everett O. Alldredge to H. G. Jones, March 27, 1968.
3. Angel is now Deputy Archivist. Alldredge is Assistant Archivist.

So it came to pass that the availability of professionally trained archivists who had added to their credentials the skills of modern records management gave the federal records program its unique strength of unified purpose in managing the nation's records from the viewpoint not of the archivist *or* the records manager but rather with an emphasis on the entire life cycle of the records. This lesson has been learned not only by the states with good archival and records management programs but also by foreign governments, particularly those in the developing countries.

The recommendations of the second Hoover Commission in 1955 resulted in strengthening the NARS program.[4] Its area of responsibility grew to "total paperwork systems." It no longer was concerned primarily with records disposition and the waste of the past; it became more involved in the record-making process, because only through controlling the production of records can the waste of tomorrow be curbed by the creation of fewer but better records. While improved measures for the maintenance, disposal, and preservation of records lead to economies, NARS in the late 1950s and early in the present decade proved that greater savings and better documentation are possible through avoiding the creation of unnecessary records and improving procedures for the creation of the necessary ones. This NARS breakthrough has colored all of the recent writing on the scope of records management.

The accomplishments of the Office of Records Management —consisting now of only about 120 staff members and an annual budget of $1,300,000—have been impressive. Most of its management analysts are located in Washington and work directly with agency headquarters, but about 30 are stationed in the ten GSA regions for service to the field offices.

One of the earliest techniques employed by the Office of Records Management remains a fundamental emphasis of its program: staff training. By the mid-1950s NARS had devel-

---

4. The findings and recommendations of the second Hoover Commission are contained in two publications by the Commission on Organization of the Executive Branch of the Government: *Task Force on Paperwork Management; Part I—In the United States Government* and *Paperwork Management; Part I—In the U.S. Government* (both published by the Government Printing Office, Washington, 1955). Leahy again directed the task force.

oped workshops, handbooks, and study materials on subjects such as the management of correspondence, reports, forms, mail, and files. From 1956 to 1963 alone, workshops were given by NARS personnel to 93,000 federal employees, and 147,000 additional workers participated in workshops conducted by agency personnel who had been trained by NARS.[5] Through 1967 more than 350,000 persons had participated in 14 major workshops, and 16 handbooks had sold about 100,000 copies each, not counting those distributed free to government employees. Congressmen—not noted for liberal compliments to government programs—estimated that 36 man-hours were saved for each hour spent in the workshops.[6] It is worthy of mention that NARS has generously assisted state and local officials through these workshops, and a number of states have adapted the federal literature and visual aids to their own specialized use.

Impressed by the results of the records system of the Navy Department involving machine-language records—paper tape, punched cards, etc.—the Bureau of the Budget in 1960 assigned to NARS the promotion of source data automation—known as "SDA" by government officials. By starting at the source of the data, SDA provides a vehicle for a self-perpetuating data system that facilitates the transmission and storage of data so that information can be used over and over again, recaptured in the many forms that management and operation may require. As early as 1961 NARS conducted workshops and issued publications on the subject, and since that time SDA workshops have been given to 10,000 federal employees. These workshops have brought into existence almost 300 applications releasing over 1,900 employees to other work. At the present time most of the cost of computers is in the input area, generally the cost of keypunching. Source data automation aims to eliminate as much keypunching as possible. It has thus been instrumental in hold-

5. *Annual Report of the Administrator of General Services for the Fiscal Year Ending June 30, 1963*, p. 52. Some of the NARS workshops are described in an 8-page booklet, *Technical Workshops to Help Federal Agencies Manage Their Paperwork*, issued in August 1967.

6. 89th Cong., 2nd Sess., *House Report No. 2197* (Committee on Post Office and Civil Service), *How To Cut Paperwork* (Washington: Government Printing Office, 1966), p. 13. This source will hereafter be cited as *How To Cut Paperwork*. For a brief review of the committee report, see Rodd S. Exelbert, "Communique from the Front: Uncle Sam Is Winning the Battle of the Bulging Files," *Information and Records Management*, I (June-July 1967), 15–16.

ing down computer costs in many installations.

Among other NARS activities along these lines have been symposia such as "Putting Information Retrieval to Work in the Office" and "Mechanizing the Information Process," which were conducted for both government and nongovernment personnel in Washington in 1967 and 1968, respectively. Mechanization is fast replacing manual record-making in many federal programs: in letter writing, preparing reports, addressing mail, and processing data from forms. There is a great need for the development of additional workshops to meet the challenges of the new technology. To the historian the titles sound forbidding —office information retrieval, data bank networks, correspondence automation, management information systems for computer input. However, he is prepared to admit that the revolutionary changes in documentation in the past decade are but a portent of greater changes to come, and he can find comfort in the fact that the National Archives and Records Service has knowledgeable specialists at work in a field of such great concern to the researcher of the future. He is even more comforted by the caliber of the leaders of those forces, many of whom had their beginnings as archivists and thus are fully conscious of the obligations of archivists to records managers and vice versa. Furthermore, he is acutely aware of the absolute necessity for a continued crossbreeding between the two specialties lest an artificial chasm evolve between the two that might, in time, disrupt the flow of documentation from its origin to its ultimate cultural usefulness.

Through program evaluation the Office of Records Management reviews the status of the paperwork management and automated program within an agency, measures that program against requirements and standards, determines its effectiveness in meeting management and operational needs of the agency and cultural needs of the community, and recommends improvements. The end result is a report containing a plan of action. This report is one of the most significant of NARS productions:

In addition to providing a critique on the agency's paperwork management program, the evaluation serves as a prime promotional device for informing agencies of NARS interests and responsibilities in Federal records management. . . . These officials receive a broad insight as to the nature of paperwork management and the role it can play in the overall agency management scheme. These officials are informed as to the meaning of a "paperwork management program" as envisioned in the Federal Records Act of 1950 and the GSA regulations.[7]

Such evaluations usually result in "organization changes, new and revised functional assignments, realinement [*sic*] of management relationships, and initiation of projects to improve the planning, coordination, and administration of paperwork management in the agency." There is an important by-product: The agency will look at data and document needs in the perspective of its assigned mission. In the event evaluation proposals go beyond the capabilities of the agency, NARS staff members may be assigned to give technical assistance.

Present funds provide for evaluations of only six agencies per year, a rate that will require from 20 to 30 years for surveying programs of all agencies. Potential savings in terms of improved documentation as well as dollars justify a speed-up of these evaluations.

The NARS technical assistance staff is available for direct assistance to agencies requesting aid in solving specific problems. At present only about 80 such projects are conducted each year, and a disappointing backlog of requests cannot be filled. Such assistance may involve a particular isolated problem or a study of complex procedures. Most technical assistance projects are designed to achieve three goals: less time for paperwork processing, better quality of documentation, and reduced costs. Dollar savings were estimated by a Congressional committee to have totaled more than $17,000,000 in 1965 alone.[8]

The following studies—five among many mentioned in the NARS budget hearings for fiscal years 1966 and 1967—demonstrate more specifically how the Office of Records Management assists agencies: (1) A study of the correspondence tasks in certain correctional institutions in the Bureau of Prisons, Department of Justice, indicated that 85 percent of the letters could be answered by well-designed form and guide letters.

7. *How To Cut Paperwork*, p. 14.
8. *Ibid.*, p. 15.

These letters were packaged in an easy-to-use, numbered form, and the official now needs only to indicate which form or guide letter is to be used, then instruct a typist. By applying the new procedure to only three federal correctional institutions in Texas, five correspondence drafters were eliminated. Adoption of the procedure on a nationwide scale will result in much greater savings. (2) A review of the processing of work requests at the Marine Corps Base, Twenty-Nine Palms, California, indicated that 80 man-years were being consumed. NARS reduced 31 work request processing steps to eight, replaced thirteen manually prepared forms with four machine-prepared tapes, and mechanized planning and estimating work request actions, enabling the base commander to abolish 26 positions. (3) Previous to a NARS study, record-keeping in the Office of Education, Department of Health, Education, and Welfare, relating to funds for school districts in "federal impact" areas, was done manually. NARS worked out an automated procedure that made data available weeks earlier and reduced the clerical force by six clerks. (4) A review of the mail and correspondence practices of the New York and San Francisco offices of the Defense Contract Administration Services resulted in the abolition of letters of transmittal, the introduction of window envelopes, the preparation of a routing guide, establishment of messenger routes and work measurement guides, and the elimination of one level of clearance on outgoing correspondence. Eleven mail clerk positions were eliminated in these two offices alone. (5) The Bonneville Power Administration's office copying machine operation, microfilm program, and system of handling correspondence and engineering drawings were revised with a resulting saving of more than 25 man-years to date.

The activities of the records manager are, by and large, no less analytical in nature than historical research. He gathers information, studies it, evaluates it, draws conclusions. But he also goes a step farther: He proposes solutions to problems and improvements for conditions. Those proposals are wise only insofar as he has accurately evaluated his information. In his own way, therefore, the modern records management specialist is no less a scholar than are those who objectively study the social or physical sciences or any other field of knowledge. His breadth of interest must be wide—it must reach the entire spectrum of documentation—and his competence must be continually

197

sharpened by mastering an incredible amount of literature flowing from the presses. Like the archivist of two decades ago, the records manager has struggled for professional status; he has now earned it, and historians, archivists, and other professionals should recognize him as their ally through whose hands the nation's documentation will reach them. Just as the archivist is no longer a librarian who hordes manuscripts, so the modern records manager of the caliber found in the National Archives and Records Service is no longer a technician in charge of records disposition. The image of the records manager, like that of the archivist, has been enhanced immeasurably within a few years. Through the further professionalization of the work of the records manager, and through the establishment of better training courses, particularly in the National Archives [9] and in academic institutions, that image will have a significantly favorable influence upon an improvement in the future documentation of the organization and functions of the federal government.

The Office of Records Management is understaffed. Its sense of mission is infectious; its sense of urgency is frustrating. The nature of the records manager's work need not be repeated except to emphasize that his effectiveness is dependent upon the amount of time available for him to carry out his mission. Every delay in a potential improvement is costly, both to the agencies concerned and to the taxpayer. Each dollar spent brings many dollars in savings, a fact demonstrable to Congress, which doles out public funds. The NARS records management program is one of the government's model undertakings, but increased staffing is needed immediately to permit it to make its assistance available to those agencies whose requests now cannot be fulfilled. This need was stressed by a 1966 Congressional committee that stated simply, "Greater support should be given to the National Archives and Records Service management program." [10]

Beyond the additional resources needed for the existing activities of the Office of Records Management, two new programs should be provided for: (1) a system for documenting machine-readable archives and (2) a records research program in methodology, technique, and hardware.

9. See pp. 218 ff.
10. *How To Cut Paperwork*, p. 14.

1. *A system for documenting machine-readable archives.*[11] Machine-readable archives were discussed at some length in Chapter IV. To bring such an archives into existence, however, requires an even earlier step on the part of the federal records managers—namely, an adequate documentation of what information is on the magnetic tape, how the information may be processed, and how it may be retrieved. Considerations of this kind are called "software"[12] by computer specialists, to distinguish them from the operation and design of the machines, usually called "hardware."

Software documentation is a problem that deserves more attention than it is given. Too often when a program encounters unanticipated circumstances or needs modification, a user finds that those who prepared it are no longer on the scene. In such a case any effort to discover what is in the software package in order to modify it or salvage it necessitates a painful unraveling process. Therefore, information on how software packages are developed and on standards for documentation are essential to efficient computer operation.

A magnetic tape record is data recorded on magnetic tape and identified by a subject title. A record may require the use of one or more magnetic tapes; also, one or more individual records may be located on a single reel of tape. Tape records are generally classified under nine headings: scratch tape, raw data input tape, working tape, interim master record tape, final master record tape, source printing data tape, printing tape, program tape, and test tape. Only the largest installations will have all of these types. Whether these nine headings are used is not so important as establishing categories, dependent upon firm definitions. It is important to distinguish between the kinds of tapes because this will have a bearing on whether a security copy needs to be made, and if so, where it is to be kept. It certainly has a bearing on retention periods.

11. The following proposal is discussed in greater detail in Everett O. Alldredge, "Tape Documentation and Maintenance," *Systems,* (January 1967), 43–46. For the layman one of the best reviews of the development of a complex data-processing system in the federal government is United States Department of Health, Education, and Welfare, *Data Processing in the Social Security Administration: Nine Lectures by Joseph L. Fay* (Washington: Government Printing Office, 1967).

12. Defined as "an arcane shorthand of codes, languages, programs and systems" (*Time,* August 18, 1967, pp. 75–76).

A full study is needed to determine the feasibility of a standardized method of identifying, filing, storing, and scheduling tape records throughout the federal government. Such a study involves highly complex considerations necessary as a prelude to the planning of a successful archives of machine-readable records. It requires the unique training and experience of the records management personnel of NARS—personnel acquainted with the new technology and its vocabulary and also with the needs of the archivist, the eventual custodian of the records being processed. Archivists and their clientele will stand amidst the chaos of mountains of unusable tapes if the problem of software documentation is not brought under control now. The problem is infinitely greater than anything ever faced in the preservation of paper records; the mass is staggering (there are now several million reels of tape in the government), and the possibilities are chilling. Yet, through prompt study and planning, these fears can be allayed, and the computer can be harnessed to become the most beneficial information retention and retrieval device ever developed by man. The choice at the moment is simple: The federal government may ignore the dangers and within two or three years be forced at great expense to try to bring order out of chaos; or it can spend a little now, provide a guided program of information-recording on tapes, and utilize the new technology for economy and efficiency in current government operations as well as for researchers of the future.[13]

2. *A records research program in methodology, technique, and hardware.*[14] The federal government spends almost $17

13. See, e.g., Jerome M. Clubb and Howard Allen, "Computers and Historical Studies," *Journal of American History*, LIV (December 1967), 599–607; Samuel P. Hays, "Quantification in History: The Implication and Challenges for Graduate Training," *AHA Newsletter*, IV (June 1966), 8–11; *Computers and the Humanities* (September 1966–   ), Queens College of the City University of New York; *Historical Methods Newsletter* (December 1967–   ), Department of History, University of Pittsburgh; and various chapters in Dagmar Horna Perman (ed.), *Bibliography and the Historian: The Conference at Belmont* (Santa Barbara, Calif.: Clio Press, 1967).

14. This proposal is based upon two papers written by Chester L. Guthrie, then Deputy Assistant Archivist for Records Management, titled "Need to Establish a Paperwork Research Program Covering Methodology, Technique and Hardware" and "Need to Make Study in Depth on Microminiaturization Techniques as Apply to Government Records and Information Systems," both of which were transmitted as enclosures to a

billion on research and development, practically none of which is devoted to records systems, procedures, methods, and other components of what is often referred to as "paperwork." This is an oversight that becomes increasingly difficult to understand and accept. Government is dependent upon its records, and the field of scientific and technical information is closely tied into the records systems that capture and process the data.

Record-making costs the government $8 billion per year.[15] This annual cost is so high that it would rate a research program in any other context. Yet none has been established for paper-work. The loss in potential efficiency in government and indus-try—not to count the loss to the cultural community dependent upon records for its research—goes much beyond the internal savings possible in the actual records operations as such, be-cause missions and accomplishments are directly affected.

In 1966 the House Committee on Post Office and Civil Serv-ice strongly recommended that a "broad-gaged, organized pro-gram of research into all fields of paperwork practices and systems" be authorized, and proposed an expenditure of $500,000 for that purpose. It repeated its previous recommen-dation that the records management program of the National Archives and Records Service "should be vigorously supported by the Congress and in the executive branch and should be expanded in the areas of paperwork simplification, standardiza-tion, and research." [16] Especial attention was given to the need for research as a result of the rapidly evolving automated data-processing technology. This technology for the most part is

---

memorandum, June 1, 1967, from Everett O. Alldredge to Andrew A. Aines, Technical Assistant, Office of Science and Technology.

15. The House Committee on Post Office and Civil Service gave the following examples of annual costs of various types of records: 360,000 forms in 15 billion copies at a cost of more than a billion dollars; a billion letters at a cost of about $1.5 billion (President Johnson alone received almost a million letters); a million pages of directives at a cost of $400 million; and reports costing about a billion dollars annually. Noting that if one sheet of federal records were thrown away every second, it would take 2,000 years to discard them all, the Committee concluded, "Al-though the situation is better than it was 15 years ago, there are still (a) too many records—nearly one-fourth of the total volume—designated by the agencies as permanent, (b) too many permanent records scattered and intermixed with temporary records, and (c) too many temporary records being kept beyond their usefulness" (*How To Cut Paperwork*, pp. 1–2).

16. *Ibid.*, p. 46. See epigraph, p. 189.

hardware-oriented; an orientation toward the record-making process itself is sorely needed. The Bureau of the Budget has twice turned down NARS requests for funds to provide for this research program.

The need is for a small focal group of highly qualified persons organized to provide a systematic program of research to address itself to the records requirements of an office in the following categories: (1) record-making systems (internal, intergovernmental, public-private sectors, etc.), (2) paperwork specialties, (3) record-making equipment, and (4) documentation standards and operation conventions. Some examples of such a program would include the study of users of information for decision by management and relate to most timely and economical inputs; better source data input methods to eliminate keypunching, especially in the field of scientific and technical information; development of university curriculum and behavioral objectives for office systems and managerial specialists; delineation of operating conventions, permitting easier interchange of data between government and industry and within industry; development of high-speed data retrieval models relating to substantive transactions; and efficient utilization of machine language in relation to mass data storage.[17]

The focal point would be to (1) identify and define research needs; (2) relate specific projects to research needs; (3) maintain active contact with federal agencies to reevaluate research needs, consult on research projects, and promote needed projects; (4) review and collaborate with ongoing research projects in fields that have possible relation to paperwork; (5) administer grant funds and promote the use of such funds to accomplish necessary research; (6) provide for appropriate dissemination of the results of research projects; and (7) maintain a council of government research people who could help develop and advance paperwork management.

The nation deserves a review of whether this is an area where

17. Records management officials are of necessity giving increasing attention to changing modes of record-making. See, e.g., John W. Porter, "The Effects of EDP on Records Management," and Everett O. Alldredge, "Documenting Computer Operations," *Records Management Quarterly*, I (April 1967), 9–12 and 13–17, respectively; and J. R. Buckingham, "Records Management Problems Transported to the Computer," *Records Review*, VII (August-September 1966), 1–5.

industry should be relied upon solely as the source of ultimately saleable ideas. In most other areas research funds are being used to *speed up* the innovative process, because from the acceleration comes new products, new employment, new advances that put America in the fore. If the federal government will explore the records research problem, it might well conclude that it cannot afford to leave the present rate of progress to happenstance.

Particularly needed is a study of microminiaturization techniques. Records are of value for their contents, not for their physical form or condition.[18] The search for alternate and economical means of recording information, therefore, is compelling. Progress is being made in this field, and several microminiaturization techniques suitable for recording data bases are becoming available.[19] One of these can theoretically put nearly 50,000 rolls of magnetic tape on one roll of new tape (metal film over mylar). If this and similar techniques prove satisfactory, the preservation of data now on magnetic tape will become easier and far less expensive. What is needed is a study group within NARS that will (1) conduct a reconnaissance study on record data bases and a feasibility study on the alternative microminiature recording systems available; (2) prepare logic charting to cover the data bases selected to give an adequate sample of the program; (3) prepare programs that will convert machine language used by clients to the new machines and will permit limited interagency access; (4) develop professional safeguards to protect the data base in regard to record integrity, confidentiality, and losses; and (5) organize and direct an operations group to provide services to clients.

This, of course, is just one example of research projects needed, but it may be the most pressing one. Automation will not wait for practical and logical systems to be devised looking to the over-all picture of records management and preservation. Automation is already here, and its impact can be for good or ill. Only through a concerted effort on the part of the archival and records management agency of the federal government can its potential be realized. The recommendation of the House Com-

18. There are, of course, many exceptions to this generalization.
19. An excellent summary of recent research in microminiaturization is contained in *10th Annual Report [of the Council on Library Resources, Inc.] for the Year Ended June 30, 1966*, pp. 25–30.

mittee on Post Office and Civil Service that NARS be given sufficient funds to conduct a "broad-gaged, organized program of research" into all areas of record-making and record-keeping, with particular attention to the problems of source data automation, should be heeded. Otherwise each agency and department will continue unguided into increasingly complex systems, each going its own way at great public expense and without a concern for the over-all purposes and uses of documentation.

It is evident from the foregoing that the claim of archivists that records management was an extension of their own areas of interest cannot imply that a new species of paperwork specialists has not evolved. In fact, the Archivist, Wayne Grover, was one of the first to admit that, while he hoped there would always be much overlapping between current records management and archival activities, ". . . each has a basically different emphasis and requires different qualifications, no matter how closely the activities and individuals involved are related to each other in common purpose." [20] Only after years of give and take between the Civil Service Commission and NARS was there established a series of job classifications (known as "management analysts") generally satisfactory to the specialized functions of the new vocation.

By applying better judgment at the point of production, a built-in form of segregation of the permanent from the temporary record is possible, a potential of vital importance to the archivist. Thus paperwork management has as its main purpose fewer but better records in conditions that permit easy and prompt disposal of those of short-term value and efficient preservation of the permanent records. Therein lay the basis for the development of archival interests in records management long before there was a records management program *per se*. Therein also lies the philosophy that archival administration and records management are but two links in one unbroken chain of documentation.

20. Wayne C. Grover, "Recent Developments in Federal Archival Activities," *American Archivist*, XIV (January 1951), 7–8. One records manager writes: "Records Management is by nature a hybrid. It is both art and craft. The Records Manager draws upon the knowledge, insights and techniques of both the archivist and the systems practitioner" (Belden Menkus, "The American Records Manager: A Critique," *Records Management Journal*, V [Autumn 1967], 10).

A few examples of how this interrelationship works are the following. (1) The records manager develops a directives system (the promulgation of orders, regulations, and instructions from superiors to subordinates) for his agency. It is an integrated, coordinated, codified system. It is thus one, not many. The master set of these directives becomes the archival core to be easily set aside and saved. This simplifies the job of the appraisal archivist. (2) The records manager establishes a classification system under which all correspondence is filed. This makes for orderly, subject-arranged files. What needs to be found can be easily located. When the files of top officials eventually are transferred to the Archives, they are much more searchable by the historian or other user than they would otherwise be. (3) The records manager organizes a management information system, so that information flows in to officials, making it easier for them to administer their organizations, control costs, meet problems in the bud, identify problem areas in serving the public, and provide the necessary career development for employees. When the records of senior executives are accessioned by the Archives, the user finds a well-arranged, easily understood mass of detailed information available to him. (4) Without the records control schedules initially prepared by agency records management personnel, the appraisal task of the archivist would be magnified a thousand times. This is especially true when it is realized that most of the NARS archivists are concentrated in Washington, whereas federal records are found everywhere the millions of federal military or civilian personnel are located—which is throughout the world. (5) The form and guide letter program, by further routinizing what are already routine communications, aids the archivist by removing from the files thousands of pieces of ephemeral material. (6) The filing station concepts of the agency records manager enable the important records to be clustered into key files, easier to maintain whether in the office or in the National Archives. (7) By specifying what papers go into case files—dossiers organized by name or number—the records manager keeps down the size of the case file by excluding papers of low information value. (8) Reports are essential guides to management in making decisions and plans; records management is constantly working to remove nonessential reporting requirements, thus making the files more usable. (9) Form designers in developing multiple-copy forms—and most forms are made in more than one copy—specify the "file" copy to be the first carbon, thus making the files more legible for the user.

In these and in many other ways the records manager who has had archival training or experience, or who has close liaison with the archivist, serves not only the needs of economy and efficiency but, equally as important—and perhaps ultimately more important—the cause of historical preservation. He is the expert who, if he does not determine what records are to be created, suggests how and in what form they are to be created and how they are to be maintained while in the possession of the creating agency. He interprets the needs of the archives to the agency, and he serves as an indispensable bridge between agency management and the archival authority. Just as an effective archivist needs to know something of the rudiments of modern records management, so the records manager must have a basic understanding of archival principles and techniques if he is to do his job without neglecting the cultural implications of record-making and record-keeping. The coordination of the archival authority with the staff leadership in records management within the National Archives and Records Service is a happy solution to this problem.

Perhaps the nation's record-making machinery can be compared with a conveyor belt moving at an ever-greater speed from the initial loading to the final disposition of its cargo. All along the belt various workers are trying to accommodate the cargo consisting of nearly 5,000,000 cubic feet of new records annually—equivalent to the contents of more than 750,000 filing cabinets. Appraisal archivists are at the source of the load attempting to tag each package. Agency personnel are snatching off those marked for rejection as having no further value. Records center personnel are grabbing most of the remaining load. The National Archives stands at the end of the belt taking what is left. This production process continues, faster and faster. It will overwhelm all the work crews along the line unless the machinery is slowed. This task—that of the mechanics who seek to improve the quality but reduce the quantity of new records—is the job of the records managers, nearly 9,000 of them, in various government agencies. Many of these analysts are highly skilled and trained in systems, procedures, and paperwork management. Each, however, is a specialist in the records and systems of his own agency, and he may have little concept of the over-all problem of the government's paper empire. He needs guidance and assistance from the "factory representative"—the paperwork specialist who studies the whole machinery of government and sees record-making and record-keeping in its entirety. It is this latter guidance and assistance that the trained records management staff of the National Archives and Records Service gives.

[10]

GENERAL ADMINISTRATION: PERSONNEL, TRAINING, AND PUBLIC RELATIONS

*In order to deal effectively and responsibly with its public
NARS must significantly increase its investment in the
recruitment and development of a staff that will command the respect and attention of the academic world.*

*A lack of research and publishing by archivists creates
a gulf between themselves and their most important
public, the scholarly writers.*

*The true educational and cultural accomplishments of an
archives are impossible to quantify accurately. Some of
the most important objectives of Federal archival services
are more qualitative than quantitative.*
—NARS Program Memorandum, *1967*

THE UNIQUENESS of the work of the National Archives and
Records Service results in extraordinary complications in its
administration. In the federal government it is a one-of-a-kind
institution. But more than that, it is the foremost institution of
its type, dwarfing in size and breadth of mission all similar
establishments. It thus occupies a status of leadership. But that
status adds to its problems, for there is no model from which it
can draw lessons. State archival agencies, in developing programs or classifying professional personnel, use the experience
of NARS to great advantage; many of their practices are
adopted as a result of the federal experience; their personnel
agencies often accept without question policies in effect in
NARS. In scores of ways they look to the National Archives and
Records Service.

Yet the status of primacy is a formidable handicap for NARS.
Its administration gets little help from smaller, sister institutions. Its personnel policies and salaries must be set without
comparison with those institutions, because there is none compa-

rable to it. Its public image must be built without drawing upon the techniques used by other archival institutions, again because none is comparable to it. Thus every new move is an experiment not new just to itself but new to the profession.

Because the National Archives and Records Service is a unique institution, its work is strange to the most knowledgeable administrative officer and personnel analyst. The duties of the archivist and records manager cannot be easily explained to the most conscientious administrator. The work of an archivist arranging the records of the Continental Congress may appear to be a simple task; his preparation of finding aids to a body of State Department records may appear also to be a task that could be performed by any good clerk. Communicating the complexities of these and other activities of an archivist, an editor, or a records manager is not easy. Even translating the term "a wide knowledge of American history and government" to a personnel analyst is virtually impossible.

Just as difficult is the task of acquainting the American people with the purposes of NARS. Its programs are so varied, so complex, so unique, that few citizens have any real understanding of them. These formidable obstacles, however, can and must be overcome.

PERSONNEL AND TRAINING

THE fulfillment of the missions of the National Archives and Records Service depends, in the final analysis, upon the ability, training, commitment, and productivity of its staff. While the contributions toward that end by nonprofessional staff members are highly important, they are, in large measure, dependent upon effective professional direction. For that reason these comments apply mainly to the professional personnel—archivists, historians, editors, records managers, and paperwork specialists.

Two new American professions owe their birth chiefly to the National Archives. When R. D. W. Connor assumed the post of first Archivist of the United States, few people had ever heard of the title "archivist." To be sure, there were a few administrators of state and private historical agencies who used the title, and there were historians who for more than three decades had met and discussed archival principles and procedures as handed down from European archivists. But there was no ready pool from which Connor could draw a large staff to man the new institution. Instead, he turned to historians. Perhaps the National Archives was fortunate in having been founded during a period of economic depression, because the oversupply of academicians resulted in the accumulation of many scholars in the Archives. Besides, the 1930s developed an entente between government and the scholarly community unprecedented at least since Jefferson's Presidency and not matched again until 1961. From these scholars came the founders of the modern archival profession in the United States—historians who formulated the principles and practices upon which the new profession was based. They then trained others who in turn became practitioners and teachers of another generation. Their influence was felt throughout the nation, and the mark of the National Archives may still be seen in every significant archives and manuscript repository in the country.

As the horizons of the archivist expanded, those with greatest perception saw the need for specialists in prearchival stages of record-keeping, and the more adventurous archivists began talking of "records administration" and "intermediate depositories." Within fifteen years after the establishment of the National Archives its staff members had implanted in many agencies of the federal government the seeds of a new field—records management—and among its leaders were ex-archivists and some who simply referred to themselves as archivists-records managers. They trained others, many of whom had no archival background but still recognized the kinship between the two specialties. Other forces were of course at work, and by the mid-1950s the field of records management had come into its own as a specialty if not yet a profession. Now, a decade later, it has earned its claim to full membership among the professions. The mutual interests of modern-day archivists and records managers are thus less evidences of a marriage than of a blood relationship, and the complementary emphases of the two groups within the National Archives and Records Service constitute one of the happy developments of recent times. Interestingly enough, archivists and records managers are well-known for their pronouncements of the superiority of the one over the other, but such claims to primacy are characteristic of young-sters—and both archivists and records managers fall into that age group.

It is refreshing, therefore, for one to observe in the National Archives and Records Service a spirit of cooperation and mutual respect among the responsible archivists and records managers. Only where the duties of subadministrative professionals have put them out of touch with the over-all functions of the institution has there been detected a sense of aloofness or unconcern. Only on the lower levels has any noticeable amount of separateness been observed, and almost without exception it appears among young history scholars whose experiences have been limited to research in pretwentieth-century documents, or among new recruits in records management whose training and experience have been limited to the new technology.

This commendable spirit of inclusiveness undoubtedly results from the continuity of leadership in NARS, and some apprehension is felt that in the not too distant future new leadership may permit a chasm to develop. This is a real danger, and it must be resisted by continued close coordination on the policy-making level, by a liberal policy of interchange of personnel between the archival and records management functions, and by broadly conceived formal training courses.

The quality of the staff of any institution depends in the long run upon the salaries paid its employees. This is a fact of life. And it is a sad fact that the professional positions of the National Archives and Records Service have not always paid enough to enable the institution to attract generally the caliber of personnel that its functions demand.[1] The nature of the work of the archivist requires a broad academic education in history and government plus the peculiar talents of the mature scholar. The recruiting ground, therefore, lies in the field of scholarship. This puts NARS squarely in competition with the academic teaching field, and in this competition it has sometimes been at a considerable disadvantage, for the opportunities and salaries in college and university teaching have in recent years become increas-

1. For statistics on academic attainments of members of the staff, see p. 76.

ingly attractive.[2] This disadvantage, fortunately, has been somewhat ameliorated in the past two years, as is shown in the following breakdown of the grade levels of 143 employees in the NARS central office whose titles are archivist, historian, or comparable designation:

Grade	Number in Grade	Entering Salary as of May 1, 1968	Comments
Ungraded	3	—	
GS-16	3	$20,982	
GS-15	4	18,404	
GS-14	12	15,841	
GS-13	15	13,507	
GS-12	22	11,461	
GS-11	37	9,657	Journeyman level. Median grade.
GS- 9	16	8,054	
GS- 7	30	6,734	Entering grade for professionals.
GS- 5	1	5,565	

An applicant with a master's degree is usually hired at an initial salary of $6,734. After two years on the job and upon completion of staff training courses he may qualify for the journeyman level at $9,657. By equating the holder of the master's degree with Grade 7 and that of the doctorate with Grade 11, a comparison is possible with similarly qualified professionals in the academic field. Though teaching salaries vary greatly, an assistant professorship—frequently the minimum rank acceptable to the holder of a Ph.D. degree—will often carry a beginning salary of at least $9,000 for a nine-month term. These academicians have the option, of course, of earning additional sums during the summer or of devoting three months per year to their private endeavors. Most academic institutions provide annual increases, periodic sabbaticals, and considerable opportunities for the teacher to conduct research and to write for publication. The beginner in the National Archives receives a lower per-month salary and faces a dubious chance of going above Grade 11 or 12. Only if he is selected for supervisory or administrative duties or is designated a subject-matter specialist is he likely to go higher. This clustering of professionals in the

2. For a study of archival and records management salaries in the United States, see Philip P. Mason, "Economic Status of the Archival Profession, 1965–66," *American Archivist*, XXX (January 1967), 105–122.

vicinity of Grade 11 is a discouraging hurdle for some promising staff members. If the complement of higher grades is filled, the journeyman may remain at Grade 11 indefinitely. The result is that some assume a stationary role, accepting their situation and looking only to Congressional salary increases or administrative grade adjustments. A few of the most promising men and women leave for better opportunities, especially in the academic world; a few drift in other directions; but many just stay. It is in the GS-11 and 12 range that morale appears lowest among the archivists. There are two means of remedying a good part of this problem: (1) by opening up the grade ladder to give greater hope to the most competent aspirants, and (2) by stimulating interest by giving professional staff members more opportunities to conduct research, write articles, and participate in professional activities.

NARS has not had an identifiable recruitment program, though in 1967 it belatedly began announcing employment opportunities in professional journals, with encouraging results. While GSA does have a recruiting office, it is staffed by personnel with little understanding of the unique problems of the professional archivist. By far the greatest number of the members of the GSA staff are nonprofessionals in fields such as transportation, maintenance of buildings, protection of property, and supply and procurement. Most of its employees, therefore, are in "occupations," not professions, and most of its professionals are in disciplines far removed from the cultural and managerial interests of NARS. While "archives" and "records management" are listed in GSA's booklet titled *Career Opportunities*, no evidence has been found to indicate that significant numbers of professional-level recruits have been obtained through its offices. Here is another instance of a vital function being centralized in an already overburdened office that cannot be expected to maintain effective liaison with the academic community from which NARS must draw most of its professional employees. There should be in NARS a program of direct communication with the academic institutions that train prospective applicants,[3]

3. Through NARS initiative a special training agreement with the Civil Service Commission was recently worked out, and this may offer some remedy to the problem of recruitment by reopening the lines of communication between the National Archives and the academic community. See also epigraph, p. 208.

and there should be one or more field representatives to visit college and university campuses, interview graduate students, talk to seminars, and promote an interest in archival and related professions. These field representatives could be more than recruiters; they could serve the institution in broader areas of public relations, the existing need for which is discussed below.[4]

One of the most vocal complaints within the National Archives concerns the poor record of literary productivity of professional staff members, a fact that was effectively discussed in the 1967 NARS Program Memorandum.[5] A review of the writings and organizational participation of the staff indicates that only a relatively few top-flight professionals are active. Yet, among the staff are outstanding historians, editors, attorneys, records managers, and other professionals, who should be encouraged and given time to contribute to the learning and enjoyment of their colleagues and the public at large, as well as to improve their own competency. Obviously an institution the size of NARS cannot send planeloads of employees to every professional meeting, nor can it allow employees to devote unrestricted time to projects of personal or even professional concern. Still, neither can this cultural institution afford not to give greater encouragement to such activities. The interest and enthusiasm of professionals are directly related to the recognition given them in their chosen fields.

Educational institutions, historical societies, libraries, and other cultural establishments gain their public image, and consequently their prestige, largely through the professional standing of their staff members. Conversely, the institution that does not encourage scholarly writing and active participation in professional organizations is usually without prestige or popularity. It is commendable, therefore, that since 1967 the official policy of NARS has been to allow professional staff members up to 10 percent of their official on-duty time for approved research projects. But this enlightened policy has not been accompanied by

4. See pp. 225 ff.
5. The Program Memorandum stated: "NARS staff members do not write and publish the number of articles and books that they should, considering that (a) NARS is the leading archival institution in the world and (b) as professions, archival management and records management should need and sustain a professional literature." See also epigraph, p. 208.

an increase in the size of the professional staff. Without additional personnel the policy is hollow and exists only on paper, for it can be carried out only by further deterioration in those functions that are so badly understaffed. The very people who are most likely to undertake research and writing are usually those who most conscientiously try to conduct their official responsibilities in a superior manner. They are the people who do government work at home at night.

More NARS scholars should attend, participate in, and read papers at meetings of scholarly and cultural organizations. At present reimbursement for travel and subsistence is generally provided only for those who are officially listed on the programs of such meetings or who hold offices in the organizations, though official leave with pay is allowed to other approved attendees. The result is that the National Archives is often insufficiently represented at the meetings of some of the leading scholarly organizations. In the words of the 1967 Program Memorandum, "Archivists need to keep abreast of developments in their respective fields and establish scholarly reputations on levels comparable to those of the public they serve."

When compared with archival salaries, records management and paperwork professionals fare better, as is indicated in the following analysis of 71 of these latter positions assigned to the central office in Washington:

Grade	Number in Grade	Entering Salary as of May 1, 1968	Comments
GS-17	1	$23,788	
GS-16	1	20,982	
GS-15	5	18,404	
GS-14	12	15,841	
GS-13	36	13,507	Median grade.
GS-12	12	11,461	
GS-11	2	9,657	
GS- 9	1	8,054	
GS- 7	1	6,734	

The difference between the median pay grades of archivists and records managers reflects the nature of a small staff group in a highly competitive field. It is a field in which competency is gained less from formal academic education than from specialized training and experience. Recruitment is largely from other government agencies and private business. The disparity in salaries thus reflects the law of supply and demand. These grade figures, then, which may look quite appealing to archivists, do not lend themselves to a neat comparison with positions involving only liberal arts training. As a matter of fact, it is a wonder that NARS has been able to attract and hold as many able records managers as it has, for there is little doubt that many of them could find higher paying jobs in other agencies and in business if they but made themselves available. The grade structure of this specialized function of NARS may be in need of revision to keep pace with increasingly attractive competition, though it is probable that the nature of paperwork management is such that its needs are more readily understood by personnel and budgetary officials, and, consequently, may tend to receive priority.

Opportunities comparable to those suggested for the National Archives employees should be afforded also to records management personnel. Because of their special interests, not many records managers below the policy-making level are interested in historical and literary publication and participation, but they are vitally concerned with maintaining close relationships with their colleagues and keeping current with the literature in their own fields. Just as the historian-archivist should be active in scholarly organizations and should read their journals, so the records manager should be expected to show the same type of interest in various management and technological associations. In view of the revolutionary developments in space-age technology, the need for updating their knowledge is as critical as that of the archivist.

One of the most remarkable feats of the National Archives has been its on-the-job training of embryonic archivists. In-service training, however, is not sufficient, and to provide an academic base for formal training, the Archives in 1939 established a joint archival education program with the American University in Washington. Some time later, courses in records management were added, and the program then offered the only comprehensive battery of such courses available in the United States. Scores of today's leading archivists and records managers benefited from the program, and hundreds more participated in the subsequently established summer institutes.

Since the retirement of Ernst Posner early in the 1960s the

216

cooperative program between NARS and the American University has diminished somewhat in stature. Posner's leaving was a double loss in that the famous teacher was no longer in the classroom and his influence as Chairman of the History Department and later Dean of the Graduate School in persuading graduate students to take these courses could no longer be exerted. Although the full-year courses are still offered,[6] they are not well attended, and the university appears to contribute little to them. The summer archives institute has been shortened to only two weeks—far too little time for adequate orientation for beginners. Considerable emphasis is now placed upon short, specialized symposia instead of upon general-information institutes, and the tuition is so high—up to $150 for a five-day workshop—that some prospective participants are discouraged from entering. This relative decline, plus the fact that there are in the United States only three other institutions offering as much as a full academic year in archival training,[7] results in a disappointingly low status of archival education. Thus at the very time when the archival and records management professions have reached a measure of maturity, they are in danger of backsliding into specialized skills handed down haphazardly rather than acquiring them through formal academic preparation. The increasing number of publications, workshops, and symposia cannot fill the need for comprehensive education in archival administration.

The real hope for remedial action lies in the National Archives and Records Service. NARS is the one institution with the human and physical resources to provide the level of education required by rapidly changing conditions in archives administration and records management, and it has the capability of

6. The course in archives administration is currently taught by Frank B. Evans, a NARS division chief, and the records management course is taught by Seymour J. Pomrenze of the Adjutant General's Office, Department of the Army. Evans conducts an additional course each week for professional trainees in NARS, supplementing his own lectures with others by senior specialists on the staff.

7. University of Denver, North Carolina State University, and Wayne State University. For a survey of archival courses, see H. G. Jones, "Archival Training in American Universities, 1938–1968," *American Archivist*, XXXI (April 1968), 135–154. NARS and the American University also cosponsor a summer institute on records management and another on genealogical research, as well as several special workshops and symposia.

tapping other resources. Furthermore, Washington, D.C., is the only location in the United States that can furnish the broad setting needed for a full experience in a training program of this sort. The National Archives itself provides a training ground for most areas of archives administration and records management; the Library of Congress and other manuscript repositories provide opportunities for teaching methods of handling private papers; the Smithsonian Institution offers facilities for audio-visual and other special types of instruction; the various federal agencies provide advanced systems and procedures for the instruction of prospective records managers; and Maryland and other nearby states carry on successful programs of public archives and records administration. These and other resources in the nation's capital cannot be matched elsewhere in the United States. Finally, the National Archives and Records Service, as the official organ of the United States government in matters relating to archives and records, has an obligation to the nation as a whole for the improvement of the state of the art in which it has few if any peers.

A remedy may be found in a bold and perhaps visionary plan for the training of archives and records personnel. The plan concerns itself chiefly with the education of a few promising young professionals for service in state and private archival and records management agencies, as well as in NARS itself and other federal agencies. The proposal is that the National Archives and Records Service, in collaboration with one of the universities in the Washington area, establish a graduate-level Institute for Archives Administration and Records Management. The program would provide elementary and advanced training in both fields and would grant a master's degree. It would be limited to 35 students already holding bachelor's degrees in appropriate fields who would be selected on a competitive basis after having been nominated by their employing agencies or institutions. Fifteen of the students would be from NARS and other federal agencies. These 15 would continue to receive their usual salary for up to 12 months while completing the course,[8] and they would be committed to continuing in

8. The continuation of salary would be the cost to their respective agencies. This cost would be more than compensated for in the quality of work to be expected from the program participants upon their return to the employing agencies.

federal employment for a minimum of three years after receiving their degree, a commitment supported by a binding agreement to refund to the government a fixed amount if they should not fulfill it. Five students would be selected from foreign countries and each would receive a stipend of $500 per month for a period not to exceed 12 months, the payment to be made by the federal agency charged with cultural exchanges between the United States and foreign countries. The other 15 students would be chosen from state, local, institutional, and private archival, manuscript, and records management agencies. To provide reasonable geographical coverage, one each of the latter would be selected from the ten NARS districts and five would be selected without regard to geography. These 15 selectees would receive from the Institute stipends of $500 per month for up to a total of 12 months while satisfactorily passing the courses. Upon completion of the course of study each would be required to work for a minimum of three years in the institution sponsoring his or her application.

The dollar cost to the Institute of such a program is estimated to be $175,000 per year—$90,000 for stipends to state, local, institutional, and private agency personnel, and $85,000 for costs of instruction, including professorial salaries. The latter would include the creation of three adjunct professorships: one designed to be filled by an eminent scholar with special knowledge of the growth of historical and archival activity within the United States; one by a distinguished archivist capable of teaching the evolution and application of archival principles and techniques; and the third by an outstanding records management expert cognizant not only of the development of traditional record-keeping systems but also of current trends in the development of more sophisticated systems. These positions would carry titles to reflect their dignity [9] and salaries commensurate with their importance. By special agreement with the degree-granting university, the advisory board of the Institute could be made up of the three faculty members plus one designee of the American Historical Association, one designee of the Society of

9. One might conceive of the designation of Jameson Fellow, Leland Fellow, and Leahy Fellow to illustrate the three areas of specialty; or titles such as Distinguished Archivist and Distinguished Records Manager might be envisioned.

American Archivists, and one designee of the Interagency Records Administration Conference or the American Records Management Association, with the Archivist of the United States as chairman. Funds would also be available for special lectures by recognized leaders in the field of archives and records management. The human resources of the National Archives and Records Service, the Library of Congress, and other institutions around the country could thus be drawn upon.

Subject content of the course of study, as well as specific requirements for the master's degree, would be determined by the advisory board. Certainly there would be included studies in the development of documentation from ancient times to the present, the history of record-making and record-keeping in America from colonial times to the present, principles and practices of archival administration, documentary preservation and reproduction, modern records management, and information storage and retrieval systems. The year should include advanced courses in American history and government, taught by a distinguished historian, to compensate for the weak undergraduate training received by some of the participants. Thirty semester hours of course work plus an acceptable thesis would be required for the master's degree.[10]

One of the first questions to arise in connection with the proposal relates to the source of funding. This is an undertaking that should be sponsored by the federal government and financed largely through appropriations to the National Archives and Records Service. The field of archives administration and records management is one of the very few in which the government is not now spending large sums for training purposes, either directly through the federal agencies or through grants to states and academic institutions. Yet few fields offer

10. While this proposal concerns itself with a one-year program leading to only the master's degree, the advisory board, following a year's experience, should consider the feasibility of extending the course of study to the doctoral degree. The latter plan would of course need to consider additional sources of funds. The program suggested here proposes an unusual relationship between the Institute, the National Archives, and the cooperating university, with a degree being granted by the latter. Should such an arrangement prove impracticable, the Institute could be established as an adjunct of the National Archives and Records Service, and could award certificates of fellowship that would, in time, become a mark of distinction in the profession.

greater potential benefits to government itself. Even so, it is believed that funds for the financing of the proposed Institute for the first two years can be obtained from one or more private foundations once the program has been worked out in greater detail.

The question may arise as to the justification for such a training program under sponsorship of the federal government. That justification is best explained by a reminder that in a very narrow sense the word "archives" refers to public records, and the greatest producer of public records is the federal government. NARS conducts the only really large and complex archival and records management program in the country. The state with the largest staff devoted to this work employs fewer than 60 persons, and most get along with far less than that number. In fact, except for the Library of Congress, there are few libraries, private historical societies, and other repositories of historical manuscripts with substantial staffs and resources. Many business archival and records management programs are one-man affairs. Thus there is in the United States no other institution approaching the National Archives and Records Service in terms of resources and commitments. That agency is supported by the taxes of all American citizens. It exists to serve those citizens. Providing training for state, local, and private archival and records personnel is a means of contributing immeasurably to professional improvement in those fields. Well-trained young professionals can influence greatly their sponsoring institutions, most of which at present are without staff members competently trained to assume positions of leadership. Potentially 75 such promising archivists and records managers from nonfederal institutions, 75 from the federal government, and 25 from foreign countries can be trained and returned to their places of employment in five years. They in turn would be in a position to train their colleagues, thus extending the influence of the education provided in NARS.

The National Archives and Records Service is the only institution with an archival obligation to the entire country; and it is the only institution that can command the resources needed for top-flight training. The federal government pours billions of dollars into education each year; the assumption of a training role by the National Archives will cost an infinitesimal amount of public funds—no more than is currently being spent on a federally financed preschool program in one small American community. The benefits to be derived from the proposed training program will make an immediate impact in fields where specialized education is absent. It is believed that such a program will be endorsed by many professional groups, such as the American Historical Association, the American Management Association, the American Records Management Association, the Organization of American Historians, and the Society of American Archivists. The American Library Association and other allied organizations can be expected to give support. It is further believed that a grant in the sum of $350,000 for the financing of the proposed program for two years can be obtained from one or more private national foundations upon endorsement by these and other professional groups.

The seriousness with which such a program would have to be undertaken is not to be underestimated. Its inauguration would not be without problems. But the fundamental idea is worthy of adoption. Above all, the primacy of the National Archives and Records Service dictates its responsibility for offering archival and records management training to state, local, and private agencies and institutions, as well as to personnel in federal employment.

The establishment of the Institute for Archives Administration and Records Management should not interrupt other training activities of NARS, such as its splendid battery of workshops, seminars, and symposia being given both in Washington and the regions.[11] These would continue to serve vital needs for short, specialized training sessions both for federal employees and for state and local representatives. Nor should such a school interfere with the development of other proposed training programs, such as the creation of fellowships to permit selected American and foreign archivists and records managers to spend a year on the staff of NARS, where they could learn while preparing specialized finding aids or conducting other useful work for the institution. There is much merit in the suggestion that experts in specific areas of history, political science, economics, and similar fields be brought into the National Archives to work on records

11. See p. 184.

relating to their areas of competence. These scholars could bring extensive knowledge of their particular subjects that might well prove invaluable in the analysis, arrangement, and description of the records. Members of the NARS field organization could profit from a year's assignment in Washington, where they could perform useful work and at the same time obtain a broader understanding of the mission and functions of their parent agency. Likewise Washington-based personnel might be assigned for a limited time to Federal Records Centers and Regional Archives for the same purpose. Finally, an exchange program might be worked out between the National Archives and selected foreign, state, local, and private agencies and institutions whereby staff members of the latter organizations might change places for a year with employees of the National Archives. Such exchanges should have a favorable effect on professional standards and work performance. In short, the opportunities appear limitless, and the nation will benefit if NARS is permitted to take advantage of more of them.

It is to be hoped that GSA's requirement that the National Archives and Records Service prepare monthly "manpower utilization reports"—a requirement that was terminated in 1967—has been ended for all time. These quantitative measurements of employee outputs created a serious morale problem among the staff. Obviously quantitative norms can and should be established in many projects. For instance, materials to be microfilmed may be divided into several classes based upon the difficulty of the task, and one employee's accomplishments can be compared reasonably with another's; so can assignments like moving boxes, flattening documents, typing labels, and sweeping floors. "Targets" can be set for these and many other jobs of a repetitive, manual nature. But there is something belittling to the intellectual tasks involved in much of the professional-level work when an attempt is made to judge the employee's performance largely on the basis of quantity. Professional activities such as reference service, documentary editing, records management surveys, and the preparation of finding aids must be judged by other standards, all of which add up to quality of performance.

While these monthly reports were being required, genuine anxiety arose among members of the staff over the quality of their work. This anxiety did not represent a lack of appreciation for work measurement controls in a public agency, for, after all, one of the chief objectives of the archival and records management programs is efficiency, and NARS is obligated to give the taxpayers the best possible service in return for their support. But a series of records wisely appraised, accurately arranged, conveniently described, effectively preserved, clearly reproduced, and promptly and courteously brought to a researcher are what the National Archives should expect of its archivists. Documents carefully handled, accurately copied, edited in a scholarly manner, correctly printed and proofread, promptly and well printed, and properly distributed are what NARS should expect of its editors. Records safely and economically housed, conveniently located, quickly retrievable, and promptly produced for reference or disposal are what NARS should expect of its records center personnel. And records systems thoroughly analyzed, maturely studied, logically changed, and proposals clearly written are what NARS should expect of its records managers. Many of these tasks are not quantifiable.[12] An attempt to make them so will lead only to inferior workmanship. NARS should never have been forced to agree to the submission of the regrettable "manpower utilization reports," and the experience gained through their use should be lesson enough to prevent their imposition again.

Finally, several of the organizational units within NARS are seriously understaffed. These conditions have been pointed out in the discussion of the various functions, and they need not be repeated in detail. It appears, however, that the shortage of human resources is most critical in records appraisal, arrangement and description, and documentary publication. It is in these areas that fundamental decisions are made that determine the usefulness of documentation. They are not glamorous functions, but they are essential ones. Without their efficient performance the remainder of the archival program will be seriously handicapped and eventually crippled. All professions and organizations recognizing the importance of these and other programs should lend their full support to efforts to obtain the necessary funds to provide for the essential services of the National Archives and Records Service.

12. See epigraph, p. 208.

PUBLIC RELATIONS

IMPLICIT in much of what has thus far been written is the need for an improved public image for the National Archives and Records Service. At this point some comment may be appropriate concerning an improved educational program that is essentially a public-relations program.

One of the most important objectives of the National Archives and Records Service is education. This objective is fulfilled through various means: furnishing information from and about records to inquirers who phone, write, or come to the National Archives or a branch repository; preparing and distributing photocopies, microfilm copies, and documentary publications; issuing records management handbooks; conducting correspondence, files, and forms workshops; and displaying charters of American freedom—to mention only the most obvious. These and many other services of NARS, however, are effective only insofar as they are known to be available.

Millions of Americans, if they have ever heard of the National Archives and Records Service, have no concept of its role in American life. To many it is just another bureau of federal government with a name that means nothing to them; to some it is only a huge building that protects the Declaration of Independence and a few other old documents; to others it is a place where aging historians and genealogists pore over manuscripts; to still others it is a warehouse on the outskirts of Atlanta or Chicago or San Francisco. Even to many scholars it is an accumulation of government records so great in volume as to discourage their use. Finally, even to the average government employee it is no more than an institution to which all of their "useless" records are sent.

Because of its unique purpose and its specialized clientele, the National Archives cannot be compared easily with the other federal cultural institutions. With its incomparable array of exhibits appealing to all ages, it is not surprising that the Smithsonian Institution's museums across the street draw many times the 1,200,000 persons who view the great documents of American history—the Declaration of Independence and the Constitution of the United States, for instance—on display in the National

Archives.[13] With its millions of printed volumes, the Library of Congress understandably serves many times more researchers. It is even not surprising that individual historic sites administered by the National Park Service throughout the country are often better known than the National Archives Building in the heart of Washington. It is not so easy to understand, however, why the Library of Congress publishes a highly reputable *Quarterly Journal* [14] and the Smithsonian Institution issues an attractive *Journal of History* while no comparable publication has been issued by the National Archives. The simple fact is that millions of Americans pass the National Archives Building without ever knowing that the most precious national documents of freedom are on display and that the bulk of the documentary heritage of the nation is shelved in the core of the building.[15]

There are available to individuals, who are informed enough to ask for them, leaflets on NARS and its activities. There are also available, again for those who have learned about them, facsimiles of certain important historical documents, published finding aids of the National Archives, documentary publications of the NHPC, legal publications of the Federal Register office, descriptive folders on the Presidential Archives, and handbooks

13. I hope that the public acquaintance with the National Archives is not indicated by a poll that I took in my classes in archives administration and records management. Of the total of my 18 students in 1968, 13 had visited the Smithsonian museums; not a single one had been in the National Archives across the street to see the Declaration of Independence and the Constitution of the United States.

14. The July 1967 issue of the *Quarterly Journal of the Library of Congress*, attractively illustrated and printed, contained a symposium on "Manuscripts on Microfilm" as well as interesting articles on colonial imprints, rare books, and facsimile maps and atlases.

15. During the preparation of this book it was noted that the National Archives was the only major cultural agency whose attractions were not included in the "places to visit" periodicals in Washington. To cite three such publications, *The Washingtonian* of May 1967, made no mention of the National Archives under "Museums & Libraries;" the *Town Tattler* of May 6 made no reference at all to the institution; and the May 14 issue of *This Week in the Nation's Capital* listed the "Archives Building" but made no mention of its attractions. In the 411-page *A Directory of Information Resources in the United States: Federal Government* (Library of Congress, 1967), the National Archives and Records Service, under the General Services Administration, is allotted just 3½ pages, including only a half page devoted to the National Archives itself. The Library of Congress entry covers 12½ pages and that for the Smithsonian Institution 8 pages. The word "archives" does not appear in the 100-page index, nor is the National Archives mentioned under the entries for "manuscripts," "films," or "photography."

on records management. But the circulation of these materials is numbered in the thousands, not the millions, and their general availability is unknown to the vast majority of the citizens. In short, NARS, with a potential as unlimited as that of any federal cultural agency, is directly serving only a tiny percentage of the American people.

This situation can be—indeed, must be—corrected. It cannot be done overnight, or within a year, or perhaps within a decade. Its correction will require ingenuity and perseverance. No pat solution to the problem can be suggested. Nonetheless, greater consideration and determination must be given to public relations and the dissemination of information. The most recent reorganization within NARS may be a portent of greater efforts along these lines. A plan has been approved, for instance, to convert *National Archives Accessions* into a more useful publication that will carry articles relating to the Archives and to the institution's interests. This plan should be carried out, for an attractively printed publication containing scholarly, lively, and interestingly written articles is long overdue.[16] NARS needs vehicles through which it can reach the people, and a prestigious journal can become one such vehicle. Such a publication can also help allay the complaint often heard within the organization concerning the present literary unproductivity of many professional staff members.

There are other improvements that can be made within NARS to better its public image. Its literature can be printed more attractively and distributed more widely. It can develop mailing lists of institutions not now receiving its materials. It can stimulate interest on the part of graduate-school faculties who in turn can acquaint students with the resources available. It can produce and lend motion pictures that portray these resources and their potentialities. It can furnish effective speakers for public meetings. And it can be host to conferences, symposia, and workshops for historians, social scientists, econo-

16. The first issue of the journal tentatively titled *Prologue* was scheduled for publication in October 1968, to be financed from the National Archives Trust Fund. It is hoped that the fact that the journal will not be paid for from appropriated funds will permit it to be printed by letterpress, for one of the chief complaints about NARS publications has been that they have not been produced in a style and format commensurate with the dignity of the institution.

mists, and other scholarly groups. There are myriad ways of making known the importance and availability of the nation's archival resources, and they all must be explored.

Not the least problem is that of effectively reaching the news media. The quality of current news releases, all of which emanate from GSA, which stresses its own name rather than that of the National Archives and Records Service, is unworthy of a cultural institution.[17] There is a tone in many such releases that is unmistakably governmentalese, a characteristic that, like the pompous tenor of too much scholarly writing, marks the release for the trash can instead of the linotype or radio or television script.

Prior to 1950 the *Annual Report of the Archivist of the United States* served as the most valuable governmental publication in promoting the national archival and related programs. It was a source document in itself; it told the story of the year's activities and described new facilities, theories, techniques, and programs. Except for the *American Archivist*, the quarterly journal of the Society of American Archivists, no other publication was as influential in archival development in the United States. Bound copies of these reports from 1935 through 1949 remain an essential part of the bookshelf of today's archivists. The *Annual Report of the Administrator of General Services* superseded the report of the Archivist beginning in 1950, and for several years an abbreviated report on the National Archives and Records Service, as contained in the Administrator's report, was reprinted and distributed to archival and historical agencies. Beginning in 1958, however, the NARS report had become so brief—only ten pages—that reprinting was discontinued. Since that time the portion allowed NARS in the Administrator's report has degenerated to just four pages of text plus a photograph or two, hardly more than enough to identify NARS as a bureau in GSA.

17. As an example, GSA News Release 3916, dated April 1, 1968, announced a program to publish on microfilm certain federal court records. Not until the third paragraph was there a mention of the National Archives and Records Service. Furthermore, the release was poorly mimeographed, was single spaced, and left no room at the opening for the writer of headlines. One needs little experience in newspaper work to recognize the shortcomings of the release. See also Justin G. Turner, "Archives, Manuscripts & Collectors," *Manuscripts*, XIX (Fall 1967), 20.

For all intents and purposes, therefore, there is no public report of the nation's archival and records management program, nor is there one to the professions that it represents. Archivists and records managers, who need to be informed of the federal activities in the field, can do so only by reading occasional news items in professional journals or by dropping in at the National Archives when they are in Washington. Even members of the GSA components have few means of learning what their sister bureau is all about. Finally, the staff of NARS itself finds it difficult to keep informed of the activities and accomplishments of the organization. All of these handicaps— and others not mentioned—can be partially overcome by the revival and distribution of the *Annual Report of the Archivist of the United States.* The printing cost for a 100-page report would not exceed $2,000 per year, and most of the information for the text and tables is readily available from various reports required by GSA. Editorial and indexing costs would not be significant. Yet the usefulness of such a report to the agency itself and to state, local, private, and business archivists and records managers would be incalculable.[18] It could go far to enhance the stature of the National Archives not only in the United States but also in the world.

The implications of reinstating the *Annual Report of the Archivist* should not be underestimated. While it is true that most such publications tend to become organs of self-commendation, the Archivist's *Annual Report* should be much more. It should, of course, record accomplishments; but more than that, it should objectively evaluate the status of the institution and its programs, pinpoint deficiencies and needs, criticize hindrances to its better performance, project both short-range and long-range plans, and appeal for public support. It should be, in effect, a sort of "Program Memorandum" for public release, for the present annual Program Memorandum is prepared only for government purposes. Just as the latter is a sort of appeal to the

18. The disadvantage under which NARS operates in informing the public of its programs can readily be seen by comparing its 4-page entry in the Administrator's report with the latest *Annual Report of the Librarian of Congress*, an interestingly written 204-page document. The biennial report of the North Carolina Department of Archives and History for 1964–66 covered 211 pages, and the annual report of the *Archivist of the [Maryland] Hall of Records* for 1965–66 contained 63 pages of narratives and statistics.

General Services Administration and the Bureau of the Budget, the former can direct the public's attention to the needs of the Archives. It can, in effect, encourage a dialog between the institution and its clientele.

Some of the "how to do it" publications issued by the National Archives in its earlier years deserve to be revised and reprinted. Between 1936 and 1956 eight numbers of *Bulletins of the National Archives* were issued. They included titles such as *Buildings and Equipment for Archives* (1944), *Historical Editing* (1951), and *The Appraisal of Modern Public Records* (1956). During about the same period 20 numbers of *Staff Information Circulars* (called *Staff Information Papers* after Number 16) were published. These included such valuable leaflets as *Repair and Preservation in the National Archives* (1939), *What Records Shall We Preserve* (1940), *Principles of Arrangement* (1951), and *Archival Principles: Selections from the Writings of Waldo Gifford Leland* (1955). The discontinuance of these educational booklets has been a perceptible loss to archivists in the federal government and elsewhere. The publications demonstrated the professional role that the National Archives should be expected to play in improving the state of archival science. The National Archives is the archival training ground in the United States, and as such, it has a duty to share its experience with other archivists. Other special publications of archival interest should be issued from time to time. Archivists look with admiration upon such publications of other cultural agencies as the Library of Congress' magnificent little book, *Papermaking: Art and Craft*, published in conjunction with its exhibition of the same title in 1968.

There appears to be almost complete absence of liaison between the National Archives and Records Service and the legislative branch that holds in its hand the fate of all government agencies. Its only direct access to the Congress is through GSA's legislative liaison unit, which appears little attuned to the unique needs and problems of NARS, particularly its educational functions. Unlike the Library of Congress, which has a Congressional committee to keep watch over it, the Smithsonian Institution, which develops its own channels, and the National Park Service, which maintains strong regional ties, the National Archives and Records Service is without a champion. Thus it suffers immeasurably in the competition for the attention and recognition of the nation's lawmakers and budget-makers. Yet, without sympathetic consideration by the Congress, the nation's archival program faces an uncertain future. A complex program such as that of NARS, combining cultural and managerial functions, can be effectively portrayed only by persons intimately connected with those functions. The National Archives and Records Service needs its own spokesman, a spokesman who uses the language of the scholar, the administrator, the citizen, and the lawmaker.

One of the saddest results of his loss of independence in 1949 has been the erosion of the influence of the Archivist of the United States. He cannot communicate with the White House except through GSA, and he is no longer invited to appear at many Congressional and executive discussions relating to educational and cultural affairs. For instance, he was not asked to testify at hearings on the Mutual Educational and Cultural Exchange Act, the Higher Education Act of 1965, the Elementary and Secondary Education Act of 1965, or the International Education Act; nor was he invited to give his views relating to the National Cultural Center and the National Foundation on the Arts and Humanities. The National Archives, which serves as a historical agency of the federal government, has not been represented on the James Madison Memorial Commission, the Civil War Centennial Commission, the Abraham Lincoln Sesquicentennial Commission, the Woodrow Wilson Memorial Commission, the Lewis and Clark Trail Commission, the Alexander Hamilton Bicentennial Commission, the Theodore Roosevelt Celebration Commission, the National Monument Commission, the Commission to Observe the 175th Anniversary of the Adoption of the United States Constitution, and many other commissions created for historical purposes.[19] Nor has there been representation by the National Archives on such commissions and

19. Only after personal remonstrances by historians to members of Congress was the Archivist named in a bill to establish a National Commission on the Bicentennial of the American Revolution, although the records of the Continental Congress are in his custody. The Archivist is not included among officials listed for membership on the board of trustees of the Woodrow Wilson International Center for Scholars that S. 3174 proposes to be established across the street from the National Archives. See *Congressional Record*, March 15, 1968, p. S2914.

boards as the Federal Council on the Arts and Humanities, the National Council on the Humanities, the Advisory Council on Historic Preservation, the Advisory Council on Library Resources, the United States Advisory Commission on International Educational and Cultural Affairs, the Battle of New Orleans Sesquicentennial Commission, the Interagency Council on International Educational and Cultural Affairs, the President's Task Force on International Education, the President's Council on Pennsylvania Avenue, the National Visitor Center Study Commission, and others.

These examples may be multiplied many times. The simple truth is that in recent years the Archivist of the United States has been deprived of one of the most valuable means of familiarizing the government and the public with the archival and records resources of the nation. Even sadder, his service has thus not been available to these official commissions, boards, and agencies, where it would have contributed greatly to the successful performance of their duties. Thus not only NARS and its objectives but the nation as a whole has been shortchanged as a result of organizational subjugation.

Finally, the public image and consequently the effectiveness of NARS have suffered from the tendency of GSA to substitute its own name for that of NARS in the minds of both government employees and the public. While this issue may be viewed by some as picayunish, it is indeed an important consideration to a cultural agency. The omission of the name of the National Archives and Records Service on the Federal Records Centers has already been mentioned, as has the playing down of the NARS name in news releases. Grants from the National Historical Publications Commission are made and announced in the name of GSA. The Presidential Archives are usually identified as being operated by GSA, not NARS. Regional Directors of NARS cannot use stationary bearing the name of the National Archives and Records Service, and the reader of a letter can determine that the writer has such affiliation only if the stenographer types in "National Archives and Records Service" below the Regional Director's title.

It is in no sense insubordination for an archivist or editor or records manager to be proud of his identity with a professional organization. The Marine Corps, the Coast Guard, the National

Park Service, the Forestry Service, the Bureau of the Census, and the Internal Revenue Service are but a few examples of bureau-level governmental units that the public identifies by their own names without prejudice to their parent agencies. If there is a sense of separateness, it is based upon a recognition of unique functions and a pride in professional associations. Without that recognition and without that pride no cultural organization can put forth its best effort. Given both, and given credit for its accomplishments and blame for its failures, it will carry out its responsibilities with a remarkable spirit of dedication.

PART THREE

THE FUTURE OF THE
NATIONAL ARCHIVES
AND RECORDS SERVICE

[11]

WHY THE FUNCTIONS OF THE NARS

MUST NOT BE DIVIDED

*. . . it would be a grave mistake to tear the records
management function away from the archival function.
Records managers and archivists are a team working
toward the same basic objectives. It has taken more than
two decades to reach the level of efficiency at which we
are now operating. It would be a tragedy if, by the stroke
of a pen, this team which has been producing so effectively were dissolved. Logic and common sense dictate
against such an action.* —Ollon D. McCool, *1967*

THE OFFICES of the National Archives, Presidential Libraries, Federal Register, Federal Records Centers, and Records
Management, and the National Historical Publications Commission—collectively known as the National Archives and Records
Service—form an immense and unbroken continuum of historical, archival, editorial, legal, and records management activities. This unique agency brings nonpartisan and professional
services to the records of the executive, legislative, and judicial
branches of the federal government. It protects the priceless
records of the past, it serves governmental and scholarly needs
of the present, and it is conscious of its many responsibilities
to the future. It correlates two important functions—efficiency
in government and service to both government and the public;
it is a cultural as well as a service organization. The fact that
these various functions represent one indivisible whole cannot
be exaggerated. A benefit to one part is felt by all; a danger
threatening one function threatens the entire fabric.

Throughout this book has run the thread knitting together
the many facets of the national archival program. That thread
must not be broken lest the entire cloth become unraveled. The
inseverability of the programs of NARS is so obvious that the
Joint Committee on the Status of the National Archives, representing the American Historical Association, the Organization

of American Historians, and the Society of American Archivists, concluded that the preservation of the integrity of the entire program must be its first desideratum.

From its inception the National Archives was a bifunctional institution—to serve governmental efficiency and to serve the cultural needs of the people. It is around these magnets that the subsequently assigned functions have been drawn. Each of them performs a specialized part of the over-all mission of the National Archives and Records Service. None operates in a vacuum; none can operate efficiently separated from the others. The NARS functions may be infinitely subdivided. They include, for example, the evaluation of records to determine their right to continued existence; the physical preservation of the permanent records and the economical housing of those of short-term value; the availability of the records to government and the people; the dissemination of information from the records; the publication of the laws of the land and of primary source materials; and the planning of programs for improved documentation.

Not all of the relationships between the varying emphases need be repeated, but inasmuch as the inseparability of the existing NARS programs is a fundamental conclusion upon which agreement is complete, a review of its most obvious justifications may be appropriate. Such a review requires a focal point at which all of the functions are bonded. That focus is the National Archives itself.

The mission of the National Archives derives from the reasons for its establishment. The literature on the founding of the institution clearly reveals those two reasons.

The first and most impelling reason was the practical need for improving governmental efficiency. Public records are created not for historical purposes but out of administrative necessity. If those records are not readily accessible for official purposes they cannot serve the primary function for which they were created. For nearly a century and a half after the establishment of the United States of America the government provided no effective program for the orderly maintenance of its records. Consequently, the records were cared for or neglected in accordance with the attention given them by the individual agencies. Lack of staff, space, and proper maintenance practices eventually led to a chaotic condition in many departments. Records that had outlived their usefulness were stored side by side with important documents in attics, basements, and other out-of-the-way places. The need for additional space was largely responsible for the first proposed remedy, a "hall of records"—that is, a warehouse to which records could be removed, thus freeing space in offices and work areas. Historians, however, recognized that the problem was too complex to be solved by wholesale storage, and they promoted the idea of an archival program that would (1) identify the records deserving continued retention, (2) provide properly designed space for the preservation of the permanent records, and (3) facilitate the disposal of the useless ones. The historians' interest in efficiency was based at first upon the assumption that the absence of a practical program discouraged government action in preserving the archives essential to the documentation of the nation's past. They also recognized, however, that a program of historical preservation would be more appealing to congressmen if it could be coupled with a program of economy in government operations. On the other hand, government officials were far less interested in the "old" records than they were in solving their administrative problems of records availability, space, and personnel. These two interests—efficiency and preservation—were merged to form the most convincing argument for the establishment of a National Archives.

The second reason was strictly a cultural one—the preservation and availability of the documentary resources, particularly to serve the political historian. Records are the grist of the historian's mill, and the records of the federal government constitute the most important body of documentation in the United States. They contain the story of the founding and growth of the nation. From them and from the private papers of statesmen comes the evidence upon which the historian builds his case, upon which the economist constructs his theories, upon which the other social scientists form their generalizations. The preservation of these sources is essential to scholars upon whom the citizens depend for a knowledge of the past.

Next to the obligation of the federal government to provide for the identification and preservation of the permanent records, their availability to the citizenry is important. The United States of America is a government of the people, and the records of that government belong to the people. In this respect the American attitude toward records differs fundamentally from that found in most other countries, where the records are considered the property of the governmental machinery and, consequently, the people have no access to them except by the grace of the government. Hence a unique philosophy of archives has developed in the United States, and Americans jealously guard their "right to know" by demanding access to their records. The National Archives is the people's strongbox, to which each citizen has free access. American archivists were never more proud than in 1966 when, during the Extraordinary Congress of the International Council on Archives in Washington, their proposal for greater freedom of access to the records of the world community was presented as an American *practice* rather than as a theory. How different was the verbose camouflage submitted by the delegates from some countries in which the national records are hidden from their citizens and from the world's scholars.

One additional point needs to be made. Never since the founding of the nation has there been a greater need for guarding the source materials of American history. The nation may be on the verge of an iconoclastic era comparable to that faced by the people of France in the early days of their Revolution, when the documentary heritage of that great nationality was threatened by those who wished to wipe out the memory of the past. "All the old documents with gothic script are presumably . . . only legal titles to feudalism, of the subjection of the feeble to the strong," wrote Minister Garat, who suggested, therefore, that they be burned without hesitation.[1] But cooler heads prevailed, and out of the years of political and social chaos emerged the first modern national archives. It is to be hoped fervently that Americans too will resist the shrill advocates of national masochism who denigrate the unique American experience in self-government and progressive adaptation to the needs of the time. The most powerful force in maintaining the principle of impartial preservation of the documentary resources of the United States will continue to be the National Archives. That great

1. Quoted in Ernst Posner, "Some Aspects of Archival Development Since the French Revolution," in Ken Munden (ed.), *Archives and the Public Interest: Selected Essays by Ernst Posner* (Washington: Public Affairs Press, 1967), p. 26. See also Carl Lokke, "Archives and the French Revolution," *American Archivist*, XXXI (January 1968), 23–31.

institution must remain free to carry on its mission without regard to prevailing notions of the rightness or wrongness of past generations, for history is the story of what was, not what should or should not have been.

These latter two principles—freedom of access and impartial preservation—are basic to the mission of the National Archives. Yet, in times of strong domestic dissention, they may be forgotten by the public. They must not be. They are bulwarks of a free people.

Historians in particular have long felt that the early Presidents of the United States were exceedingly remiss in failing to recognize the records of the Presidency and of the Cabinet members as public records. That tradition has been costly to the nation, for many of these significant records have been lost to posterity. The decision of President Franklin D. Roosevelt to offer his records to the government for public use was, therefore, of far greater importance than the nation was prepared to admit at the time. Similar actions by succeeding Presidents have assured the future preservation of presidential records, provided the trust is not abused.

The evolution of the Presidential Archives, which are constructed by private funds and then turned over to NARS for administration, came at a propitious time, for the increase in the quantity of presidential records would otherwise have resulted in either the destruction of many or the invention of some other means of disposition. As has been noted, President Franklin Roosevelt received 140,000 letters a year, several times that of his predecessor; but by 1965 President Johnson was receiving nearly six times more. The preservation of such quantities of records is possible only through some extraordinary provision, and the Presidential "Libraries" offer that solution. These institutions are really Presidential Archives, and should be so designated. Archival principles and techniques, rather than traditional library or private manuscript techniques, must be employed in the arrangement and description of the records. Problems of confidentiality are inextricably linked with the obligations of the archivist in servicing the materials. The security and interests of the nation depend upon the application of archival integrity and protection. And the commitment of the government in accepting a President's records is a binding one for all time.

The Presidential Archives are also authorized under statute to accept (1) public archives authorized for transfer by the Archivist of the United States, and (2) papers of Cabinet members and others whose careers or interests were related to the particular President. Thus the Presidential Archives are but branches of the national archives system. Their relationship to the total archival picture is clear: They are an integral part of it.

Created by the act establishing the National Archives, the National Historical Publications Commission is now the most obvious link between the scholarly community and the national archival program. Its concern is the publication or encouragement of the publication of documentary resources. It does not produce narrative histories. It does not serve as a government historian. It seeks to make available for wider use the original sources that otherwise can be studied only in the National Archives, the Library of Congress, and in hundreds of other repositories. One of its chief purposes is the editing and publishing of the records of the government itself; and currently projects are under way to issue in letterpress form the significant records relating to the adoption of the Constitution and the Bill of Rights and to the First Federal Congress. It proposes to edit and print other important federal records and to make available on microfilm many others. It also encourages and assists other projects both publicly and privately sponsored. In effect, the NHPC promotes the dissemination of the archival resources of the nation, thus serving all segments of the government and the population. It is a vital link in the archival chain, for it takes the archives—and to some extent the Archives—to the reader who cannot come to the repositories in person.

By statute the Office of the Federal Register is archival in function. It is required to receive, preserve, and publish all presidential proclamations and executive orders having general applicability; Congressional bills, resolutions, orders, and votes; certificates of appointment of presidential electors; certificates of the electoral votes for President and Vice President; and other important documents. It thus is something of a miniature archives with custodial, editorial, and distributional responsibility over the most vital documents of the government. Furthermore, its task of accurately and promptly publishing the laws, orders, and regulations of the government personally affects every citizen. The Archivist of the United States is appropriately Chairman of the Administrative Committee for the Federal Register.

The Federal Records Centers are different things to different people. This is because they have at least four very definite functions. They serve: (1) to accommodate records that regularly accumulate in the government and that must be held for varying periods of time; (2) to accommodate special accumulations of records of defunct agencies or of terminated activities; (3) as places for the concentration of all past accumulations of records—regular and special, valuable and valueless—while they are seasoned, appraised, checked against schedules and retention plans, and eventually disposed of or transferred to the National Archives; and (4) as Regional Archives for the permanently valuable records.

Records centers, like the National Archives itself, contribute to both archival preservation and efficiency and economy in government. Their role in the latter is evident to all and has been credited by a Congressional committee with having saved the government a quarter of a billion dollars during a fifteen-year period. Efficiency too has been served, for records are more easily serviced in a records center than they are in cluttered storage rooms in obscure places. On the other hand, the relationship of records centers to the national archival program is often overlooked by management personnel, a curious oversight in view of the original concept of the records center as an intermediate depository.

These relationships, already discussed,[2] need not be fully repeated, but it is pertinent to note that the Federal Records Centers serve both as a purgatory where the records are given their final evaluation and as a sieve and funnel through which the permanent records are directed into the Archives. The records are in limbo, ready for use for government purposes but not yet ready for general public access. Their legal title remains

2. See pp. 181 ff.

with the creating agency, though their physical custody has passed to NARS. In effect, custody is in flux; the records are moving from administrative to research purposes, or to uselessness for either purpose and therefore, in time, to destruction. This matter of custody is crucial. Under centuries-old archival principles a public record may have but two custodians—the agency or department in which it was created (or its legitimate successor), or the archival establishment to which custody must pass directly without an intermediary. In other words, the public archives is the successor custodian for all records leaving the creating agency or its successor. An important principle long recognized by legal authorities is that the integrity of records is protected only when they remain in continuous custody. The notion of a third party becoming involved in this custody is in direct conflict with archival theory and practice.

Thus while economy and efficiency are among the first justifications for the Federal Records Centers, these purposes are complementary to the existence of the centers as an extension of the archival arm that reaches out and prepares for the transmutation of the records into archives.

The planned Regional Archives within the Records Centers [3] should not be confused with the matter of the archival orientation of records-center operations. The title to holdings of a Federal Records Center remains with the creating agencies, but the records have acquired a second influence: They have come into the physical province of the archival agency, which begins applying additional measurements and evaluations designed to prepare them for their ultimate fate. They are not generally available for public use except with the permission of the creating agency. The concept of the Regional Archives, on the other hand, involves the conversion of the permanent records into their final status as archives of the nation. The Regional Archives will accept the records only after the title of the creating agency has been relinquished and legal as well as physical custody has been transferred to NARS. In other words, an agency's records under schedule for retention in the Federal Records Center for 20 years do not become archives—and therefore their *legal* custody is not transferable to the Regional Archives or the National

3. See pp. 183 ff.

Archives—until that period has expired. At that point they are eligible for the Regional Archives, where control over their use (subject to restrictions formally agreed upon between NARS and the creating agency) passes from the agency to NARS. Thus the creation of Regional Archives in no way affects the Federal Records Centers as intermediate repositories. "Regional" in this sense is geographic; "intermediate" is legal and physical status. The tendency for some management personnel to view Federal Records Centers as only warehouses for dead records raises the question of whether, in the late 1940s, archivists may have seriously erred by adopting the term "records center" instead of "intermediate archives." Such a question is now academic, but far from academic are the organic relationships of the Federal Records Centers and the archival programs—relationships so vital that one without the influence of the other would revert to a monodic purpose, the avoidance of which has been the unique feature and most powerful strength of the archival program of the United States from its beginning.

Third parties often stand by amused as they listen to archivists, brandishing their academic degrees, and records managers, dropping new technological terminology, extol their comparative virtues. These family arguments have misled some persons outside the paperwork field to assume that there has been a domestic break-up and that each—the archivist and the records manager—wishes to go it alone if he cannot make the other simply a lackey in his own field. There have been all sorts of attempts to explain the difference between the modern archivist and the records manager. For instance, one writer concluded "that an archivist is a records manager who has specialized or that a records manager is an archivist who has become a general practitioner." [4] That definition, however, will not satisfy the neophyte who dominates the convention bull sessions. The discourses are characteristic of two specialties so closely related in purpose as to involve many gray areas of overlapping authority, and they serve at least to keep each aware of his respective

---

4. J. J. Hammitt, "Government Archives and Records Management," *American Archivist*, XXVIII (April 1965), 219. A useful discussion of the subject will be found in Frank B. Evans, "Archivists and Records Managers: Variations on a Theme," *American Archivist*, XXX (January 1967), 45–58.

primacy in other areas. The simple truth is that the archivist and the records manager are coworkers on the same line. What is important is not where the golden spike is driven, or if it is driven at all, but that they do come together, thus linking the life-giving transcontinental rail that provides an unobstructed movement of records from their conception to their ultimate destination.

The suggestion of a divorce between archivists and records managers in the government's central staff program reveals the common interests and aims of both. As a means of provoking discussion on the point, many practicing archivists and records managers were queried by the Joint Committee. These discussions revealed a remarkable unanimity: In every single case deliberate provocation brought an immediate defense of the organizational relationship of the two. The defense was almost as strong among lower-echelon personnel as among leadership, and somewhat surprisingly, the most sophisticated reasoning was given by nationally recognized records management experts outside of NARS.

The records officer of the Department of the Treasury says: "The responsibility of the National Archives and Records Service for the records of the Federal Government is an all-inclusive one which is properly concerned with the complete life cycle of records from creation to final disposition. This function could not be properly exercised if the archival and the records management programs were separated." [5] Another leading federal records manager says that it would be "extremely cumbersome" to have to deal with more than one agency in matters relating to records management.[6] And a veteran of 25 years in federal records work warns that it would be a "tragedy" if the unified archival-records management program were dissolved.[7] The very thought of divorcing records management from archives suggested to the editor of the *Records Management Journal* that

5. William H. Collins, Departmental Records Office, Treasury Department, to H. G. Jones, June 15, 1967.

6. John J. Shurman, Chief, Communications & Records Management Division, Agency for International Development, to H. G. Jones, June 12, 1967.

7. Ollon D. McCool, Chief, Office Management Division, Department of the Army, Office of Adjutant General, to H. G. Jones, June 6, 1967. See also epigraph, p. 237.

"What is needed is not separation, but closer and more effective inter-relation of the control and operating aspects of these programs." [8]

These expressions—and those of other outstanding records management people of the country—are convincing evidence that leaders of the cultural community have been unaware of or unwilling to admit the significance of the emergence of the modern records manager as a professional who is potentially their most valuable ally. Too often scholars have viewed records management as comprising a horde of file clerks and efficiency experts bent upon destroying every paper not needed for current operations. By the same token, too many people dealing with paperwork have viewed scholars as insisting upon the retention of every scrap. The observer must be impressed not only by the fallacy of any such views but also by the relatively small amount of serious professional snobbishness on each side. The competent archivist should be the first to recognize his limitations and the resultant need for the records manager, and the latter should be aware of his deep commitment to the improvement of documentation and of record maintenance for the ultimate purpose of the national good, not for dollar savings alone.

The Office of Records Management is the government's staff agency responsible for the coordination and promotion of improved records programs and for assistance in developing those programs. It is small, having only slightly over a hundred employees, and was never intended to displace the individual records programs in the agencies themselves.[9] Thus the federal records program is a multifaced one. Some 9,000 agency records officials—largely management analysts and technicians—carry out the day-to-day programs, which vary in sophistication and effectiveness. Except in the large agencies with comprehensive programs, records management is viewed as little more than the actual creation of documentation and its short-term storage in the agency itself. Here specialization is the rule, each analyst concerned with a particular system, a particular procedure, a particular machine. Too often "records management" as practiced within an agency is confused with "records management"

8. Belden Menkus, Editor, *Records Management Journal*, to H. G. Jones, May 31, 1967.
9. See pp. 190 ff.

in the government's staff agency—NARS. The latter by training and outlook comprehends and is concerned with the entire life span of records. Though NARS records management personnel too may have individual specialties, they are more than management analysts; they are records management officers, which means that their concern is so broad as to encompass archival considerations. They form, in effect, the bridge—a vital link—between the agency records officer and the Federal Records Centers and the Archives. They are the couriers of archival messages to the former and efficiency messages to the latter. Their credentials give them entree into every office. Their essentiality to both archivists and agency management is so obvious to both government and the public interest that it cannot be overstressed.

The NARS records management officials are the instruments through which archival concerns in current practices are brought to bear in the agencies. Why is the archivist so interested in those practices?

In the first place, the archivist is interested in the adequacy of documentation of the government's organizations and activities. While the agency management analysts are concerned with information for day-to-day operations, the long-range outlook of the archivist and his knowledge of broader than administrative interests allow him to observe the adequacy or inadequacy of the nature, quantity, and forms of the records created. The archivist does not often exert influence on what records are to be made, but the records manager will often find the suggestions of the archivist useful in improving documentation by the omission or inclusion of certain data or by manipulating it differently. On the other hand, the records manager who is thoroughly cognizant of the documentation of his agency can often assist the archivist in locating alternate sources of desired data.

Second, appraisal practices involve the archivist and records manager in an indissoluble partnership. Public records are created for administrative use, not for historians and other researchers. Thus there are two types of "values" in records appraisal: a "primary" value to the agency itself for administrative, legal, fiscal, and other uses, and a "secondary" value for research use by the government or by the citizenry. While the competency of the agency records officer is paramount in the former, the final determination of the latter rests with the archivist. Both, however, must coordinate their appraisals, for records do not easily categorize themselves as having one value to the exclusion of the other. Oftentimes the official in the creating office will have a better notion of the research potential of a particular series than will the archivist; conversely, the archivist may recognize potential administrative value of a series that the specialized agency records personnel is not aware of. This anomaly explains and justifies the need for mutual agreement between the records officer and the archivist before any record is recommended to Congress for destruction.

Furthermore, the way in which records are created and kept by the agency determines the facility with which the appraisal archivist can carry out his duties. Information possessing permanent value recorded on impermanent media poses a serious and expensive problem. Information of permanent value recorded in forms not lending themselves to easy public use cause similar problems. In this area the records manager needs the archivist and his knowledge not only of the values of records but also of the lasting qualities of various recording media. But of perhaps even more concern to the archivist is his hope that records are created and maintained in the agency in such a way that after appraisal they can, in bulk, be either destroyed or retained. Correspondence files of high officials, for instance, in which impermanent materials have been filed alongside important documents, pose a demoralizing dilemma for archivists. The records manager's failure to segregate short-term materials from records of permanent potential can be costly both in terms of money and the loss of vital documentation. Ideally, records retention and disposition schedules should be established *prior* to the creation of a particular group of records; in this way the original arrangement can provide for a built-in disposal feature that will eliminate much of the expense of ex post facto segregation.

Third, current records practices affect the archivist's policies of arrangement and description. One of the cardinal principles of archival science dictates the retention of the original arrangement of public records wherever possible, because the arrangement itself reveals the organization and the relationships of activities of the agency. The joint principles of provenance and original order, for theoretical justification, require a logical system of creation and maintenance. The archivist attempts to leave undisturbed the arrangement given the records by the creating office, for he expects that that arrangement was designed to facilitate their use for current business and that the researcher will generally find that it reveals the office's functions, effectiveness, and efficiency. The archivist initially describes his records according to the condition in which they are received, though he will later prepare more detailed finding aids. In effect, records are kept in their original arrangement, and through finding aids they are made more usable for researchers by means of a system of cross-manipulation of significant information.

Finally, the successful preservation of permanent records by the Archives is dependent upon the records manager's decisions at the time of their creation. Not only are the lasting quality of the media and the retrievability of the information important, but other considerations, such as size, color, and texture, are problems familiar to the archivist. As a result of his experience in archival preservation he can predict storage trends and suggest improvement in the physical size and form of documentation. As a result of his familiarity with microminiaturization and other copying methods he can advise on the reproduction capability of certain textures and colors. He can, in effect, often give the records manager a lesson in saving public funds by looking beyond the period when the records are of concern only to the creating agency.

Though the formal contacts between the archivist and the agency records officers are relatively infrequent, they are vital. It is this recognition of mutual interest that accounts for the archivist's appreciation of and interest in the records officers and their responsibilities. It also accounts for the management official's dependence upon the archivist for advice and assistance in matters relating to records of continuing value. This interchange of information and assistance is performed largely through the Office of Records Management. Once this picture is pieced together, one can see the extension of the influence of both archivists and records officers: the interests of the former working through the central staff of records managers, who have daily contact with the individual agency records officers, who directly supervise the records programs; and the concern of the records officers for efficiency working through the archivist, who makes determinations on what has lasting value, how it is to be preserved, and how it is to be made available for government and public use. These relationships make it clear that if the archival and records management functions were separated, the symbiotic connection between the two would be destroyed. Liaison between the two elements is easy and natural when they have a common head—the Archivist of the United States. Given different heads, the National Archives would still have to satisfy its interests in the record-making, record-keeping, and records disposition practices of the various federal agencies. This would require the institution to establish its own external relations group to secure the necessary liaison arrangement with the agency records management officers. Not only would this be expensive, but it could never be as valuable as the present arrangement. Furthermore, the records management staff is too small—only about 120 employees—to have an independent existence. It would have to be attached to some other, larger unit, perhaps a management office. It would inevitably take on the orientation of that unit, whatever it might be, thus ending records management as presently practiced in the federal government. All of the concern would be with management information, source data automation, mechanized information retrieval, records creation systems, and the like. The present records management program includes these areas, but it goes much further. Because of its National Archives connections, it still keeps feeding archival considerations into all of its work, and it in turn feeds records management considerations into the archival work.

Taken together, the functions of the National Archives and Records Service constitute an unmatched comprehensive program of public records management, preservation, and disposal. Indeed, NARS serves all the free world as an example of the advantages of an integrated program encompassing the entire range of records activities, both managerial and cultural. The best state programs have been modeled after NARS, and its influence can be seen not only in the developing countries but also in the programs of nations that established archival programs a century and more ago. This integrated archival and records management program also has had its impact upon business, organizations, and institutions. Its full import, however, is not known to some segments of the citizenry. It has failed to receive the continuing interest and support of important groups because its significance and contributions have been hidden by its organizational subversion.

[12]

AN APPEAL TO STATESMANSHIP

. . . a national archival agency will greatly profit from being subordinate to the head of the Government rather than to any particular ministry or department. Such was the status of the National Archives during its formative years, and in my opinion this contributed immensely to the National Archives' stupendous success in concentrating the Nation's record in its custody, a success that must seem a miracle to European archivists, many of whom have struggled for 150 years to achieve what the National Archives had largely achieved by the beginning of World War II. —Ernst Posner, *1955*

THROUGHOUT this book both strengths and frailties of the National Archives and Records Service have been noted. An attempt has been made to weigh objectively the existing program against its *potentials* and to identify the areas in which it shows weaknesses. Recommendations for improvements have been made liberally.

The nation has reason to be proud of its program of archival preservation and records management, and no criticism should be allowed to obscure that fact. Yet the United States is not a country to accept the status quo; it wants not only to have the best but to maintain its leadership. In matters relating to archival and records management it is a pace-setter, but it can remain so only by accelerating its progress in documentation and education. The many recommendations contained in this study are intended to encourage that progress.

The General Services Administration today comprises the Public Buildings Service, Federal Supply Service, Transportation and Communications Service, Defense Materials Service, Property Management and Disposal Service, and the National Archives and Records Service. Its responsibilities, according to the Administrator's *Annual Report*, include:

providing and maintaining office and related working space for *the executive agencies which it serves;* procuring and

253

distributing supplies; transferring excess property among agencies for further Federal use and disposing of property surplus to Government needs; managing stockpiles of materials held for national emergencies and disposing of excesses; operating centralized telecommunications and motor pool systems; *storing and administering records* [emphases added].[1]

In that characterization of the duties of the General Services Administration lies a fundamental handicap of the nation's archival program. A great cultural and service program, responsible to the nation for the records of *all* branches of government, is simply an activity called "storing and administering records" in an agency whose primary responsibilities are in the areas of property, supply, communications, and transportation for *one* branch of government. To suggest that this position represents a sharp decline in stature from the independent status of the National Archives Establishment in 1949 in no way denigrates GSA, which has justified its creation many times over and which needs no defense from archivists and historians. Nor does it allege that GSA has always been a restrictive force upon the national archival and records program, for the growth of that program into several new areas has indeed been assisted, especially in the provision of physical facilities. It does imply, however, that the submersion of a cultural and service organization into an agency concerned with procurement and supply was illogical in 1949 and is infinitely more so in 1968.

The task force on records management of the first Hoover Commission proposed the relegation of the National Archives Establishment to a subordinate position within a "Federal Records Administration." The proposal was based upon the premise that the records centers that it advocated presented "primarily a management rather than an archival problem," that their operation involved "administrative rather than archival" techniques, and that the handling of the records should be done "for the most part by clerical and administrative employees rather than professional archival assistance." The fallacy of those assumptions need not be repeated here.[2]

1. *Annual Report of the Administrator of General Services for the Fiscal Year Ending June 30, 1966*, p. vii.
2. See pp. 181 ff.

The full Hoover Commission rejected the suggestion of an agency-level "Federal Records Administration," but instead proposed that the National Archives Establishment and responsibility for records management and records centers be thrown into a general service agency concerned with property, supply, and housekeeping activities of the executive branch. This merger, with the consequent loss of an independent archival organization, was adopted by Congress within months after it was proposed, and archivists, historians, and others outside of the National Archives had little chance to present their arguments against it. The decision, based strictly on management considerations, was made in spite of the beginnings of a program of records administration in the National Archives and the contention of the Archives that it could expand those activities to encompass the major recommendations of the Hoover Commission.

The lumping of the nation's archival and records program into the new General Services Administration was an illogical union in the first place and would not have happened if there had been greater opportunity at the time for consideration of all interests. The former is a program with dual purposes. While one of its main functions is advice and assistance to *all three branches* of the government in the creation and management of official records, it is equally committed to the service of research organizations; to the writers of history and the purveyors of information on government, economics, and other subjects; to state, local, institutional, and private archival and records management organizations; and to the public in general. It does not act as an official government historian, but it serves as the source of history insofar as that history is derived from federal documentation. Its mission is directed toward both education of the people and service to the government. The General Services Administration is, on the other hand, the government's "business manager." Its functions are managerial; it accommodates the executive branch of government by providing facilitative services; except incidentally, it is not a *public* service agency; it certainly does not presume to have a cultural or educational function. The end results of the work of GSA are measured in dollars and statistics; the end results of the national archival and records program are measured in governmental efficiency *and* the cultural enrichment of the American people.

It is to the credit of both the General Services Administration and the National Archives that this unnatural marriage has worked as well as it has. The major credit, of course, is due the first Administrator of General Services, Jess Larson, who, in the face of the recommendations of the first Hoover Commission, resisted the further subordination of the National Archives to a proposed records management bureau within GSA. Instead, he established the National Archives and Records Service with the archival and records management functions as coordinate divisions. The task force of the second Hoover Commission tried to remove the management of paperwork from NARS, but the new Administrator wisely rejected the effort. In effect, the bureau-level National Archives and Records Service was organized in almost the precise manner proposed earlier by the National Archives Establishment, with the total archival and records programs under the Archivist of the United States. But there was an important difference. The Archivist was stripped of his substantive statutory authority and he became merely a head of a bureau in a larger agency, chosen by and responsible to the politically appointed head of that agency. Even the Archivist's responsibility for recommending to Congress the disposition of public records was transferred to the Administrator of General Services.

This transfer of the records-appraisal responsibility from a professional archivist to a politically appointive office—whose occupant can never be expected to come from the archival or historical fields—violated a principle as old as archival science. Even the redelegation of the authority by the Administrator to the Archivist has failed to alter the inherent danger, for in any conflict of opinion the basis on which an objective and independent appraisal can be made has been completely removed. The evaluation of records in terms of their future administrative, legal, research, historical, or scientific or other value is not a routine, clerical, or housekeeping function. It requires the special kind of competence of the archivist. In a democracy this evaluation must be carefully, impartially, and competently made, for in addition to protecting the civil rights of individuals and protecting the government against unjust claims, the records of the federal agencies, selected and preserved by the

256

Archivist of the United States, must, in a larger sense, constitute the evidence by means of which the people can judge the performance of public officials and agencies. The service of the Archivist cannot be considered an unnecessary cultural luxury; neither should it be regarded as a housekeeping service of the type performed by the General Services Administration.

Fortunately for the National Archives and Records Service, the successive Administrators of General Services have been men of competence and character who, to the extent possible in the face of their backgrounds, have either encouraged the archival and records program or have at least not discouraged it. But a continuation of this luck is not assured. The Administrator is presumably selected on the basis of his ability as a businessman or politician, or both. He in turn appoints the Archivist of the United States. Thus there is no protection against an ill-advised appointment by an Administrator who himself has credentials in areas far removed from archives and records management and who may change with administrations. Hence there is no insulation whatever between the Archivist and the winds of politics. The potential danger is particularly frightening when the Presidential Archives are considered. It would be disastrous if even one instance of misuse of these records—in violation of restrictions placed on them by a President or his associates—were to occur as a result of political pressure from any source or through the carelessness or irresponsibility of a newly appointed Administrator of General Services coming in after a bitter election contest and change of administration. In a nation prone to fierce political partisanship, addicted to sensational journalism, and never wholly free from demagoguery, the possibility of such an occurrence is very real. This is one of the weightiest arguments for keeping the National Archives free from politics. Up to this time it has succeeded in staying free, but its dependent status since 1949 has increased its vulnerability, and its responsibility for the records of all future Presidents will make it more vulnerable still unless it regains and strengthens its independence.

By the very nature of his other responsibilities an Administrator is not very likely, despite all good intentions, to know much about archives or to understand the duties and responsibilities of the Archivist of the United States. In fact the better equipped he is for administering other services of GSA the less is he likely to understand the substantive mission and great importance of NARS and the interests of its special constituency. This is no criticism of GSA or of any Administrator. It is inherent in the present relationship. In the 19 years of GSA's existence there have been six Administrators, each of whom had to be, to some extent, educated in the elementary principles of archival administration by the Archivist and his staff. By the time they left office each had gained some understanding and appreciation of the "general services" side of archival and records work, but they could not be expected to have had much understanding of the educational and research aspects. The disproportionate growth of the "general services" phases of the NARS program is sufficient evidence that the cultural side has not had the understanding, interest, and support that it deserves.

But it is not only the head of the agency who needs to understand and appreciate the mission of NARS. It is the top echelon of his advisers in the central office—his assistants, his legal advisers, his legislative liaison staff, his budget and fiscal staff, his administrative and planning staff, his public-information staff, and most important of all, his personnel staff, which is concerned with classification, recruitment, and personnel policy in general. All these are facilitative services, intended to help the Archivist perform his duties, yet at present all are geared to the other services of GSA, which are business services. In the entire history of GSA only one member of the National Archives staff has served as a high-level adviser to an Administrator. Hence NARS has had in the central office but a single liaison official, and this one only for a short time.

Under the present organization, the educational and research side of NARS can hardly expect to receive much attention in budget discussions in the Administrator's own office or in the Bureau of the Budget or in Congress. Its GSA association means that NARS comes before examiners that may be little acquainted with the government's educational and cultural programs. Again the "general services" end of NARS gets most attention. The Archives is deprived of the more understanding hearing it might receive from examiners more knowledgeable about and sympathetic toward educational programs. This process is often repeated in the hearings before the appropriations subcommittees in Congress. Before congressmen known to be more interested in business services and management functions, it is not surprising that the Administrator and the Archivist restrict themselves largely to a discussion of the money-saving programs of NARS rather than its educational purposes. It is not in the nature of the present GSA association that NARS can get as satisfactory a hearing as it would before a subcommittee more concerned with educational activities of the government. Hence NARS often suffers from not being within the purview of the divisions of the Bureau of the Budget or the committees of Congress that are concerned with educational and cultural matters.

One of the most unfortunate results of the loss of independence by the National Archives in 1949 has been its fading image as one of the great cultural organizations of American government. Not only has the Archivist been virtually forgotten in the shaping of educational and cultural policies of the nation,[3] but the National Archives itself, by suffering a demotion in the governmental hierarchy, has lost the active interest and support of much of the portion of the community that it serves. Scholars and educators themselves must share the blame for the deterioration of the lines of communications, but the loss of image on the part of the National Archives has increased the distance between the archival program and its constituency. The aloofness represents less indifference than unreachability—the feeling that NARS has been stripped of its rightful authority and that it can speak only through higher bureaucracy. Not only have the channels between the Archivist and his constituency been closed, but also those between him and the Congress and the White House. The Archivist of the United States no longer speaks for his institution and its program; he does not communicate directly with the Congress or the President,[4] but only through his

3. See pp. 231 ff.
4. The special kinship felt toward the National Archives by President Franklin D. Roosevelt is demonstrated in the following words on a bronze plaque at the Franklin D. Roosevelt Memorial near the National Archives:

In September 1941, President Franklin Delano Roosevelt called his friend, Supreme Court Justice Frankfurter, to the White House and asked the Justice to remember the wish he then expressed.

"If any memorial is erected to me, I know exactly what I should like it to be. I should like it to consist of a block about the size of this

superior. He cannot initiate, he cannot propose, and he is even restricted by his organizational status in the promotion of his program. He cannot issue invitations to formal functions, because he is not head of the agency. He is limited in his cultivation of the public, and he is restricted in his cultivation of the executive and legislative branches. He cannot even issue his own news releases or, in his official capacity, ask for a conference at the White House. How different things were in the early, independent years of the Archives has been repeatedly shown above. It is a striking irony in the history of the government that the office of one of its principal cultural programs has been downgraded in the era when national administrations have stressed the need for educational and cultural development.

The fact that programs of management of current records have grown to their present preeminence under the General Services Administration is not a convincing argument that they could not have developed similarly under an independent NARS. It is incontrovertible that these programs have received benefits from the GSA relationship. Records management and records centers contribute to the twin purposes of GSA, economy and efficiency. It was, therefore, to the interests of the agency itself, as well as of the government as a whole, for these programs to be encouraged. They fitted into GSA's role as a managerial agency, and their being in the same agency as the Public Buildings Service undoubtedly contributed to more fervent pleas for Congressional funds for space. The Administrator's authority to shift limited budget percentages from one service to another helped out these programs from time to time, an example being the current movement of records into the Suitland Records Center, the cost of which has been taken care of outside the NARS budget. Even so, it would be unfair to the General Services Administration to doubt that it would have given equal support to a sister agency of government serving the same ends of economy and efficiency. After all, GSA is the service agency of the executive branch. Its concern is not just for economies

---

(putting his hand on his desk) and placed in the center of the green plot in front of the Archives building. I don't care what it is made of, whether limestone or granite or whatnot, but I want it plain, without any ornamentation, with the simple carving, 'In Memory of ———.' "

within its own organization, but in all executive agencies and departments.

Some apprehension has been expressed that a separation of NARS from GSA might make more difficult the securing of necessary appropriations from Congress and support from the other agencies. The experience of the National Archives in its formative years dispels such apprehension. Then the archival agency had its own following, its own constituency, which took pride in working for its welfare. This following dwindled only after the establishment was taken away from the professionals and submerged in GSA, where it has been deprived of direct contact with its constituency. But its friends and well-wishers are standing in the wings, and their numbers are potentially much greater in 1968 than they were two decades ago. The story of the National Archives and Records Service is one that, if properly told, will rekindle the pride and enthusiasm with which the original National Archives was viewed, not just by historians and other scholars but by legislators and administrators. A formidable public, appreciating that it is one of the great cultural agencies, will rally around it. Its friends, having once observed the fate that befalls such institutions when they are caught off guard, will see to it that the National Archives and Records Service is provided with the things essential to make it an even more useful servant of the government and of the people.

As has been said, when the National Archives Establishment was created in 1934 it was an independent agency responsible immediately to the President. In 1949 this time-honored principle, grounded in a thorough understanding of the fact that archives must serve both the current requirements of government and the cultural needs of the citizens, was abandoned. The aims promoting the incorporation of the National Archives in the new General Services Administration—economy and efficiency—were laudable, but good intentions do not necessarily make good law. This sharp and sudden development brought dismay to concerned historians, to archivists, and to the informed public. In the name of efficiency it placed the cultural records of the nation, which in other countries are given the same dignity of status accorded to national libraries and national galleries of art, in the same category as articles of office equipment and transportation vehicles.

The ironic fact is that this sharp break with past experience came at the very moment that the National Archives Establishment was setting standards of professional excellence for the nation and for the world.[5] It was on the eve of its greatest achievements, just about to confront all of the problems and possibilities that came with maturity. It could not have needed the position of an independent agency and the responsibility of accounting directly to the President more than at this moment, when it was suddenly reduced to the level of a bureau and placed in one corner of an agency whose concerns, important as they are for the orderly administration of government, have little relation to the preservation and dissemination of the national cultural heritage. Had a similar decision been made about the Library of Congress, the friends and supporters of that great institution would have made an irresistible clamor. The friends and well-wishers of the National Archives, however, had little opportunity to be heard prior to the decision, and a spirit of hopelessness gripped them afterward. For nearly 20 years they have awaited the propitious moment to rally their forces in order to return the national archival and records program to its proper status as an independent agency in the federal government.

Thus the time has come for the establishment of a "National Archives and Records Authority" in the executive branch. The new agency should succeed to all of the archival and records management authority now vested in the Administrator of General Services. Since the National Archives and Records Service already has a workable organization, the divorce would be attended by few administrative problems. The substitution of the title "Board of Regents" for that of "Administrator" in the statutes, orders, and regulations pertaining to archival administration and records management can be made easily. Only details such as the reestablishment of central service functions in the new NARA and the realignment of chains of command with the regional directors would present problems of consequence.

5. See epigraph, p. 253, for a former European archivist's comments on the independence of the National Archives, the "hallmark of its dignity." The quotation is from Ernst Posner, "The National Archives and the Archival Theorist," *American Archivist*, XVIII (July 1955), 208.

At present approximately $700,000 per year is deducted from the NARS budget and returned to GSA for these services, a sum fully ample for their performance by the new independent agency, which could use the funds, it is believed, to greater purpose in carrying out its functions.

The reorganization should—indeed, must—be carried out with the good will of the General Services Administration. It will be essential that GSA recognize that the separation works to the advantage of both, freeing one to work out its own destiny while freeing the other of functions with which it had illogically been forced to concern itself since 1949. The cordial relationships between the present NARS and the constituent services of GSA must be extended to the new NARA. The National Archives and Records Authority will need GSA, just as other departments rely upon it for assistance in all matters relating to space and supplies.

The new National Archives and Records Authority should be governed by a Board of Regents, which would succeed to the archival authority, now vested in the Administrator of General Services, to prescribe rules and regulations, establish basic policies, and delegate authority to the Archivist of the United States, who would serve as the chief executive of NARA. The Board should be authorized to establish, or to delegate authority to the Archivist to establish, advisory committees, chaired by a member of the Board but representative of professional organizations and interests, in such fields as documentary publication, records management, machine-readable records, training, and the like. There should be a statutory requirement that the full Board meet at least two times per year.

Once the principle of a Board of Regents has been agreed upon, careful consideration should be given to the composition of the Board. In order to insure representation by parties most intimately concerned with the national archival program, a board under the *ex officio* chairmanship of the Archivist of the United States and made up of the following members would have much merit: *ex officio*—all living former Presidents of the United States, the Attorney General of the United States, the Administrator of General Services, and the Public Printer; *appointive*—one member of the Senate appointed by the President of the Senate, one member of the House of Representatives appointed by the Speaker of the House, one representative of the judiciary appointed by the Chief Justice, one member elected by the Council of the American Historical Association, one member elected by the Executive Board of the Organization of American Historians, one member elected by the Council of the Society of American Archivists, one member elected by the Board of Directors of the American Records Management Association, and three public members appointed by the President of the United States. A board with this composition would insure representation by all three branches of the government and by the three professions most directly concerned with the mission of NARA. Former Presidents would add prestige to the board, and they also would bring to it the unique experiences and interests of the men around whom modern history has been made; the Attorney General, the Administrator of General Services, and the Public Printer would provide representatives particularly interested in the Federal Register system, the program of records management and centers, and the publication of documentaries; the three professions most concerned with the over-all functions of NARA would be represented by members of their own designation; and the presidential appointees might reasonably be expected to represent other groups having considerable professional interest in NARA.

An alternate composition—and one worthy of consideration— would be the following: the Archivist of the United States as *ex officio* chairman, all former Presidents, the Chief Justice of the United States, the President of the Senate, the Speaker of the House, the Attorney General, the Administrator of General Services, the Public Printer, and eight distinguished citizens who would be appointed by the President and whose basic qualifications would be prescribed by law. Prescribing the latter qualifications would pose a difficult but not impossible task of bill drafting.

This appeal is to reason and logic—and the best interests of the nation—for the separation of the National Archives and Records Service from the General Services Administration and its reestablishment as the National Archives and Records Authority. The proposed transition will in years to come be viewed as the most important archival development since the founding of the original National Archives thirty-four years ago. The

National Archives Act of 1934 represented the country's commitment, at long last, to the development of an archival program; the reestablishment of an independent NARA will represent its commitment to forge ahead with renewed vigor at precisely the moment when new technology is revolutionizing systems and procedures of documentation. Only by such a bold commitment can policies and programs be adopted that will prepare governmental machinery and the professions for the new era when macroscopic media may virtually disappear in the recording of the day-to-day life of the American government.

This is a time for the spirit of the Jamesons and the Lelands to reassert itself. It is also a time for the nation to awake to a new realization of its documentary heritage. The creation of a new, strong, independent, and professionally administered National Archives and Records Authority—composed of the offices of the National Archives, Presidential Archives, Federal Register, Records Management, Federal Records Centers, and Archives of Machine-Readable Records, plus the National Historical Publications Commission—is the surest way of guaranteeing that the American story will be told and that it will be told accurately and objectively.

BIBLIOGRAPHICAL NOTE
APPENDIX & INDEX

BIBLIOGRAPHICAL NOTE

THE footnotes throughout this book illustrate the variety of sources required for a review of the development of the national archival program and for a report on the present status of the National Archives and Records Service. They also reveal the absence of a published comprehensive history of the National Archives.

The most ambitious effort to prepare a documentary history of the records of the government to 1934 was undertaken by Percy Scott Flippin who compiled twenty-four (plus several supplementary) typescript volumes and scrapbooks of source materials titled "The Archives of the United States Government: A Documentary History, 1774–1934." These volumes are in the Search Room of the National Archives. Useful published references concerning the interest of historians and others in the establishment of a national archival program are found in the reports of the Public Archives Commission, organized within the American Historical Association in 1899. Most of these reports are printed in the *Annual Reports* of the Association. Especially useful is V. H. Paltsits' article, "An Historical Resumé of the Public Archives Commission from 1899 to 1921," in the *Annual Report* for 1922. Occasional articles in the *American Historical Review* and the *American Archivist* touch upon the subject, and there are glimpses of Jameson's energetic activities in Elizabeth Donnan and Leo F. Stock (eds.), *An Historian's World: Selections from the Correspondence of John Franklin Jameson* (Philadelphia: American Philosophical Society, 1956).

Published materials on the National Archives, 1934–49, and on the National Archives and Records Service since 1949, are more numerous, but none of these is comprehensive in scope. For the period of independence, the fifteen numbers of the *Annual Report of the Archivist of the United States* are extraordinarily rich. These reports, it is not surprising to observe, are self-commendatory in tone, but they nonetheless chronicle the story of the completion of the National Archives Building, the slow and arduous development of archival principles and techniques, the frustrating effects of World War II upon the archival program, and the gradual extension of archival interests to the administration of current records. They also often discuss the problems facing the institution and outline programs for the future. But these valuable reports were a casualty of the loss of independence, and since 1949 the *Annual Report of the Administrator of General Services* has devoted progressively less space to NARS—so little that the report for 1967 contains only four pages of encomia. Special publications of the National Archives, such as *Bulletins of the National Archives* and *Staff Information Circulars*, issued during the period 1934 to 1956, reveal the evolution of principles and practices, as do T. R. Schellenberg's two books, *Modern Archives: Principles and Techniques* (Chicago: University of Chicago Press, 1956) and *The Management of Archives* (New York: Columbia University Press, 1965). Also revealing are minutes of the "Open Conference on Administration," 1944–46, and the "Seminar Conference on Archives Administration," 1946–47.

Blueprints for the development of the NARS records management program were published in several reports of the Commission on the Organization of the Executive Branch of the Government (the first Hoover Commission, 1949, and the second Hoover Commission, 1955). Numerous articles on records management in NARS have appeared in the *American Archivist*, *Records Management Journal*, *Records Management Quarterly*, *Information and Records Management*, and other professional journals. Minutes of the meetings of the Interagency Records Administration Conference and reports of Congressional committees looking into the problems of records management are also useful.

Customarily the *American Archivist* carries annually a bibliography of writings on archives, current records, and historical manuscripts. A more comprehensive bibliography on these subjects is Frank B. Evans (comp.), *The Administration of Modern Archives: A Select Bibliographic Guide* (Washington: National Archives and Records Service, 1968, mimeographed).

The most revealing manuscript sources are, not surprisingly, the voluminous records of the National Archives. Especially pertinent to this study is a fat file titled "Transaction: 049–106. Formulation of recommendations with respect to the Hoover Commission Report on Records Management in the United States Government." Statistical information furnished by the Office of Administration and Technical Services was used extensively, along with supplemental data made available by heads of offices and divisions within NARS. Personal interviews were helpful, but they also revealed discrepancies between memory and contemporary documentation.

APPENDIX

REPORT OF THE JOINT COMMITTEE

ON THE STATUS OF

THE NATIONAL ARCHIVES

INTRODUCTORY NOTE

At its meeting on December 27, 1966, the Council of the American Historical Association adopted a resolution, introduced by Julian P. Boyd, inviting the Organization of American Historians and the Society of American Archivists to join with the AHA in creating an ad hoc *committee to "report upon the status of the National Archives in the Federal Government, particularly with reference to the question whether it should exist as an independent agency. . . ." Both organizations accepted the invitation.*

Thus was formed the Joint Committee on the Status of the National Archives, which was composed of the following: Julian P. Boyd, Editor of the Papers of Thomas Jefferson *and Professor of History at Princeton University, and Kent Roberts Greenfield, former Chief Historian, Department of the Army, representing the American Historical Association; Fletcher M. Green, Kenan Professor of History at the University of North Carolina at Chapel Hill, and David A. Shannon, Professor of History at the University of Maryland, representing the Organization of American Historians; and William T. Alderson, Director of the American Association for State and Local History, and H. G. Jones, State Archivist of North Carolina and Adjunct Professor of History at North Carolina State University, representing the Society of American Archivists. Dr. Boyd was elected chairman and Dr. Jones was named secretary of the Joint Committee. Louis Morton, Professor of History at Dartmouth College, was appointed to the AHA vacancy following Dr. Greenfield's death in the summer of 1967.*

273

Notwithstanding the emphasis of the resolution and its preamble upon the organizational status of the National Archives and Records Service, the Committee at its first meeting on April 15, 1967, focused its attention upon the various functions of NARS and upon the importance of having these kept together in a single unified system. What was needed, the Committee recognized, was a detailed staff study of the National Archives from its inception to the present. To provide for this study, the Council on Library Resources, Incorporated, made a grant of $2,500 to the American Historical Association, and to conduct the staff study the Committee engaged its secretary, Dr. Jones, who was given leave of absence by his department. He began his task on May 1 and completed it in October. The study pointed to the inseverability of NARS functions, the need for greater resources for the educational and cultural functions, and the desirability of independent status for the National Archives and Records Service. A revised version of the staff study became the text of The Records of a Nation.

On November 18, after having analyzed the staff study, the Committee met and adopted in principle a summary report which, following minor revision, was unanimously approved, signed, and forwarded on December 14 to the secretaries of the three participating organizations.

In February 1968 the Archivist of the United States, Robert H. Bahmer, in a statement titled "Comments on a Report on the Status of the National Archives," *took exception to certain parts of the report. Upon receipt of the Bahmer statement, the Council of the American Historical Association asked for clarification, and the chairman reconvened the Committee on April 11. After an all-day meeting during which various comments by Dr. Bahmer were discussed, the Committee unanimously reaffirmed the substance of its report and recommendations as previously submitted. Nevertheless, the Committee felt that the language of the report, including that employed in stating its recommendations, should be modified at various points. Some revisions were made in committee and, because of lack of time and a desire to give Dr. Bahmer's views full and fair consideration, the Committee invited Dr. Morton to restudy the text and to submit any recommendations for further changes. Late in April Dr. Morton submitted a revised version of the report, and in May five of the six members by mail ballot approved the revision as a substitute for the report as adopted in December.*

The final Report on the Status of the National Archives *and the dissenting statement of the chairman are given here in full, as follows:*

REPORT OF THE JOINT COMMITTEE

THIS report, based largely on a careful and detailed staff study prepared for the Committee and soon to be published under separate auspices, seeks to focus the attention of historians, archivists, other scholars, and informed citizens on the archives of the nation as a matter of vital public importance. It is grounded on the simple proposition that no nation can be said to have a prudent regard for its own interest, or a civilized nation hope to rise to greatness, if it neglect the records that are indispensable to the orderly conduct of government and serve over the centuries as the embodied memory of the aspirations and achievements of its people.

The desirability of a study of the National Archives was recognized at the 1966 annual meeting of the American Historical Association, when the following resolution was adopted without dissent:

> *Resolved*, that the Organization of American Historians and the Society of American Archivists be invited to join with the American Historical Association in creating an *ad hoc* committee to be composed of not more than two representatives of each organization and to be directed to investigate and report upon the status of the National Archives in the Federal Government, particularly with reference to the question whether it should exist as an independent agency, with the Archivist of the United States appointed by and accountable to the President, and, if so, whether authority for determining general archival policy should be vested in a Board of Governors under the chairmanship of the Archivist and composed of representatives of the three branches of government, the archival and historical professions, and the public at large.

The two other societies concerned, the Organization of American Historians and the Society of American Archivists, promptly accepted the invitation of the American Historical Association. As a result, the Joint Committee on the Status of the National Archives was created, the first joint committee ever to be established by these three national organizations.

It is only natural that historians should have prompted such an inquiry. Through more than a quarter of a century they were in the forefront of a movement to persuade the government to establish, as other nations had long since done, a systematic means of administering public records. The work of their own Public Archives Commission and their annual conferences devoted to archival problems gave them an intimate knowledge of many aspects of the subject. Having conducted and published in 1904 the first survey of federal archives, historians realized that without wise planning the building of a splendid archival repository would do little toward solving the fundamental problems of the public records—their orderly care, maintenance, and preservation or disposal. They saw in clear perspective the importance of a single, unified, and impartial administration of the nation's records; they believed that the agency bearing responsibility for the records should have an independent status, and that it should be under the direction of an independent Archivist of the United States charged with the duty of giving equal care and protection to the records of all three branches of government.

This concept, which laid the basis for the American solution to an old problem, was given statutory endorsement by the Congress in the Act of 1934 creating a "National Archives of the United States Government" as an independent agency. The National Archives Building, a great structure equipped with all of the facilities for the care and preservation of records that science could devise, was a major achievement and a monument to the patient labors of Jameson, Leland, and other scholars. Perhaps the founders' greatest archival service to the nation lay in their insistence upon an idea—a comprehensive public records program to be professionally directed and independently administered by an agency having separate status.

The historians not only played a major role in the creation of the National Archives, but they also supplied the first incumbents of the office of Archivist, occupied most of the principal posts, and furnished much of the personnel of the new agency. These historian-archivists became the guiding force of the newly created National Archives. They made the facilities of the national repository the model by which all subsequent archival buildings and equipment have been measured; they developed

276

principles and techniques for the administration of public records that have been largely adopted by both public and private archival institutions in the United States and have exerted influence on long-established archival systems throughout the world; they instituted and laid emphasis upon the value of a training program; they took the lead in founding the new archival profession, helped define its canons, and, through its excellent scholarly journal, assisted it in setting disciplinary standards that have been acclaimed by archivists everywhere. Theirs was an outstanding achievement, and in the seven brief years that ended with the retirement in 1941 of R. D. W. Connor, the first Archivist of the United States, they laid a firm and enduring basis for the success of the new agency.

The importance of the concept of an independent, unified archival system became evident when the Archives during its early years was inundated by a flood of records—a confused, disorderly mass containing worthless flotsam as well as records of imperishable value. The problem was most cogently stated by Ernst Posner, who wrote in 1940 that if the public records of the nation were to be regarded as a single entity, the archivists responsible for receiving and caring for them should be consulted in all questions of record-making and record-keeping besides being the trustees of "the written monuments of the past, of the present day, and of the future." The progressive enlargement of this concept from a mere assertion of the right of archivists to be consulted to the ultimate affirmation of the right to a responsible voice in such matters was amply confirmed in the ensuing years.

Solon J. Buck, the second Archivist of the United States, gave this idea the status of official theory. Throughout his tenure, he insisted that archivists could assist public officials in the handling of modern records and that improvements in record-keeping practices would enhance the quality and provide safer techniques for separating records of permanent value. The result, he asserted, would be increased economy and efficiency for government as well as greater value for posterity. With audacity and skill, Buck led the National Archives into the uncharted wilderness of records administration, thereby creating the fundamental distinction between the American archival administrator and his European counterpart. This program of assistance in records management problems, based initially upon the National Archives' right of inspection, was given official approval by President Truman's Executive Order #9784 in 1946.

The importance of this pioneering exploit cannot be exaggerated. The government's records in 1943 totalled sixteen million cubic feet with another million accumulating annually. Caring for these records was likened to keeping an elephant for a pet: "its bulk cannot be ignored, its upkeep is terrific, and, although it can be utilized, uncontrolled it is potentially a menace." The key to the solution was a partnership between the National Archives and the various governmental agencies. Administrators were receptive and soon experienced personnel trained in records management by the National Archives were being drafted throughout government. Others, fired with the zeal of missionaries, carried the lessons learned in the hard school of archival experience into the profession and later into business. Thus the concept that only through an orderly program of records creation and maintenance in governmental agencies could the archival establishment properly carry out its responsibility for all records became generally accepted throughout the government.

This major accomplishment was not without its inner travail for archivists. Involvement in records management, some thought, might lead to abandonment of the archival tradition of scholarship and research, an undue emphasis upon a mechanized efficiency, and a wholesale destruction of records in order to reduce storage and maintenance costs. This concern was understandable, for the scholarly tradition among archivists was rooted in centuries of experience and found its finest expression in the *Ecole des Chartes* in Paris, for which no counterpart was to be found in the western hemisphere. But Solon J. Buck and his successors, Wayne C. Grover and Robert H. Bahmer, though they understood the importance of economy and efficiency, did not forget their archival birthright, the ultimate justification for their existence as Archivists of the United States.

A profound change in the status of the National Archives occurred in 1949. In that year the Commission on the Organization of the Executive Branch of the Government under the chairmanship of Herbert Hoover (the Hoover Commission) gave its endorsement to the recommendations of a report prepared by a committee headed by Emmett J. Leahy. This report held forth the promise of immense economies. An estimated billion dollars was being spent each year on salaries of personnel engaged in handling records, $154 million was tied up in equipment, and annual rentals for storage of records amounted to $20 million. To reduce these expenditures, the committee proposed the creation of a new agency to administer federal records, of which the National Archives Establishment would be an integral part. This recommendation came as a surprise to most of the archival profession, many of whom viewed it as a mistaken conclusion drawn from a sound premise.

The substance of the Leahy Report, if not the form, was accepted by the Commission with the result that the National Archives lost its independent status and became part of the newly-created General Services Administration. A dozen years earlier the Archivist of the United States had encountered a comparable threat. He had met this threat with the emphatic declaration that the concept of an independent archival establishment was not only the expressed intent of Congress but also one tested by the experience of other nations and many of the states as "the most efficient plan of archival organization and administration." With the support of President Roosevelt, he had been able to defeat the proposal. But when the threat was renewed in 1949, those who had been instrumental in establishing the National Archives fifteen years before had passed from the scene. The then Archivist made a valiant stand, but lacking adequate support, lost under overwhelming pressures, pressures, ironically, that sought to achieve the kind of economy and efficiency that the archivists had so successfully demonstrated to be both necessary and feasible. Thus was sacrificed the independence of the National Archives Establishment, created by the Congress after several decades of thoughtful planning on the part of historians and others.

The final irony is that predictions used in the Leahy Report to support this move proved to be erroneous. It was argued, for example, that management of a system of regional records centers—an idea long advocated by Archivists of the United States—was an administrative not an archival task and that the undeniable economies in cheap storage space could be augmented by

279

the use of unskilled personnel instead of trained archivists. But these centers did not and could not develop as predicted for the simple reason that records management and archival functions are integral and inseparable. The great national system of Federal Records Centers developed since 1949 have become intermediate archival repositories as well as economical storage centers. The archival function of appraisal of records for disposal or permanent preservation is inseparable from them and can only be performed by professional archivists. Furthermore, these centers are already functioning in some degree as regional research repositories and are bound to have an increasing influence upon the study of history and government in the various parts of the country in which they are located. They have the unique advantage of appealing alike to archivists, to scholars, to administrators, and to legislators. But their foundations and their promises for the future lie in the concept of archival policy formulated earlier by Archivists of the United States, not by the proposals that destroyed the independence of the National Archives Establishment.

Despite the erroneous nature of the argument advanced in the Leahy Report, these records centers have been managed in an extremely effective manner since 1949 by the National Archives and Records Service. No longer independent and acting under authority delegated by the Administrator of the General Services Administration, to whom the Federal Property and Administrative Services Act of 1949 and the Federal Records Act of 1950 transferred the Archivist's statutory authority, the Archivist of the United States achieved considerable success after 1949 not only in the records management program, but also in the work of the National Historical Publications Commission, in the operation of the presidential archives, and in the unique combination of editorial, archival, and legal functions of the office of the Federal Register.

For permitting the loss of the independent status of the archival system they had done so much to create and for failing to make their voices heard at a critical moment, the historians exhibited a state of apathy unworthy of the successors of Jameson and Leland and for which the surprise and swiftness with which the change came offered little by way of extenuation. The loss of independence was a serious blow to the morale of the staff of the National Archives Establishment, to the pride of the archival profession, and to the standing of the institution among the cultural agencies of the world.

Everything thenceforth depended, of course, upon the incumbent of the office of the Administrator of General Services to whom the authority of the Archivist of the United States had been transferred. If he recognized the importance of a unified program of records management and archival functions under professional guidance, then the loss of independent status might not be as disruptive as some feared. That the union of an archival institution with a vast managerial operation having no manifest obligations to learning or inherited cultural values has succeeded at all has been due to the fact that successive Administrators have respected the need for professional leadership of the National Archives and Records Service. Twice they have rejected recommendations that would have adversely affected the professional coordination of the archival and records management programs: in 1949 by refusing to establish a Bureau of Records Management, and in 1955 by placing under the administration of the Archivist of the United States, instead of in a separate service, an expanded paperwork management program. Thus far none of the archival authority previously vested in the Archivist of the United States has been delegated by the Administrator to individuals not professionally competent to exercise it. But all of this offers inadequate safeguards for the future dignity and security in the exercise of powers once adhering to the office of Archivist of the United States.

Loss of independence brought as one of its first casualties the cessation of the *Annual Report of the Archivist of the United States*, an indispensable medium for the discussion of policies, principles, and techniques of archival administration. This loss has deprived the government, the learned world, and the public at large of an adequate accounting of the manner in which its public records are preserved and managed. In place of the *Annual Report of the Archivist* are a few pages in the *Annual Report of the Administrator of General Services*, in the midst of extended accounts of business operations, addressed for the most part not to broad questions of archival policy but to economy in expenditures. The archival reports of some of the states put those of the national government to shame both in form, in length, and in substance.

Another effect of the loss of independence has been the lessening of emphasis on the publishing of finding aids, such as final inventories to replace preliminary inventories. Still, despite budgetary shortages, NARS has continued to extend its program of finding aids in an effort to control the constantly increasing flow of records. According to the Archivist of the United States, "at least 95 percent of the archives of the United States are under inventory or comparable control. . . ." Unfortunately, not all these inventories have been published, and many of them are hardly adequate for the scholar and researcher. Also, the 1948 *Guide to the Records in the National Archives*, giving a summary description of over two hundred record groups going back to the founding of the nation, is obsolete, out of print, and has not been replaced, though efforts to do so have been going forward somewhat slowly for the past three years. Specialized guides to specific bodies of records have been published or are in preparation, but much remains to be done. The pace is slow and the records grow at an alarming rate. There is urgent need for greater efforts and the assignment of additional manpower to arrange and describe the present holdings of the National Archives. In the face of growing demands, an unprecedented proliferation of federal records, and constantly rising costs of services, supplies and equipment, the resources allocated to the National Archives for these purposes need to be greatly augmented. Historians and others have an obligation to do all they can to assist the Archivist in securing these resources.

What is needed is a bold and open statement of policy for the future to supplement the annual "program memorandum" prepared by the Archivist for his superiors. Such a statement would provide a basis for discussion by scholars and the interested public of the way in which the NARS was meeting their needs as well as providing support to the Archives for needed programs. The need for such statements of policy and future planning is all the more imperative because of the impact of the computer upon the record-creating process and upon the fundamental nature of records themselves. Already the federal government has several million reels of magnetic tape. Many of these will be kept for long periods of time, especially those containing statistical data valuable to the American economy. But the magnetic tape is an expensive medium and it can be used again and again. The obvious implications for an agency head conscious of the need for economy and for the Archivist who has to appraise records for disposal or permanent preservation emphasize the importance of this problem. For these are as much federal records as the millions of cubic feet of paper records, microfilms, and sound recordings held by the government. They come under the same statutory provisions for public records. Already the need for an archives of machine-readable records is evident and its fulfillment soon or late is probable. These and other questions touching the fundamental nature of public records and their proper management need to be examined and fully discussed. This is a task for professional archivists.

There are in addition important archival programs whose effect might well be enhanced if the independence of the National Archives were restored. One of these is the National Historical Publications Commission. The immense potentialities being released through the microfilm publication program of the Commission will benefit research in colleges and universities throughout the land. This is a program designed to create equal opportunities for scholarship everywhere. The phenomenal success of the Commission in the past decade and a half is a tribute to the liberal policy of the National Archives in its own microfilm publication program—"basically a final break with the archivist's proprietary attitude toward his records." These are achievements that have already influenced other nations. Another such program is the system of presidential archives. Inaugurated by Franklin D. Roosevelt, the Presidential libraries represent an achievement unprecedented in archival history and the decision of President Kennedy and President Johnson to locate the records of their administrations in great university centers is a recognition of the essential research purposes of these institutions. In no aspect of the Archivist's responsibilities is it more imperative that he be given authority over an independent agency than in the administration and protection of these repositories of the records of the presidency.

In these and many other respects the staff study on which this report is largely based provides evidence that the loss of the authority and influence of the Archivist of the United States since 1949 has seriously affected the administration of the nation's records. These, therefore, are the major conclusions to which these findings point:

1. *The integrity of the entire archival program of the nation in all of its varied functions as now constituted must be preserved.*

To attempt to separate records management from archival responsibilities would be a disavowal of the lessons learned from the accomplishments of the National Archives Establishment and the National Archives and Records Service. It would create two separate, conflicting, and overlapping authorities and impose an artificial shackle upon the responsibility of the Archivist of the United States to insure the efficient creation, maintenance, and preservation of today's records which are the source of tomorrow's archives. The symbiotic relationship between the professional archivist and the records manager would be destroyed, seriously endangering the interest of the historian with no advantage to either economy or efficiency. The National Archives would become a passive recipient of unmanageable accumulations of records while records management would be absorbed by and lost in management services having no interest in or concern for the documentary heritage of the nation. To this conclusion the Committee found no disagreement among scores of archivists and records managers consulted. This unanimity is evidence that the concept of a unified archival and records management program for the federal government, first enunciated by the National Archives Establishment, supported by the Hoover Commission report, and developed to its present effectiveness by the National Archives and Records Service, has been demonstrated to be not only successful but essential as a means of administering the records of the nation.

2. *The cultural and educational functions of the National Archives and Records Service, which have failed to receive the attention and support they deserve, must be strengthened.*

While it is perhaps inevitable that new programs designed to save money and improve efficiency more readily attract both

284

support and recognition, it does not follow that traditional cultural and educational aspects of a national archival program must be neglected. The record shows that too little has been done to promote these cultural and educational responsibilities of the National Archives. The appraisal function is seriously understaffed in the face of the heavy responsibility of identifying adequately the permanently valuable records among the some five million cubic feet of new records being created each year. Arrangement and description of records long in the National Archives have proceeded too slowly; ideally from the historian's point of view there should be descriptive, as distinct from title, inventories of all record groups, but there are today such descriptive inventories of only about half of the approximately 400 record groups in the Archives. Moreover, because of lack of funds, according to the Archivist of the United States, no substantial progress against a major backlog of document repair work is projected through 1973. The discontinuance of significant publications such as bulletins, staff information papers, and the Archivist's *Annual Report*, has markedly reduced the contributions of the National Archives to the scholarly community and to the public at large. And finally, the publication of documentaries has been seriously hampered by penurious appropriations.

But the needs of the National Archives and Records Service are not limited to existing programs. They extend also to functions not now being performed, or if so, performed inadequately. It is time to review programs designed to educate the historical profession and the public in the purposes and services of the National Archives. Existing programs need to be strengthened and new programs developed to encourage staff members to participate more actively in scholarly research and activities. The classification system and pay scales need to be reexamined and, if necessary, revised to attract additional competent personnel, retain those already on the staff, and provide greater incentive for professional employees. Consideration should be given to the establishment of fellowships and exchange programs as a means of maintaining liaison with the learned professions and of utilizing the human resources available; to a graduate-level Institute for Archives Administration and Records Management to provide a high order of training for a limited number of promising scholars who can be drawn into the rapidly-expanding field of archives and records administration; and to an archives of machine-readable records as a part of the NARS program.

These are but a few of the specific programs to which the National Archives and Records Service should give serious attention. To do so does not imply that less attention and support should be given to the records management and records center programs; these programs too require increased staffing if they are to operate at peak efficiency.

3. *The national archival and records management system should be restored to independent status as the National Archives and Records Authority, administered by an Archivist of the United States appointed by the President and responsible to a Board of Regents.*

The Archivist of the United States should be appointed on the basis of professional qualifications by the President of the United States by and with the advice and consent of the Senate. The independence of this office and its establishment on a level comparable to that of the Librarian of Congress and the Secretary of the Smithsonian Institution is an imperative necessity. Under the present arrangement the Archivist is rarely if ever made an *ex-officio* member of any cultural commission. Only after protest from historians and others was the bill creating the commission to celebrate the bicentennial of the American Revolution amended so as to make the Archivist a member, though he has custody of the greatest body of records of the Revolution and his advice and assistance in the planning of the commemoration will be indispensable. It is only through intermediaries that the Archivist has access to the White House and to the Congress. He is now the head of a relatively small bureau in an executive agency with little save a title to maintain a remnant of the former prestige of the office. The subordination of the office in 1949 has long been a source of distress to a worthy profession. Today, at a time when the nation is experiencing an awakened sense of its cultural responsibilities, the status given to this office stands as a comment upon our professed concern about our heritage and our historic values.

The Archivist should be responsible to a Board of Regents in performing his duties with respect to the records of all three branches of government. The composition of this body should be given careful consideration and study. The Committee suggests, as a means of stimulating such consideration, that the Board be composed of, *ex-officio*, all of the living ex-Presidents of the United States, the Attorney General of the United States, the Administrator of General Services, and the Public Printer; and, *appointive*, one member of the Senate appointed by the President of the Senate, one member of the House of Representatives appointed by the Speaker of the House, one representative of the judiciary appointed by the Chief Justice, one member designated by the American Historical Association, one by the Society of American Archivists, one by the Organization of American Historians, one by the American Records Management Association, and three public members appointed by the President of the United States.

The elevation of the national archival and records management program to the status it once held would rectify the error that in 1949 placed the records of the nation, which in other countries are accorded the same dignity as national libraries and national galleries of art, in the same agency that was responsible for such items as office equipment and transportation vehicles. All that need be done to achieve this result is to transfer to the new agency all the authority for records management and archival functions now vested in the Administrator of General Services.

The importance of this matter to the national interest, as well as reason and logic, call for a separation of the National Archives and Records Service from the General Services Administration and its reestablishment on such a footing as it was once given by the Congress after long and careful planning on the part of those most concerned about the administration of the public records. Such an independent agency is best suited to our constitutional system. Once restored to the status and dignity it originally enjoyed, it could be expected to release new energies, to invigorate every aspect of its varied operations, and to focus all of its talents and resources upon the vast problems and changes now being produced by the revolution in the form and nature of records. Such a restoration, in the years to come, will undoubtedly be regarded as the most important archival development since the nation belatedly recognized its responsibilities by founding the National Archives more than three decades ago.

The opportunity presses and should not be delayed.

The American experiment in self-government that began in 1776, under the influence of one of the most potent ideas in history, is a miraculous and moving chapter in the annals of mankind. The records that embody this great achievement lie in the hundreds of millions of documents in the National Archives, in the presidential archives, in the regional archives, and in the scores of federal agencies. The national archival program is an indivisible continuum dedicated to the objective, impartial, and professional administration of this immense body of the records of a people on their march to self-fulfillment. These records, somewhat like the people themselves, have right to equality of treatment, equality of protection, equality of access. In them successive generations will search for the benchmarks of their greatness. These are the records by which they will judge and be judged, openly and impartially as only a free people dare to be. They deserve a place of dignity and a measure of attention worthy of their great role.

Representing the American Historical Association:
> Louis Morton

Representing the Organization of American Historians:
> Fletcher M. Green
> David A. Shannon

Representing the Society of American Archivists:
> William T. Alderson
> H. G. Jones, *Secretary*

DISSENTING STATEMENT

IT IS with profound regret but with deep conviction that I find myself unable to join my colleagues in signing the present revision of the Report that was transmitted on December 14, 1967 to the American Historical Association, the Organization of American Historians, and the Society of American Archivists as the final summation of our study.

That Report was the product of a serious and objective investigation by responsible scholars. It was a summary of findings and recommendations made in an extended Draft Report that had been developed through several stages and to which several members of the Committee and many distinguished archivists and scholars in and out of government contributed. Considering the circumstances under which this inquiry was carried on, including pressures for haste generated by the justifiable fear that a parallel study being conducted in the Bureau of the Budget might bring forth recommendations or a *fait accompli* diametrically opposed to the fundamental principle which governed our inquiry, the construction of this solid factual foundation was indeed a remarkable achievement.

As my colleagues well know, I considered it unnecessary, ill-advised, and contributory to misunderstanding for the generalized summary of findings and recommendations to be embraced as our Report and thus separated from its natural matrix of fact and argument, the more so since there was no evident disagreement on matters of principle or substance but only a mere procedural distinction between a staff study and a committee study. The technical distinction in this instance was not entirely applicable and certainly less so to the Draft Report than to the present Revision. Yet, with a reluctance of which my colleagues were fully informed, I signed the Report in order to achieve unanimity for our recommendations, particularly the first and most fundamental of them. The present Revision, however, is a compounding of the original mistake which separated the summary of findings from its solid basis of fact. It weakens an argument that was by no means overstated in the Report. It invites unfavorable comparison with its prototype and thus will provide the opening for misunderstandings and misrepresentations even more egregious than those which greeted the Report and thus prompted the Revision.

The Revision departs from the Report in a number of ways that I cannot accept, particularly in respect to excisions of statements which are demonstrably supported by fact and against which no persuasive allegation of error has been offered. But for the sake of brevity, I confine myself to the single most important recommendation made in the Report: that *"The integrity of the entire archival program of the nation in all of its varied func-*

tions as now constituted must at all costs be preserved." On this point the Revision, to be sure, reaffirms the recommendation and retains the assertion that our investigation disclosed no disagreement among the scores of archivists and records managers consulted. But in the sentence quoted the phrase "at all costs" is deleted, an alteration immediately giving rise to the question as to the point at which the recommendation will not be defended. The Report also contained the following warning: "To attempt to separate records management from archival responsibilities would be . . . to create two separate, conflicting, and overlapping authorities and to impose an artificial *and disastrous* shackle upon the responsibility of the Archivist of the United States to insure the efficient creation, maintenance, and preservation of today's records which are the source of tomorrow's archives." The effect of this warning, infelicitously stated but deeply felt, was greatly weakened by elimination of the words underscored.

Our Report also presented a summary of the arguments advanced by the leading proponent of the shift in policy that occurred in 1949 and it was quite explicit in pointing out that this proposal was in effect an advocacy of the principle of separation. The following passage from the Report may be compared with the corresponding summary on pages 5 and 6 of the Revision to show how this essential point was blunted to the point of extinction:

If there was any doubt about the threat of exaggerated emphasis upon administrative efficiency, it should have disappeared with the profound shift in policy that took place in 1949. In that year the Commission on the Organization of the Executive Branch of the Government under the chairmanship of Herbert Hoover gave its endorsement to the recommendations of a special investigation headed by Emmett J. Leahy. Leahy had been a member of the staff of the National Archives in its early years, had been the principal mover during the war of the outstanding records management program of the Navy Department, and had founded the National Records Management Council. The Leahy report held forth the promise of immense economies. With an estimated billion dollars being spent each year on salaries of personnel engaged in handling records, with $154 million tied up in equipment, and with annual rentals for storage of records amounting to $20 million, Leahy proposed the creation of a new agency to administer federal records, of which the National Archives Establishment would be an integral but subordinate part. This came not only as an almost complete surprise to the archival profession but also as a most grievously mistaken conclusion drawn from a sound premise. For what the proposal amounted to was that the principles and techniques of records management that the National Archives had originated and carried on with such success should be taken out of its hands. The arguments advanced in its support were as illogical and as insubstantial as its conclusion.

Leahy argued, for example, that to place additional records management responsibilities on the National Archives would alter its character so radically as to make it a different kind of institution. But he failed to see or would not concede that this was precisely the effect that his own proposal would have. The course that he advocated was thus a disavowal of the nurturing theory of archival administration that had ushered in the new profession, had produced such exemplars of its principles and techniques as himself, and had wrought in the National Archives Establishment a distinctively American role for such an institution. Leahy dismissed its records management programs as being limited to the isolation of a small percentage of records having permanent value, but in doing so he quite forgot the simple principle pointed out by Buck, Grover, Brooks, and others that the responsibility for this small percentage could not be met effectively unless archivists were directly involved in decisions concerning the total mass of records from their creation to their final destiny. *He did not venture to suggest how, once stripped of any real voice in the management of records, the Archivist of the United States could meet this responsibility. Leahy was advocating, in brief, the principle of separation: the theory that a distinction could and should be made between techniques primarily administrative and those primarily archi-*

291

val in nature. His proposal was in reality a return to the old traditional view of an archival agency, a denial in the name of the new doctrine of all that the National Archives had contributed to efficiency and economy in the management of the public records. This proposal represented such a fundamental shift of policy as to amount to a virtual abandonment of the role the National Archives Establishment had assumed in its brief but spectacular career.

Yet in principle if not in precise form the new policy was written into law. This was done hastily, without the benefit of any genuine public discussion, and under the sponsorship of a powerful commission supported by an influential and well-organized group called the Citizens' Committee for the Hoover Report. The dispassionate analysis of the two main responsibilities of the National Archives that Buck had set forth in his far-reaching statement of 1941 was forgotten in the single-minded concentration upon a narrowly defined goal. . . . The independence of the National Archives Establishment, created by the Congress after several decades of thoughtful planning on the part of historians and others, was sacrificed in a moment by what the chief proponent of this monumental aberration of policy was candid enough to describe as an act of salesmanship. There was little new in his proposal save the abandonment of the idea of an independent national archival system, and the consequences of this were overlooked in the face of the glittering promises held forth. (*Emphasis added.*)

No one will contend that this language could not be improved, most especially in respect to brevity. But these revisions, placed in the context of past efforts to effect a separation of the archival system, cannot be dismissed as mere alterations of phraseology. These and other evidences of a weakening of our position on the fundamental principle are to me wholly unacceptable. If anything, our Report was not emphatic enough in calling attention to the consequences to be expected from any successful attempt at separation of archival and records management functions. I believe that such a separation would not only be a disaster. It would initiate a retrogression from the position of leadership and preeminence that our archivists have achieved through long years of trial and error. It would be a denial of archival doctrine validated by experience and by the emulation of other nations as well as by the separate states of the union. Even to provide the slightest hint of a weakening of resolution on this fundamental doctrine of inseverability would be to open the door to dangers that, ironically, inspired our inquiry in the first place.

For the simple fact is that, contrary to the basic allegation made against the Report under the aegis of the General Services Administration, a doctrinaire preconception of independence for NARS was *not* the primary factor that prompted the original resolution that led to this inquiry. The question of a less incongruous status for the national archival system was, of course, one that needed to be raised. So, too, was it necessary to call to historians' attention their neglect of and indifference to an institution which they had been foremost in creating. But overriding these and other concerns was the simple threat then existing and still apparent that the integrity of our national archival system in all of its offices and operations might be violated. This can be documented in a variety of incontrovertible ways, but let two facts suffice.

First, on the occasion of the initial meetings of the committee at which our study was benefited by testimony from able and respected archivists, discussions did not center on the question of independence but on the harmful consequences that would result if archival functions were to be separated from records management. On the question of independence there were divided opinions within the Committee, on the principle of inseverability none whatsoever. In fact the Committee, fearing that the parallel study going on in the Bureau of the Budget (inspired by the same resolution that led to our inquiry) might soon be completed and might contain recommendations in violation of this principle, "unanimously requested the Chairman to inform the Bureau of the Budget that its consensus was, thus far, only that the entire NARS program should remain together, *whether in or out of GSA*, and that the Committee would study further the question of independent status with the hope of making its findings and recommendations known at as early a date as possible" (Minutes of the Joint Committee, April 18, 1967; *emphasis added*).

293

Second, while the parallel study going on in government not only had the advantage of authority and greater staff and other resources for investigation than did our study, its findings have never been made available to the Joint Committee, though formally requested. Our proceedings and our findings as represented in the Draft Report and final Report, on the other hand, were promptly and fully transmitted to the government, along with offers of cooperation and mutual exchanges. Can it be asserted by anyone familiar with the government study that its recommendations stand as firmly and as inflexibly on the side of the doctrine of inseverability as our Report did, as unanimously as all of our archival and scholarly testimony did? Can it be said that the government study defends the integrity of the entire archival system as transcending in importance the question of status? I cannot, on my own authority, supply the answers to these questions. But I do not for a moment believe that either can be answered with an affirmative. The danger which gave rise to our inquiry is ominously present and I have no hesitancy in predicting that, the moment legislation is introduced calling both for the preservation of the integrity of the system in all of its offices and functions and for a status more suitable to the dignity and importance of our archival heritage, this known but hidden danger will disclose itself.

For these and other reasons I cannot acquiesce in a Revision which seems to me clearly to view this danger with greater equanimity and tolerance than our Report or our factual findings would justify. Neither our Report nor its supporting study was an indictment of the General Services Administration in its proper sphere of activity. Both were addressed to an important public question, every aspect of which needs to be explored in all of its ramifications. In my opinion the Revision contributes even greater confusion and ambiguity to the discussion than occurred when, for reasons which now appear somewhat inconsistent, the summary of findings and recommendations was separated from its underpinning of fact and argument. But that underpinning, constructed as a professional and public service chiefly by the able Secretary of the Joint Committee, is one with which I am proud to associate myself and one which, when published, will provide an appropriate platform for the discussion of this important matter of public policy. I regret that I cannot extend my approval or my pride to the Revision of the Report which my colleagues have seen fit to make.

But I should like to make it very clear that my dissent is offered solely to draw attention to the undeniable danger that inspired this study, that is still present, and that, unless I am very much mistaken, will eventually manifest itself. If and when it does appear, those who wish to make a judicious estimate of its nature, its force, and its implications will not be helped very much by this retreat from a position I had thought we had held with conviction and unanimity. I know of no evidence adduced in the entire course of our investigation—most certainly not in the challenge to the Report which prompted the Revision—that can justify such a departure on such a fundamental doctrine.

Julian P. Boyd, *Chairman*

INDEX

H. G. JONES

H. G. Jones lived on a tobacco farm near the extraordinarily named community of Kill Quick in Caswell County, North Carolina, until he was seventeen. At that point he left, on borrowed money, to work his way through college. World War II interrupted, with service in the Navy on submarine chasers and minesweepers. He graduated from Appalachian State University in 1949, took his M.A. at George Peabody College in 1950, and his Ph.D. at Duke University in 1965. He has done free-lance writing, edited a weekly newspaper, and taught history and political science at various colleges in North Carolina and Georgia. He is now Adjunct Professor of History at North Carolina State University.

In 1956 Dr. Jones became State Archivist of North Carolina and soon developed the largest and most comprehensive archival and records management program among all the states of the Union; for this his department won the first Distinguished Service Award ever given by the Society of American Archivists. He has been an officer of that society since 1961 and is now its president. In November 1968 he became Director of the Department of Archives and History of the State of North Carolina.

A bachelor who lives and works quietly, Dr. Jones has written three books and numerous articles on historical and archival subjects. His article "Bedford Brown: State Rights Unionist" won the R. D. W. Connor Award, and his book For History's Sake *won the Waldo Gifford Leland Prize of the Society of American Archivists.*

Dr. Jones has served as a consultant to the states of California, Florida, and Virginia with regard to their archival problems. In 1967 he was engaged by the American Historical Association to conduct the study of the status of the National Archives and Records Service from which grew The Records of a Nation.